European Yearbook of International Economic Law

EYIEL Monographs - Studies in European and International Economic Law

Volume 35

EYIEL Monographs is a subseries of the European Yearbook of International Economic Law (EYIEL). It contains scholarly works in the fields of European and international economic law, in particular WTO law, international investment law, international monetary law, law of regional economic integration, external trade law of the EU and EU internal market law. The series does not include edited volumes. EYIEL Monographs are peer-reviewed by the series editors and external reviewers.

Calliope Makedon Sudborough

Mediating Sovereign Debt Disputes

Springer

Calliope Makedon Sudborough
IESEG School of Management
Paris, France

ISSN 2364-8392 ISSN 2364-8406 (electronic)
European Yearbook of International Economic Law
ISSN 2524-6658 ISSN 2524-6666 (electronic)
EYIEL Monographs - Studies in European and International Economic Law
ISBN 978-3-031-46786-8 ISBN 978-3-031-46787-5 (eBook)
https://doi.org/10.1007/978-3-031-46787-5

This Springer imprint is published by the registered company Springer Nature Switzerland AG
The registered company address is: Gewerbestrasse 11, 6330 Cham, Switzerland

Paper in this product is recyclable.

Acknowledgments

I feel enormously fortunate that Professor Aikaterini (Catharine) Titi supervised my doctoral thesis. I am eternally indebted to her for the time and effort she invested in me, as well as the wonderful publishing opportunities she presented to me along the way. Despite the many professional and personal obstacles that I encountered as a PhD student, Professor Titi remained in constant contact. Her sound advice, immense support, and gracious patience guided me through the most difficult periods.

I would also like to thank Professors Julien Chaisse, Katia Fach Gómez, Antonis Karambatzos, and Thomas Peyroud for having accepted to participate in my thesis committee. I am very honored. I would also like to extend a special thanks to Professor Katia Fach Gómez, for sharing interesting articles with me and Professor Antonis Karambatzos who encouraged me to pursue a PhD at the very start of this journey.

Having spent many evenings, weekends, and vacations working on this thesis—often to the chagrin of my family, and especially my young children Théodore, Pénélope, and Athéna, I thank them for their understanding and their support. I will always remember their sweet gestures of encouragement and their help at home. I will cherish the memory of Athéna using her toy computer to "work" beside me as I completed this thesis. I would also like to thank my parents, Professors Fillia Makedon and Hal Sudborough, for their inspiration, coaching, and advice. I hope that I have made them proud.

I would also like to thank my dear friend, and mediator, Angela Herberholz, for her loyal friendship, dynamic problem-solving skills, motivational speeches, and unwavering support.

Lastly, I would like to honor the memory of Professor Laurence Ravillon who first accompanied me on the start of my PhD path and who, so very wisely, advised me to turn to Professor Titi.

Calliope M. Sudborough

Contents

Abbreviations

BIT	Bilateral Investment Treaty
CAC	Collective Action Clause
CJEU	Court of Justice of the European Union
EMU	European Monetary Union
EC	European Commission
ECB	European Central Bank
IBA	International Bar Association
FAA	Fiscal Agency Agreement
FSIA	Foreign Sovereign Immunities Act
ICC	International Chamber of Commerce
ICJ	International Court of Justice
ICSID	International Centre for Settlement of Investment Disputes
IMF	International Monetary Fund
IFI	International Financial Institutions
IIA	International Investment Agreement
ISDS	Investor-State Dispute Settlement
PCA	Permanent Court of Arbitration
SCC	Stockholm Chamber of Commerce
UMA	Uniform Mediation Act
UNCITRAL	United Nations Commission on International Trade Law

Chapter 1
Introduction

Particularly since the start of the twenty-first century, high profile sovereign debt crises have highlighted the need to explore new means for resolving differences between debtor governments and their sovereign bond creditors in a time-efficient manner that does not sacrifice economic recovery. The recent Argentine and Greek governments' sovereign debt crises were the first to raise legal claims by creditors under investment treaty law, sparking extensive debate amongst investment arbitration practitioners and scholars at a time when the investor-state dispute resolution system itself has been facing intense criticism from a multitude of governments.

On 23 December 2001, Argentina defaulted on its sovereign debt launching an almost-20-year period of economic crisis and austerity until it finally reached a settlement with its creditors who had been litigating against the state to recover their investments in full. Nine years after Argentina's sovereign debt default, Greece indicated it might default on the massive accumulation of sovereign debt it owed to the EU, jeopardizing the sustainability of the Eurozone itself. To avoid default, European authorities and private investors loaned nearly 320 billion euros to Greece over the course of the debt crisis. This bailout plan was the biggest financial rescue of a bankrupt country in history and, as a result, Greece has debt payments scheduled beyond the year 2060. In exchange, the EU demanded that Greece implement strict reforms and austerity measures to bolster the Greek government's finances. However, these measures also plunged the country into a recession for the better part of a decade.

Financial crises such as the Argentine debt crisis of 2001–2002 (Argentine crisis) and the global financial crisis of 2007–2008 cause immense instability often provoking sovereign bankruptcy and the resultant longstanding political and economic consequences on debtor state populations. At the same time, international law on sovereign bankruptcy has failed to develop and still provides no accepted definition of sovereign debt. Nevertheless, it is commonly understood in the legal and financial

C. M. Sudborough, *Mediating Sovereign Debt Disputes*, EYIEL Monographs - Studies in European and International Economic Law 35,
https://doi.org/10.1007/978-3-031-46787-5_1

community that sovereign default is when a government is unable to pay its debt within the time limit or grace period stipulated in the contract with its creditors.[1]

Despite mounting calls for the establishment of a unified set of international legal principles to deal with sovereign debt crises, legal scholars, financial stakeholders and governments have so far been unable to reach agreement thereupon.[2] As a result, sovereign debt crises almost invariably result in either partial or total default producing a variety of responses ranging from sovereign debt restructuring (whereby creditors agree to reduce their claims) to bailout (financial support given to defaulting countries). When economic crisis has left a state unable to repay its debt, sovereign bondholders and states must negotiate a new financing agreement. Yet various factors undermine such collective negotiations, leading many creditors to seek full collection of their investments via litigation or, more recently, investment arbitration.

Critics of these mechanisms have argued that they not only undermine future restructuring efforts but that they further deplete the state's much-needed funds at a time of economic crisis and postpone economic recovery.[3] Indeed, investment arbitration claims easily reach the hundreds of millions—and at times billions—of U.S. dollars. Yet, the financial risk is not limited to losing these enormous claims as states are often liable for millions of dollars in arbitration costs even when they have successfully defended themselves.

In parallel, investment arbitration has been facing an increasing avalanche of political backlash from governments and non-governmental organizations. As a result, investor-state dispute settlement stakeholders are advocating for alternative, supplementary dispute resolution mechanisms for investment disputes. One such complementary dispute resolution mechanism that has been gaining momentum is investment mediation.[4] Accordingly, an increasing number of international investment treaties, including model bilateral investment treaties and multilateral investment treaties have inserted mediation in their provisions on dispute resolution.[5]

The rising interest in mediation is also exemplified by the Convention on International Settlement Agreements Resulting from Mediation (Singapore Convention).[6] This novel, multilateral framework provides for the recognition and enforcement of mediated settlements and, as of September 2021, has 54 countries as signatories.[7] Although the expressly stated scope of the Singapore Convention refers to international commercial disputes, there is reason to believe that it could be

[1] Ams et al. (2020), pp. 275–278.

[2] Guzman and Stiglitz (2016), pp. 3–32; Bolton (2004), p. 707; Rogoff and Zettelmeyer (2002), p. 470; Schwarcz (2000), p. 956.

[3] Asonuma et al. (2019); Bohoslavsky (2017), paragraph 59.

[4] Claxton (2020), p. 78; 'Mediation of Investor-State Conflicts' (2014), pp. 2543–2564.

[5] ICSID (2021).

[6] United Nations Convention on International Settlement Agreements Resulting from Mediation (Singapore Convention) (New York, 2018).

[7] United Nations Treaty Collection (2021).

interpreted to apply to "commercial" investment disputes, as will be discussed in Chap. 3 of this thesis.

The convergence of the need for a more economically-sound means to resolve sovereign debt disputes and the rise of investor-state mediation has yet to be explored in depth. Therefore, this thesis examines whether, and how, investment mediation could offer an advantageous means for resolving sovereign debt disputes. This topic is an important area to explore for various reasons. To date, the literature has focused on the absence of a global framework for sovereign bankruptcy or on the legal debates generated by the mass claims filed by creditors in investment arbitration proceedings.[8] But it has generally ignored the idea of mediating sovereign debt disputes. Accordingly, investigating the potential of mediation as a dispute resolution mechanism in this domain fills an important gap in the academic research concerning sovereign debt disputes. In addition, identifying a more efficient means of resolving sovereign debt disputes could help indebted countries to rebound economically, which itself has significant social and political consequences. Moreover, as sovereign debt disputes are a subset of investor-state disputes more generally, exploring how mediation could be a valuable dispute resolution mechanism could also shed light on mediation as a tool for resolving investment disputes more generally. Therefore, the research question addressed in this doctoral thesis is: Should parties resort to mediation for resolving sovereign debt disputes, and, if so, how could such investment mediations be put into place?

To answer the research question, this thesis uses a multi-faceted analytical methodology. As a first step, to identify the stakeholders, main developments, and challenges created by the intersection of the sovereign financing and investor-state dispute settlement systems, this thesis explores (i) the available academic literature on sovereign debt and default, investment arbitration and mediation as well as (ii) Case studies of the two countries most recently plagued by sovereign debt: Argentina and Greece. Building upon this literature review and these two case studies, this thesis proceeds to conduct a comparative legal analysis of the primary judicial decisions and investment arbitration awards filed by sovereign debt creditors. Lastly, this thesis also addresses the research question using a normative component that suggests how to settle sovereign debt disputes using mediation.

This thesis is organized in five chapters. This chapter is dedicated to introducing the research topic and research methodology.

Chapter 2 establishes the underlying context for this thesis. After explaining the basic mechanics of sovereign financing, this chapter details the historical and legal framework surrounding sovereign debt disputes. This chapter traces how the lack of an international bankruptcy paradigm for sovereign debt undermines efforts to restructure sovereign debt. As a consequence of this legal vacuum, Chap. 2 argues that creditors have fewer incentives to accept the reduced payouts on their sovereign bonds and instead seek litigious means by which to recover their full investments. In addition, after reviewing the judicial decisions made in cases involving sovereign

[8] Rault (2017); Guzman and Stiglitz (2016), pp. 3–32; Waibel (2007).

bonds, this chapter observes that, whereas states once enjoyed a certain level of immunity, there has been a steady decline in sovereign immunity as creditors employed increasingly sophisticated legal tactics against debtor states, including arbitration. Chapter 2 concludes by explaining how international investment agreements work and the arbitration system that has arisen therefrom.

The purpose of Chap. 3 is to give a detailed definition and analysis of the mediation process so as to gain in-depth insight into how mediation could be applied in the sovereign debt dispute context. Accordingly, this chapter reviews past and present definitions of mediation before suggesting a working definition in the context of sovereign debt mediations. It then goes on to distinguish mediation from the seemingly similar but different settlement technique of conciliation, which is well-anchored in the investor-state domain but which has had only limited success to date. Thereafter, the chapter sheds light on the different phases of the mediation process, their purpose and how they are organized. It also describes the training and techniques mediators use to help parties agree on settlement terms. Mediators' techniques are focused on a negotiated outcome based on the parties' interests, as opposed to imposing an outcome based solely on the parties' legal positions. Such mediation techniques can lead to more efficient outcomes. Moreover, reflecting the divergent needs that might arise depending on the parties' characteristics or the circumstances surrounding the dispute, this chapter also describes the multitude of mediation styles that have developed to cater to those specific needs and describes the various criteria that the parties or the mediator can use to select the most appropriate style to resolve their dispute. In addition to having the possibility of selecting from various mediation styles, Chap. 3 also posits that parties may additionally resort to blended styles of mediation involving a combination of mediation and arbitration, which might be useful where the circumstances are not ripe for mediation or where different aspects of the dispute require different dispute resolution mechanisms. Subsequently, this chapter turns to the underlying legal framework on both a domestic and international level for mediation with regards to how parties are compelled to mediate, what procedural and ethical safeguards are put in place for the proceedings and the legal effect of an eventual settlement agreement. Most importantly, with respect to the investor-state context, this chapter also describes the Singapore Convention which grants certain mediated agreements the status of an enforceable, final judgment and the potential of the Singapore Convention to apply to sovereign debt disputes and the benefits thereof.

Having examined mediation in detail in Chap. 3, the goal of Chap. 4 is to explore the potential of mediation more specifically in the context of sovereign debt disputes. Accordingly, this chapter will discuss the advantages as well as the disadvantages of mediating in this context, particularly in comparison with arbitral proceedings. The analysis in this section of the chapter is framed on either side by sovereign bond creditors' established trend of linking their claims to investment treaties and the growing public policy concerns raised by investment arbitration proceedings in terms of cost and transparency and their effect on economic recovery. Chapter 4 also identifies the various practical aspects of mediating sovereign debt disputes, such as commencing the proceedings, choosing a set of rules to govern the procedure and selecting the mediator. Additionally, Chap. 4 identifies the obstacles that could block sovereign bond creditors and states from mediating their disputes, such as misunderstanding and a lack of information about the mediation process as well as political resistance. Consequently, this chapter examines various coercive and beneficial measures that stakeholders can put into place towards promoting mediation in the investor-state and sovereign debt dispute context. Lastly, Chap. 4 seeks to examine the empirical evidence by considering the case studies of the Argentine and Greek sovereign debt crises and the potential for mediation between the respective sovereign bondholders and debtor governments.

Finally, Chap. 5 concludes with the main findings of the thesis and some thoughts on further areas of research.

References

Articles

Bolton P (2004) Inside the black box: how should a sovereign bankruptcy regime be structured? Fac Scholar Penn Law 53:707

Claxton JM (2020) Compelling parties to mediate investor-state disputes: no pressure, no diamonds? Pepp Disp Resol Law J 20:78

Note (2014) Mediation of investor-state conflicts. Harv Law Rev 127(8):2543

Rogoff K, Zettelmeyer J (2002) Bankruptcy procedures for sovereigns: a history of ideas, 1976-2001. Int Monetary Fund Staff Pap 49:470

Schwarcz SL (2000) Sovereign debt restructuring: a bankruptcy reorganiztltion approach. Cornell Law Rev 85:956

Waibel M (2007) Opening Pandora's box: sovereign bonds in international arbitration. Am J Int Law 101:711

Books and Book Chapters

Ams J, Baqir R, Gelpern A et al (2020) Sovereign default. In: Abbas A, Pienkowski A, Rogoff K (eds) Sovereign debt: a guide for economists and practitioners. Oxford University Press

Guzman M, Stiglitz JE (2016) Creating a framework for sovereign debt restructuring that works. In: Guzman M, Ocampo JA, Stiglitz JE (eds) Too little, too late. Columbia University Press

Rault CJ (2017) The legal framework of sovereign debt management. In: Geiwitz A, Kebekus F, Knecht TC et al (eds) Schriften zur Restrukturierung, vol 9. Nomos

Official Reports

Asonuma T, Chamon M, Erce A et al (2019) Costs of sovereign defaults: restructuring strategies, bank distress and the capital inflow-credit channel. International Monetary Fund Working Paper WP/19/69

Bohoslavsky JP (2017) Effects of foreign debt and other related financial obligations of States on the full enjoyment of all human rights, particularly economic, social and cultural rights. Report of the Independent Expert to the United Nations General Assembly

ICSID (2021) Overview of investment treaty clauses on mediation. https://icsid.worldbank.org/sites/default/files/publications/Overview_Mediation_in_Treaties.pdf

United Nations Treaty Collection (Treaties.un.org, 2021) https://treaties.un.org/pages/ViewDetails.aspx?src=TREATY&mtdsg_no=XXII-4&chapter=22&clang=_en

Sources

United Nations Convention on International Settlement Agreements Resulting from Mediation (Singapore Convention, 2018)

Chapter 2
Historical and Legal Framework

Historically, a combination of political, practical and legal circumstances have largely shielded states from the enforcement of their debts to sovereign bondholders.[1] Unlike corporations, it is not possible to liquidate (*i.e.* turn into cash) the assets of a defaulting state.[2] In addition, the majority of a state's assets are located inside the country rendering it extremely difficult to compel a sovereign to pay its creditors.[3] Moreover, legal doctrine has protected debtor states until at least halfway into the twenty-first century, most notably through the principle of absolute sovereign immunity, which prevented governments from lawsuits in foreign courts.[4] As a result, creditors were constrained either to accept sovereign defaults and restructurings or to attempt (often unsuccessfully) to lobby their own governments for support through trade sanctions or military interventions.[5]

This chapter sets out the historical and legal framework of the sovereign financing system. The purpose of this chapter is to demonstrate how the development of the sovereign financing system undermines orderly debt restructuring and leads to litigation between debtor states and its creditors. The main arguments of this chapter are that the decline in sovereign immunity combined with the lack of an international bankruptcy mechanism for sovereign debt, have allowed creditors to use international investment treaties and investment arbitration against debtor governments as part of an aggressive litigation strategy to secure their full investments. With this in mind, Sect. 2.1 will describe the gradual decline in sovereign immunity that accompanied the increasingly advanced legal strategies by which creditors sought to

[1] Schumacher et al. (2021); Blackman and Mukhi (2007), pp. 49–50; Foster (2008); Fisch and Gentile (2004), p. 1043.

[2] Id.

[3] Id.

[4] Weidemaier (2014), p. 77.

[5] Id.

C. M. Sudborough, *Mediating Sovereign Debt Disputes*, EYIEL Monographs - Studies in European and International Economic Law 35,
https://doi.org/10.1007/978-3-031-46787-5_2

recover their investments and which introduced a new kind of litigious actor in the sovereign debt market. This section also depicts the lack of an international bankruptcy paradigm for sovereign debt, similar to the bankruptcy legislation which generally exists on the national level. Accordingly, Sect. 2.1 demonstrates that in the absence of an orderly manner for restructuring sovereign debt, creditors have few alternatives than to seek litigious measures against debtor states, including arbitration proceedings pursuant to investment treaties. Section 2.2 reviews the Argentine and Greek debt crises of the early 2000's and their debt renegotiation efforts. The aim of this section is to better comprehend the complications governments and creditors face in renegotiating sovereign debt to the satisfaction of all stakeholders and the resulting costs to the national economy and society. Finally, Sect. 2.3 explains the workings of international investment agreements and the specific arbitration system created thereunder.

2.1 Declining Sovereign Immunity and Restructuring Sovereign Debt

Following World War II, state-owned companies became increasingly active across borders.[6] As these state owned-companies benefitted from legal immunity they had an unfair competitive advantage over private enterprises.[7] Furthermore, in the context of the Cold War period, Western governments were worried about holding Soviet firms legally accountable for their international commercial activities.[8] Accordingly, the United States and a number of European countries began to restrict the sovereign immunity doctrine.[9] In 1976, the U.S. government passed the Foreign Sovereign Immunities Act (FSIA), which permits private parties to file litigation against a foreign state in U.S. courts for the breach of commercial contracts.[10] The United Kingdom followed suit with similar legislation, notably the State Immunity Act of 1978, as well as many other countries soon thereafter.[11]

For illustrative purposes, this section of the thesis will focus on the United States as an example of the evolution of sovereign debt and sovereign immunity. Reviewing the history of government debt litigation following the FSIA, one can observe the ongoing degeneration of sovereign immunity, categorized into three principal periods associated with prominent legal decisions: (i) erosion of sovereign

[6] Megginson (2018), pp. 13–24.

[7] Weidemaier (2014).

[8] Schumacher et al. (2021); Sturzenegger and Zettelmeyer (2007).

[9] Weidemaier (2014).

[10] Schumacher et al. (2021); Waibel (2007); Sturzenegger and Zettelmeyer (2007).

[11] United Kingdom State Immunity Act of 1978; Megginson (2018).

immunity; (ii) entry of specialized hedge funds; and (iii) asset seizures and *pari passu*.[12] These will now be considered in turn.

2.1.1 Initial Post-FSIA Cases and the Erosion of Sovereign Immunity

In the wake of the Latin American debt crisis, litigious creditors filed a wave of lawsuits seeking a better recovery than the outcome of the "London Club" negotiation process.[13] The London Club negotiation process refers to the establishment of an *ad hoc* Bank Advisory Committee to organize meetings between commercial creditors and a debtor.[14] In 1982, Allied Bank, the agent of thirty-nine creditor banks, filed the first prominent case relying on the FSIA against three government-owned Costa Rican banks after the actions of the Costa Rican government provoked the defendant banks to default on their debts (*Allied Bank Intern. v. Banco Credito Agricola*).[15] The creditors sought to recover on the promissory notes issued by the Costa Rican banks which were payable in U.S. dollars in New York City.[16] Although the New York Second Circuit ruled in favor of the creditors, the U.S. government pressured the plaintiff to settle out of court on the same terms as the other creditors.[17] Despite this settlement, the legal judgment established an important precedent demonstrating that a "holdout" strategy, meaning a strategy of refraining from cooperating in debt renegotiations, can succeed and that a government's attempted defenses under the sovereign immunity doctrine would not protect the state from liability.[18] Accordingly, the *Allied* case was a critical precedent because it established that the sovereign immunity doctrine did not protect states from liability with regard to its bond creditors and therefore this case paved the path for creditor litigation against indebted sovereign states.

The next pivotal case was *Republic of Argentina v. Weltover, Inc* in which the U.S. Supreme Court's 1992 decision confirmed that debtor governments were no longer protected from creditors' legal claims.[19] Pursuant to the judgment, the justices' held that issuing sovereign bonds on international capital markets constitutes a commercial activity and that defaulting on those bonds, if issued under

[12] Schumacher et al. (2021).

[13] Id.

[14] Vitale (1995).

[15] *Allied Bank Intern. v. Banco Credito Agricola* 757 F.2d 516 (1985); Schumacher et al. (2021).

[16] Id.

[17] Id.

[18] Schumacher et al. (2021).

[19] *Republic of Argentina v. Weltover, Inc* 504 U.S. 607 (1992); Schumacher et al. (2021).

U.S. law, establishes jurisdiction of U.S. courts according to the provisions of the FSIA.[20]

2.1.2 CIBC v. Banco Centra do Brazil *and the Entry of Vulture Funds*

In 1995, the decision of the U.S. District Court for the Southern District of New York in *CIBC Bank and Trust Company (Cayman) Limited v. Banco Centra do Brazil* marked the start of a major shift in the sovereign debt litigation landscape as the first success by a new type of plaintiff: specialized distressed debt funds, which would later be called "vulture funds".[21] Vulture funds are established with the sole purpose of investing in distressed debt with a high risk of default at a discounted price in order to consequently recover compensation at many times their investment by engaging in protracted litigation until they win or the state settles the case.[22] Using such tactics, vulture funds achieve exorbitant profits, on average obtaining recovery rates of 3–20 times their investment, or 300–2000 per cent.[23] Often, these funds are founded in tax havens and exist only as long as needed to pursue a specific case.[24]

The *CIBC* case was the first in which a vulture fund was successful in its strategy to employ litigation against sovereign bond-issuing governments to achieve a significant profit, thereby making this an attractive scheme for other vulture funds. The *CIBC* case was instigated by the Cayman Islands-based investment company, CIBC Bank and Trust Company (Cayman) Limited, run by the Dart family, which had purchased U.S.$ 1.4 billion in Brazilian long-term debt.[25] Refusing to participate with all the other creditors in Brazil's 1992 debt restructuring under the program called the "Brady Plan" led by the U.S. and multilateral lending agencies to resolve the Latin American debt crisis, the Dart family chose to file a lawsuit in court instead, where it received a favorable judgment and a considerable profit.[26]

From the standpoint of legal precedent, the *CIBC* case significantly undermined the defense under the Champerty Doctrine, which bars lawsuits on claims procured wholly for the purposes of filing litigation, after it was rejected by the court.[27] Accordingly, the *CIBC* ruling, which was followed in subsequent cases, essentially

[20] Id.

[21] *CIBC Bank & Trust Co. v. Banco Cent. Do Brasil* 886 F. Supp. 1105 (S.D.N.Y. 1995); Schumacher et al. (2021).

[22] Blackman and Mukhi (2007), pp. 49–50; Ziegler (2015).

[23] Ziegler (2015).

[24] Schumacher et al. (2021).

[25] Id; Power (1996); Schmidt (2015).

[26] Schumacher et al. (2021); Buckley and Arner (2011), pp. 49–50; Sturzenegger and Zettelmeyer (2007).

[27] Id.

made holdout strategies legally viable and made possible vulture funds' business strategy of buying discounted distressed debt with the purpose of suing for the full amount.[28] Therefore, the *CIBC* decision and subsequent rulings served to encourage vulture funds to seek out risky investments at discount prices by providing them with a legal avenue to collect on their investments with a significant profit.[29] This suggests that vulture funds are employing the investment arbitration system to override their assumed business risk.[30] Consequently, one can observe a progression between the *Allied* and the *CIBC* cases, the first neutralizing the sovereign immunity doctrine and the second establishing a favorable legal climate for vulture funds. The next case will address the issue of seizing sovereign assets to enforce favorable judgments.

2.1.3 Elliott v. Peru*: Asset Seizures and the New* Pari Passu *Strategy*

Although sovereign immunity from lawsuits is no longer a hurdle for holdout creditors, attachment, or protection from the seizure of assets, to enforce favorable judgments continues to be a hurdle for various reasons.[31] Specifically, creditors may be unable to compel governments to comply with adverse decisions for the following reasons: (i) the court system of the indebted state is insufficiently independent to do so; (ii) the sovereign holds few assets outside of the country; (iii) the sovereign property located abroad is maintained indirectly through corporations that are legally distinct from the sovereign, or (iv) because sovereign immunity laws create such narrow circumstances for enforcement that creditors are effectively left without recourse.[32]

As a consequence of this attachment dilemma, creditors developed a strategy of enforcement based on the *pari passu* clause found in the majority of sovereign debt contracts.[33] *Pari passu* means "*equal in right of payment*".[34] Pursuant to the *pari passu* principle, all unsecured creditors in insolvency processes, must share equally any available assets of the insolvent entity or individual, or any proceeds from the sale thereof, proportionate to the debts due to each creditor.[35] *Pari passu*, although subject to conflicting interpretations, is essentially meant to ensure the comparability

[28] Id.

[29] Euler (2013), pp. 560–564.

[30] Iversen (2019), p. 57.

[31] Foster (2008), pp. 666–731.

[32] Id.

[33] Schumacher et al. (2021); Gulati and Scott (2013); Foster (2008), pp. 666–731.

[34] Bratton (2004), pp. 823, 830.

[35] Id.

of the treatment of creditors and is one of the most fundamental principles of insolvency law.[36]

In *Elliott Associates, LP v. Republic of Peru*, the hedge fund Elliott Associates, LP ("Elliott") argued that the *pari passu* clause obligated Peru to give equal treatment to its creditors therefore preventing Peru from paying the participating creditors to the restructuring scheme at the expense of the holdout creditors.[37] Using this argument, Elliott successfully obtained a restraining order from a Brussels court of appeal blocking an interest payment Peru was scheduled to make on its Brady bonds.[38] Brady bonds are sovereign debt securities, issued by developing countries but denominated in U.S. dollars and guaranteed by U.S. Treasury bonds.[39] Brady bonds were introduced in 1989 to help restructure developing countries' debt as part of the "Brady Plan" which was named after former U.S. Treasury Secretary Nicholas Brady.[40] Fearing a new default now on its Brady bonds, Peru was forced to settle with the hedge fund at U.S.$ 58 million, representing a 400 per cent profit over the price of the defaulted bonds for the hedge fund.[41] Unsurprisingly, this decision opened the floodgates to a surge of analogous *pari passu*-based lawsuits and settlements.[42]

2.1.4 Challenges to Sovereign Debt Restructuring

As a result of the global COVID-19 pandemic, the increased government spending and decrease in revenue has increased government debt tremendously.[43] OECD governments borrowed U.S.$ 18 trillion from the markets in 2020, equivalent to approximately 29% of GDP.[44] For comparison, this level of government debt is 60% greater than in 2019 and 12 percentage points higher relative to GDP.[45] Dominating the international financial market for sovereign lending are sovereign bonds, debt instruments by which creditors advance money in exchange for the promise of

---

[36] Schumacher et al. (2021); Buckley and Arner (2011); Sturzenegger and Zettelmeyer (2007), p. 56; Waibel (2013).

[37] *Elliott Associates, LP v Republic of Peru* [1998] 12 F Supp 2d 328 (SDNY 1998); Schumacher et al. (2021); Olivares-Caminal (2011), p. 39.

[38] Schumacher et al. (2021); Olivares-Caminal (2011).

[39] Investopedia, 'Brady Bonds' https://www.investopedia.com/terms/b/bradybonds.asp, accessed 23 July 2021.

[40] Id.

[41] Schumacher et al. (2021); Olivares-Caminal (2011); Elliott Assocs., L.P., General Docket No. 2000/QR/92, 16 (Court of Appeal of Brussels, eighth Chamber, Sept. 26, 2000).

[42] Schumacher et al. (2021); Olivares-Caminal (2011).

[43] OECD, 'Sovereign Borrowing Outlook for OECD Countries: 2021' (2021).

[44] Id.

[45] Id.

repayment of principal (i.e. the original amount of the loan) and interest.[46] The providers of financing are either so-called 'official creditors', such as other states and international development institutions like the World Bank, the International Monetary Fund (IMF) or bilateral governmental agencies, or 'private creditors' including private banks, funds or retail commercial creditors.[47] After being issued on the primary market, sovereign bonds may subsequently be traded on the secondary market by 'underwriters' or 'intermediaries' to virtually anyone producing a large number of highly varied creditors around the world.[48]

However, contrary to the private debt market, there is no national or international bankruptcy procedure that can ensure an orderly restructuring of the debt of a sovereign that has defaulted on its bonds, despite the numerous suggestions that have been made to that effect.[49] Thus, when a state is unable to repay its debts, it is the sovereign debtor's responsibility to enter into voluntary negotiations with its numerous and diverse creditors around the world and to reach a consensus despite their different agendas in order to obtain an acceptable restructuring of its debts.[50]

Since the debt restructuring process is voluntary, a creditor may refuse to accept a 'haircut' (a reduced reimbursement of their loan) and instead 'hold out' and seek a legal strategy to enforce their contractual rights via state litigation.[51] Whenever one or more creditors agrees to relieve a country's debt by reducing its claims, the value of the remaining creditors' claims increases, creating a free rider problem in which there is an incentive for the 'holdout creditors' to benefit at the expense of the creditors who have reduced their claims by seeking full payment through various legal remedies.[52] Moreover as mentioned in Sect. 2.1.2 above, secondary sovereign debt market has attracted a specific category of hedge funds, known as vulture funds, that seek to recover compensation at many times their investment by buying distressed sovereign bonds at a discounted price with a high risk of default, refusing to participate in restructuring and then engaging in protracted litigation until they win or the state settles the case.[53] As discussed previously, by "preying" on distressed sovereign bonds, vulture funds achieve extortionate profits, often obtaining a full return on their investment many, many times over.[54]

As has been described in Sect. 2.1, the gradual decline in sovereign immunity starting in the mid-1970s to the present has encouraged increasingly aggressive litigation techniques by sovereign debt creditors. Moreover, specialized hedge funds have developed in recent years, seeking not only to recover on their

[46] Waibel (2013), pp. 7–11.

[47] Id.

[48] Power (1996).

[49] Rogoff and Zettelmeyer (2002), pp. 470–500.

[50] Wright (2012), p. 172.

[51] Id.

[52] Id; Waibel (2007), p. 722.

[53] Blackman and Mukhi (2007), pp. 49–50; Ziegler (2015).

[54] Id.

investments but to make a significant profit by specifically targeting states with weak economies. In light of the gaping hole in international law which lacks any sovereign bankruptcy procedure, the voluntary debt renegotiation process between indebted governments and their sovereign bond holders incentivizes non-participating creditors, at the expense of participating creditors, to pursue legal strategies to obtain profitable compensation.

2.2 Sovereign Debt Organization: Case Studies of Argentina and Greece

In this section, we will review the Argentine and Greek sovereign debt crises as case studies. After examining the history of Argentina and Greece's high levels of debt we will study and compare their debt restructuring negotiations. By using Greece and Argentina as case studies, we can better understand the difficulties governments and creditors face in renegotiating sovereign debt satisfactorily as well as the economic and social costs thereof. This context will be useful in examining the value of mediating sovereign debt disputes.

Argentina and Greece have become synonymous with the term "debt crisis".[55] Both countries amassed mammoth debts, which in turn destabilized their economies, provoked internal unrest, diminished wages and rising inflation.[56] As a consequence, Argentina and Greece have since had to implement measures imposed upon them by their creditors, impinging upon their sovereignty.[57] We will begin by understanding the origins of their high levels of debt.

2.2.1 History of Argentina's High Levels of Debt

There was nothing unexpected or abrupt about Argentina's default on its sovereign debt on 23 December 2001.[58] From 1972 to 1985 during Argentina's military dictatorship, many private Argentine companies were made public which coincided with a massive increase in Argentina's external debt from U.S.$ 8 billion to U.S.$ 43 billion.[59] The subsequent post-dictatorship government, under the leadership of Raul Alfonsin, attempted to correct the skyrocketing external debt and to steady the Argentine economy by introducing the "Austral Plan", which immobilized wages

[55] Butenskey (2017), pp. 164, 169.

[56] Id.

[57] Id.

[58] Schilling (2012), p. 160; Samples (2014), pp. 52, 64; Oliveri (1992), p. 164.

[59] Butenskey (2017), p. 164.

and prices.[60] Initially the Austral plan provoked a drop in inflation and a growth in GDP. Ultimately however, the Austral plan was unable to stabilize Argentina's fragile economy resulting in hyperinflation.[61] Consequently, the Argentine government adopted Ley N°23.928 attaching Argentina's new currency, the "Austral" (as well as the subsequent Argentine peso), to the U.S. dollar's value in an effort to control inflation.[62] Moreover, Argentina followed the International Monetary Fund ("IMF") policy for economic equilibrium and growth, which generally involves budget restrictions, balancing payment deficits, raising interest rates, reducing inflation, privatizing State assets and minimizing trade barriers and controlling capital flows in and out of the country.[63]

Despite the initial diminution in inflation following the implementation of these measures, Argentina's high level of public debt persisted requiring the government to seek IMF loans in order to attempt to pay off creditors.[64] As a result, Argentina had acquired U.S.$ 11 billion in loans in 1995, including U.S.$ 2.4 billion from the IMF.[65] These loans came at a cost because they were contingent upon Argentina implementing various economic reforms and austerity measures.[66] These measures included, amongst others, overhauling its social security system, improving tax compliance, trimming its budget deficit and augmenting the minimum retirement age.[67] However, the combination of these austerity measures with the IMF's above-described economic stabilization policy made it practically inevitable for Argentina's economy to fall into recession.[68]

In 1998, 3 years after their government's acquisition of the IMF loans and implementation of the austerity measures that accompanied them and suffering from unemployment, reduced spending and increased taxes, the Argentine people launched violent strikes against the restrictive economic measures.[69] Notwithstanding the public's growing discontent with the IMF-imposed economic measures, the IMF granted another U.S.$ 40 billion loan in 2000.[70] However, as Argentina's economic outlook deteriorated and funding from international capital markets shrank, the IMF's outlook on Argentina became increasingly unsympathetic.[71]

---

[60] Id; Snyder (1994), p. 102.

[61] Maute (2006), pp. 26–27.

[62] Id.

[63] Paddock (2002), p. 158.

[64] International Monetary Fund, 'The Role of the IMF in Argentina, 1991–2002' (2003).

[65] Paddock (2002), p. 158.

[66] International Monetary Fund, 'Memorandum of Economic Policies of the Government of Argentina' (2000).

[67] Id.

[68] Paddock (2002), p. 158; Gallagher et al. (2011).

[69] Linares (2005), p. 20; Krauss (2000).

[70] BBC News, 'Argentina profile – Timeline' (2015).

[71] International Monetary Fund, 'The Role of the IMF in Argentina, 1991–2002' (2003).

This culminated in the IMF's refusal in December 2001 to pay out a U.S.$ 1.24 billion loan citing the country's failure to meet budget deficit benchmarks.[72]

Soon afterward, Argentina chose to default on its U.S.$ 102 billion debt, which was the "largest sovereign debt default in history" at that time.[73] Some 500 thousand creditors around the world held this colossal debt through 152 unpaid debt instruments, denominated in "six currencies under the laws of eight different jurisdictions."[74] Overwhelmed by the amount of debt and diversity of creditors, Argentina declared a temporary moratorium on principal and interest payments (Padlock Law).[75] Conversely, faced with the moratorium and the lack of an institutional partner to assist in the negotiations, a majority of Argentina's creditors were obliged to accept a disfavorably lopsided deal during each of Argentina's two main debt exchanges.[76]

In 2005, Argentina temporarily suspended the Padlock Law and initiated its first bond exchange for a new unsecured debt at a rate of 25–29 cents on the dollar in exchange for creditors waiving certain rights for recovery.[77] Faced with the threat that Argentina would not repay creditors that did not proffer their bonds, participation in the bond exchange reached 76%.[78] In 2010, Argentina suspended the Padlock Law for a second time to launch a second bond exchange with its remaining creditors offering similar payment terms as the 2005 bonds.[79] Following the 2010 bond exchange, between 91% and 93% of Argentina's creditors participated in Argentina's debt restructuring scheme.[80] The remaining holdout creditors pursued full payment of Argentina's debt in the State courts of New York and ICSID arbitration proceedings.[81]

2.2.2 *Greece: Near-Default and Debt Restructuring*

Like Argentina, Greece can trace its high levels of debt to the 1970s, when the Greek government controlled the economy with a network of state-owned companies.[82] These economic policies failed to support high rates of economic growth and instead

---

72 Graham and Masson (2002).

73 Butenskey (2017), p. 166.

74 Id.

75 Joiner (2015), p. 94.

76 Samples (2014), pp. 49, 66.

77 Argentine Law No. 26547, art. 1, Dec. 9, 2009, B.O. 31798; Samples (2014), p. 74.

78 Butenskey (2017), p. 166.

79 Argentine Law No. 26547, art. 1, Dec. 9, 2009, B.O. 31798.

80 Joiner (2015), p. 88.

81 Butenskey (2017), pp. 166–167. See also Chap. II.

82 Macias (2012), p. 264; Nations Encyclopedia.

promoted excessive levels of debt.[83] Over the course of the following decade, Greece's sovereign debt rose from 25% of GDP to 100%.[84] The government's macroeconomic policies failed to foster economic growth or prevent high inflation.[85]

Despite Greece's high inflation and low economic growth, the nation was able to meet the strict eligibility criteria for membership in the European Monetary Union (EMU) in 2001, replacing the Drachma with the Euro as its currency.[86] In particular, the Maastricht Treaty's admissibility benchmarks for membership in the EU's common currency required, *inter alia*, that national debt must not surpass 60% of GDP and that inflation levels not surpass 1.5% more than the average inflation of the three EU member States with the strongest economy.[87] Greece's sudden economic improvement raised suspicion amongst commentators that this was only possible due to fraud, which the Greek government rejected.[88] Those who challenged Greece's entry into the EMU alleged that Greece disguised the true data regarding its actual GDP, deficit and debt using "deceptive accounting policies, in conjunction with the EMU's strict adherence to sovereignty".[89]

In any case, thanks to Greece's membership in the EMU, the government was able to obtain large amounts of low-priced debt, a temporary boon which ultimately led to worse economic troubles.[90] Despite its membership in the EMU, the European Central Bank (ECB) excluded Greek bonds from the ECB's covered bond purchase program as they were considered too risky.[91] As a result, the Greek government was compelled to seek new loans to pay off its accumulating debt.[92] Greece's staggering levels of debt along with the global financial crisis culminated in May 2010 in a EUR 110 billion (U.S.$ 145 billion) bailout loan with the "Troika".[93] The Troika refers to the amalgamation of the IMF, the European Commission (EC) and the ECB.[94] Whereas Argentina received its funding mainly through the IMF, Greece obtained

83 Id.

84 Alogoskoufis (2012), p. 4.

85 Id pp. 16–17.

86 Council Decision 2000/427/EC of 19 June 2000 in accordance with Article 122(2) of the Treaty on the adoption by Greece of the single currency on 1 January 2001 [2000] Official Journal L 167 of 7 July 2000.

87 Treaty on European Union, Protocol on the Convergence Criteria Referred to in Article 109j of the Treaty Establishing the European Community art. 1, Feb. 7, 1992, 1759 U.N.T.S. 3 ("Maastricht Treaty").

88 Macias (2012), p. 264; Nations Encyclopedia.

89 Macias (2012), pp. 263–264; Nations Encyclopedia; Little (2012).

90 Gutierrez (2013), p. 438; 'A Synopsis of the Greek Debt Crisis' (2011).

91 'ECB announces operational details of asset backed securities and covered bond purchase programmes' (2014).

92 Butenskey (2017), p. 168.

93 Thomas et al. (2011); 'IMF Survey: Europe and IMF Agree €110 Billion Financing Plan with Greece' (2010).

94 European Stability Mechanism 'Enter the troika: the European Commission, the IMF, the ECB'.

its funding from other Eurozone members as well as the IMF, but only contingent on the implementation of stricter austerity measures in Greece:

> The European Commission (EC) jointly with the European Central Bank (ECB) supervise the implementation of the program's conditionality on behalf of the euro zone creditor countries, along with the IMF. The EC/ECB/IMF are often referred to as the "Troika" of creditors, even though the funding does not come directly from these institutions.[95]

Accordingly, although the European Commission and the European Central Bank did not directly provide funding to the Greek government, they supervised the Greek government's implementation of the conditions upon which the bailout loans had been provided to Greece along with the IMF, which had provided EUR 30 billion out of the total EUR 110 billion loan package.[96] The Troika required the Greek government to transform its economic policies by reducing spending, collecting more revenues and implementing processes to increase economic growth, such as "strengthening income and labor markets policies; better managing and investing in state enterprises and improving the business environment".[97]

Notwithstanding these various economic policies, the Greek economy failed to grow sufficiently leading the private sector to participate in a debt exchange program in 2011, which provided EUR 135 billion in private financing.[98] The following year, a committee of private and public creditors entered into a "historic" restructuring agreement for the EUR 206 billion held by the private sector.[99] The creditors were motivated to accept this restructuring agreement upon realizing that they could lose 75% of their investments if they failed to participate.[100]

This debt restructuring agreement consequently opened the door for a second bailout provided jointly by Eurozone countries and the IMF of EUR 130 billion.[101] This second bailout was stipulated upon, *inter alia*, the Greek government's transformation of the country's tax system, restructuring of the banking sector, scaling down of public administration and reform of the pension system.[102] The European Commission on Economic and Financial Affairs considered these conditions for funding as "disbursement by disbursement milestones", whereas the Greek people viewed these demands as far-reaching austerity measures that significantly encroached on their nation's sovereignty.[103] Moreover, these austerity measures

---

[95] Tsoukala (2013), p. 32.

[96] Id; 'IMF Survey: Europe and IMF Agree €110 Billion Financing Plan With Greece' (2010).

[97] Butenskey (2017), p. 169; IMF Survey Magazine (2010).

[98] Zettelmeyer et al. (2014), p. 520.

[99] Rooney (2012).

[100] Butenskey (2017), p. 169.

[101] Tsoukala (2013), p. 32.

[102] European Commission on Economic and Financial Affairs Occasional Papers No. 123 of Dec. 2012; European Commission on Economic and Financial Affairs Occasional Papers No. 148 of May 2013; European Commission on Economic and Financial Affairs Occasional Papers No. 159 of July 2013.

[103] Butenskey (2017), p. 169; Rooney (2012); Lapavitsas et al. (2011).

had a significantly negative impact on the country's economic growth and human rights.[104] In June 2014, Greece's unemployment rates soared to 26.6% with outstanding debt at 175% of the nation's GDP.[105] This bleak economic outlook failed to improve despite the injection of funding because Greece used the bailout money to pay off outstanding debts rather than investing in the restoration of the Greek economy.[106]

In January 2015, stuck in a powerless status quo, characterized by oppressive austerity measures and crushing debt, Greek voters elected the radical leftist Syriza party, led by Alexis Tsipras, which campaigned on an anti-austerity platform.[107] In June 2015, the new Tsipras government, having promised voters to "un-do the strict constraints of conditionality imposed by the EU and the International Monetary Fund", proclaimed that it would default on EUR 1.6 billion because the government's coffers were insufficient to "satisfy creditors at the same time as paying wages and pensions".[108] At the same time, there were strong insinuations that Greece planned to exit from the Eurozone, a possibility coined "Grexit", which would mark the "beginning of the end of the Eurozone".[109] These two threats gave Alexis Tsipras and his Syriza government leverage to attempt to renegotiate with the EU the terms of Greece's economic reforms in June 2015.[110]

Nevertheless, the Tsipras government's negotiation game failed to meet its objectives, accepting instead a third bailout package of EUR 86 billion to be disbursed over 3 years conditioned on EU-defined radical economic reforms.[111] The Syriza government did obtain one significant concession however as the deal permitted the Greek government to avoid default on a EUR 3.2 billion debt to the European Central Bank.[112]

2.2.3 *Comparing the Argentine and Greek Debt Restructuring Negotiations*

Argentina chose to default on its debt whereas Greece chose a different path to restructuring its debt. Understanding the underlying motives for these divergent

---

[104] Housos (2015), p. 432.

[105] Leivada (2015); Georgiopoulos and Babington (2014).

[106] Shell (2015); Gallagher et al. (2011).

[107] Lakhani (2015).

[108] Smits (2015).

[109] Inman (2015a, b).

[110] BBC News, 'Greece submits new reform plan to EU and IMF' (2015).

[111] Traynor (2015).

[112] Butenskey (2017), p. 169; Rooney (2012); EuroNews, 'Greece repays ECB after tapping fresh bailout funds' (2015).

paths and their outcomes is useful in examining the value of a mediated outcome to sovereign debt disputes between sovereigns and creditors.[113]

Various analysts cited Argentina's post-default, positive economic results to encourage Greece to default as well.[114] Shortly following default, Argentina's economy rebounded with an initial reduction in its debt-to-GDP ratio.[115] However, as for any country, the costs of default would have been multiple for Greece.[116] Starting with blocked access to financial markets and an economy in nose-dive, a default could have also resulted in suppressed foreign trade due to trade sanctions resulting in financial isolation and a subsequent banking crisis.[117] When a debtor nation loses access to financial markets, creditors must also accept haircuts to recuperate on their losses, whereas if the indebted country is given time to regain access to capital it is in a better position to repay its debtors in full.[118]

In addition, those who advocated a Greek default based on the "success" of the Argentine model, failed to expose the difficulties Argentina faced following its brief economic renaissance following default.[119] Ultimately, the Argentine default and longstanding refusal to pay holdout creditors negatively affected its stock market and the country's reputation, as it was viewed as an "untrustworthy borrower in the international capital markets".[120] Moreover, a Greek default would have also likely cost Greece its membership in the EU.[121] Despite the Syriza government's populist platform and threats of a Grexit, many were still wary of such a dramatic outcome.[122] The Greek government was aware that it would have been unable to obtain new, more advantageous debt and to restructure the old debt without the Troika's assistance.[123] The Troika's involvement in debt restructuring negotiations played an important role in reassuring and incentivizing creditors to participate.[124] The debt-restructuring package itself reduced the Greek bonds' face value and prolonged their maturity dates.[125] In addition, the involvement of European institutions facilitated the signing of the multilateral Treaty Establishing the European Stability Mechanism, which directed that "all new euro area government securities with maturity above 1 year issued on or after 1 January 2013" shall include collective action

113 Cibils (2015); Elliot (2015).

114 Creighton (2015); Krugman (2015).

115 Cibils and Lo Vuolo (2007), p. 773.

116 Wright (2012), p. 158.

117 Id p. 159.

118 Gallagher (2013), pp. 41–62.

119 Schubert (2013), p. 1129.

120 Id p. 1129.

121 Georgakopoulos (2012), p. 27.

122 Angeletos et al. (2017).

123 Georgakopoulos (2012), p. 27; Thrasher (2021), pp. 103–124.

124 Chambers and Spink (2012).

125 Thrasher (2021), pp. 103–124; Chambers and Spink (2012).

clauses (CACs).[126] CACs are included into bonds to prevent holdout creditors from undermining the debt restructuring process.[127] Such clauses in sovereign bonds authorize modification and restructuring thereof provided a majority of bondholders agree to the proposed amendments.[128]

Nevertheless, the "Troika's Framework" and assistance, although instrumental in Greece's debt restructuring efforts, came at a biting cost. As detailed above, aid disbursement hinged upon the implementation of loathsome austerity measures that impinged upon Greece's sovereignty.[129] For some observers, the Troika's supervisory framework allegedly usurped "rewriting Greek laws" and even "redesigning the social fabric".[130] Nevertheless, Greece accepted this painful infringement on its sovereignty to avoid finding itself in the same isolated position in debt negotiations that Argentina found itself immediately post-crisis.[131]

Despite the parallels in the origins of the Argentine and Greek debt crises, the outlook on Argentina's debt restructuring differed from that of Greece.[132] Despite the IMF's initial lead in Argentina's debt restructuring endeavors, Argentina later decided to forego the IMF's assistance and negotiate on its own to avoid the problems presented by the fact that the IMF was itself one of Argentina's creditors.[133] However, without an institutional negotiation partner, Argentina was at a disadvantage during the 2005 and 2010 bond exchanges.[134] Lacking any assistance from International Financial Institutions (IFI), Argentina could only resort to its national law to restructure its debt.[135] As described previously, the Argentine government enacted the Padlock Law and other legal devices to pressure bondholders to participate in restructuring.[136] Despite their efforts, 7% of Argentina's bondholders persisted as holdout creditors because they possessed Fiscal Agency Agreement (FAA) bonds governed by New York law.[137] Since the FAA bonds did not possess CACs, a small minority of bondholders were able to challenge Argentina's debt restructuring with all of its creditors.[138]

As can be observed from the Argentine and Greek sovereign debt crises, the lack of a centralized mechanism for restructuring sovereign debt complicated the process

---

126 Treaty Establishing the European Stability Mechanism (2012); European Union Economic and Financial Committee, 'Collective Action Clauses in the Euro Area'.

127 Hofmann (2013), p. 549.

128 Id.

129 Housos (2015), p. 432; Dale and El-Enany (2013), p. 628.

130 Sotiris (2012).

131 Lakhani (2015), p. 115; Stevenson (2015).

132 Butenskey (2017), p. 174.

133 Joiner (2015), p. 116; Thrasher (2021), pp. 103–124.

134 Samples (2014), p. 70.

135 Butenskey (2017), p. 169.

136 See Sect. 2.2.1.

137 Joiner (2015), p. 88.

138 Id.

for the governments' debt renegotiations' with its creditors. Although Argentina and Greece took different approaches, both governments' strategies resulted in painful austerity measures at great cost to their countries' economic recovery. Furthermore, in line with the decline in sovereign immunity this paved the way for creditors to use a new litigation tool against indebted governments: investment arbitration.

2.3 Investment Arbitration of Sovereign Debt Disputes

As mentioned in the introduction, the dispute between Argentina's government and its creditors lasted close to two decades. In addition to filing lawsuits, Argentina's creditors were the first to open the door to a different legal tool for resolving sovereign debt disputes in their search for a more efficient means of obtaining a favorable outcome: investment arbitration. Section 2.3 will begin by explaining the framework of international investment law based upon international investment agreements wherein investment arbitration has become the dispute resolution mechanism of choice. Then this segment will trace the jurisprudence of sovereign debt investment arbitration cases to date before analyzing the outcomes of those cases, the potential recognition and enforcement issues they have raised, as well as the costs of investment arbitration on economic recovery.

2.3.1 International Investment Agreements

International investment law is based on international investment agreements (IIAs). IIAs are treaties signed by countries, often bilateral investment treaties (BITs), committing to accord certain protections to foreign investments.[139] BITs generally provide a definition of "investment" and "investor" thus entitling the nationals of the contracting states to the protections accorded under the BIT insofar as their actions fall within the confines of the BIT's definition of investment.[140] Almost invariably, IIAs include a dispute resolution procedure that foresees arbitration for conflicts arising from investment activity within their scope.[141] Such investment arbitration proceedings may take place under the rules of the International Centre for the Settlement of Investment Disputes (ICSID), the UN Commission of International

---

[139] McLachlan et al. (2008).

[140] Ortolani (2017), pp. 49–88; Schlemmer (2008), pp. 49–88; Schreuer and Dolzer (2008), pp. 28–43.

[141] Convention on the Settlement of Investment Disputes between States and Nationals of Other States (ICSID Convention), 18 March 1965, 575 UNTS 159; Rules of Arbitration of the International Chamber of Commerce (2021) ("ICC Arbitration Rules"); Arbitration Rules of the Arbitration Institute of the Stockholm Chamber of Commerce (2017) ("SCC Arbitration Rules"); UNCITRAL Arbitration Rules (2013); Permanent Court of Arbitration Arbitration Rules (2012); ICSID Convention Article 54; Schreuer et al. (2009), pp. 71–347.

Trade Law (UNCITRAL), the International Chamber of Commerce (ICC), the Stockholm Chamber of Commerce (SCC) and the Permanent Court of Arbitration (PCA) as well as other competent legal bodies.[142] Investment arbitration presents various advantages and in particular, it provides for heightened enforceability.[143] For example, parties that engage in investment arbitration proceedings conducted under the Convention on the Settlement of Investment Disputes between States and Nationals of Other States (ICSID Convention), to which 155 countries are parties, are guaranteed that member states shall enforce the arbitral award without appeal, subject only to the procedures provided for in the ICSID Convention itself.[144] In other words, an award under the ICSID Convention is the same as a final judgment in the territory of ICSID member states.[145]

Bondholders seeking to file arbitration claims do so by categorizing their bonds as 'investments' in order to benefit from the arbitration clauses within a particular IIA.[146] Although the language of BITs varies, most set forth that investors can initiate arbitration proceedings under the ICSID Convention.[147] However, for sovereign bond creditors to establish jurisdiction or the right to file an investment arbitration claim under the ICSID Convention, they must first persuade the arbitral tribunal that their purchase of sovereign bonds constitutes an 'investment' pursuant to Article 25(1) of the ICSID Convention as well as the underlying BIT providing for ICSID arbitration.[148]

2.3.2 Sovereign Bonds Under Article 25 of the ICSID

Pursuant to Article 25(1) of the ICSID Convention, ICSID has subject matter jurisdiction over "any legal dispute arising directly out of an investment, between a Contracting State [. . .] and a national of another Contracting State".[149] The ICSID Convention does not provide a definition of the term "investment" but simply pronounces that ICSID's jurisdiction encompasses all disputes that are directly

[142] Id.

[143] ICSID Convention art 54; Schreuer et al. (2009), pp. 1115–1150.

[144] ICSID 'ICSID Convention' https://icsid.worldbank.org/resources/rules-and-regulations/convention/overview, accessed 15 October 2021; ICSID Convention art 54; Schreuer et al. (2009), pp. 1115–1150.

[145] ICSID Convention Article 54; Schreuer et al. (2009), pp. 1115–1150.

[146] ICSID Convention; ICC Arbitration Rules; SCC Arbitration Rules; UNCITRAL Arbitration Rules (2013); Permanent Court of Arbitration Arbitration Rules (2012); ICSID Convention Article 54; Schreuer et al. (2009), pp. 71–347.

[147] ICSID, 'Database of Bilateral Investment Treaties'; Yannaca-Small (2018); Pohl et al. (2012), pp. 10–12.

[148] ICSID Convention art 25(1); Schreuer et al. (2009), pp. 71–347.

[149] Id.

related to such investments.[150] Thus, although it is evident that sovereign bonds are covered by the common meaning of the term "investment", it is not immediately apparent whether sovereign bonds fall within the scope of Article 25(1) of the ICSID Convention since the ordinary meaning of 'investment' and the meaning as intended by ICSID Convention cannot be assumed to be the same.[151] Case law has examined the issue of whether sovereign bonds are investments for the purposes of the ICSID Convention.

2.3.2.1 *Fedax v. Venezuela*

The first arbitral tribunal to tackle the issue of whether sovereign debt instruments can be categorized as investment under Article 25 of the ICSID Convention was in the *Fedax v. Venezuela* case.[152] At issue in this case were six promissory notes that Venezuela had issued recognizing its debt for contractual services provided by a private company and which had subsequently been assigned to Fedax.[153] When Venezuela failed to repay its debt pursuant to the promissory notes, Fedax filed for ICSID arbitration proceedings.[154] Venezuela then objected to the arbitral tribunal's jurisdiction, arguing that the promissory notes did not meet the definitional requirements of an investment pursuant to Article 25(1) of the ICSID Convention since (i) they did not provide a sustained transfer of financial resources and (ii) since Fedax did not have a direct relationship with Venezuela having bought the promissory notes on the secondary market.[155]

Operating under the assumption that the common meaning of investment in finance is not automatically identical to the delineation of investment pursuant to the ICSID Convention, the tribunal referred to Christoph Schreuer's Commentary on the ICSID Convention.[156] In his commentary, Schreuer described an investment as protected under the ICSID Convention on condition that it posseses a number of fundamental characteristics including, duration, a certain regularity of profit and return, assumption of risk, a substantial commitment and a significant contribution to the host state's development, this has been called the "Salini Test" and is discussed below in the analysis of the *Abaclat* case.[157]

---

[150] Id.

[151] Id.

[152] *Fedax N.V. v. The Republic of Venezuela*, ICSID Case No. ARB/96/3, Decision of the Tribunal on Objections to Jurisdiction, 11 July 1997; Martin (2011).

[153] *Fedax* paragraph 16.

[154] Id paragraphs 1–14; Martin (2011).

[155] *Fedax* paragraph 18.

[156] Id; Schreuer et al. (2009).

[157] Id.

Applying Schreuer's analysis to the *Fedax* case, the tribunal found that the promissory notes qualified as an investment under the ICSID Convention.[158] According to the tribunal, the fact that the promissory notes were purchased on the secondary market was irrelevant since the state enjoyed "continuous credit benefit until the time the notes become due" regardless of whether the investor's identity changes.[159]

2.3.2.2 The Argentine Cases

In a series of three ICSID arbitration cases involving claims brought by Italian creditors against Argentina, which issued sovereign bonds pursuant to the 1990 Italy-Argentina BIT, the tribunals' decisions on jurisdiction consistently concluded that holders of sovereign bonds could qualify as 'investors' pursuant to Article 25(1) of the ICSID Convention, thus finding that the bondholders have standing to bring investment treaty-based claims.[160] The following sections will consider these decisions.

2.3.2.2.1 *Abaclat and Others v. Argentine Republic*

The *Abaclat* case was the first of the ICSID arbitration cases following Argentina's 2001 debt default and suspended payment on its sovereign bonds.[161] In 2006, 180,000 sovereign bondholders filed a mass claim for ICSID arbitration.[162] After Argentina's second exchange offer in 2010, half of the creditors withdrew from the proceedings leaving 60,000 Claimants.[163]

The members of the arbitral tribunal were Albert Jan van den Berg (appointed by the Claimant bondholders), Georges Abi-Saab (appointed by Argentina) and the chair, Pierre Tercier (who was appointed by the parties after the original chair, Robert Briner, resigned).[164] Argentina objected to the arbitral tribunal's jurisdiction contending that the ICSID system was not designed to handle mass claims, that the ICSID Convention's investment protection did not cover sovereign bonds and that even if the tribunal were to find that the bonds constitute investments they fail to satisfy the territorial nexus requirement.[165]

---

[158] *Fedax*. See also: Martin (2011).

[159] Id.

[160] *Abaclat* Decision on Jurisdiction and Admissibility; *Ambiente Ufficio* Decision on Jurisdiction and Admissibility; *Alemanni* Decision on Jurisdiction and Admissibility.

[161] *Abaclat* Decision on Jurisdiction and Admissibility. See also Strong (2013b), pp. 266–270.

[162] Id 266–270.

[163] Id.

[164] *Abaclat* Decision on Jurisdiction and Admissibility paragraph 119.

[165] Id paragraph 130. See also: Park and Samples (2017), p. 1048.

2.3.2.2.1.1 *Abaclat: Mass claims*

In its objection to the tribunal's jurisdiction, Argentina argued that its consent to arbitration in the Italy-Argentina BIT did not include collective arbitration proceedings.[166] Furthermore, Argentina contended that the ICSID Convention's silence on the issue of mass proceedings supported the conclusion that such proceedings were outside the scope of an ICSID tribunal's jurisdiction and unacceptable under ICSID's procedural structure.[167]

The *Abaclat* case was the first time that an ICSID tribunal had to consider the issue of mass claims.[168] The majority, Pierre Tercier and Albert Jan van den Berg, rejected this objection noting that there was no logical explanation for why and how the arbitral tribunal could have jurisdiction over the claims of several individual Claimants and then "lose" such jurisdiction once the number of Claimants exceeded a certain, undefined threshold.[169] Moreover, the majority refused to treat the silence of the ICSID Convention on the issue of mass proceedings as proof that such proceedings were prohibited. The majority determined that such a conclusion would be contrary to the purpose and spirit of the ICSID Convention, stating that consent to ICSID arbitration must be considered to cover the "form of arbitration necessary to give efficient protection and remedy to the investors and their investments, including arbitration in the form of collective proceedings".[170] Additionally, the majority found that, provided ICSID arbitration proceedings could include mass claims, then there was no reason for requiring specific consent to collective arbitration proceedings.[171]

2.3.2.2.1.2 *Abaclat: Investment*

Argentina also objected to the arbitral tribunal's jurisdiction on the basis that sovereign bonds are not within the meaning of "investment" as foreseen in the Italy-Argentina BIT and Article 25(1) of the ICSID Convention.[172] To address this objection, the majority began by examining the list of criteria used to establish whether an investment exists within the meaning of Article 25(1) of the ICSID Convention,[173] known as the "Salini Test", which was established by the arbitral tribunal in *Salini Costruttori S.p.A. and Italstrade S.p.A. v. Morocco*.[174] The decision of the *Salini* tribunal was trailblazing because it distinguished between the

---

[166] *Abaclat* Decision on Jurisdiction and Admissibility paragraph 234.

[167] Id.

[168] Id paragraph 295. See also: Park and Samples (2017), p. 1048; Strong (2013b), pp. 282–88.

[169] *Abaclat* Decision on Jurisdiction and Admissibility paragraph 490.

[170] Id paragraph 490.

[171] Id paragraph 491.

[172] Id paragraph 333.

[173] Id paragraphs 362–367.

[174] *Salini* Decision on Jurisdiction.

conditions that satisfied the meaning of an investment under the relevant BIT and under Article 25 of the ICSID Convention.[175] Moreover, for the first time it also provided the elements of the definition for the latter, namely that an investment under Article 25 of the ICSID Convention should involve (i) a contribution, (ii) of a certain duration, (iii) of a nature to generate profits or revenues, (iv) showing a particular risk, and (v) of a nature to contribute to the economic development of the Host State.[176] In general, ICSID tribunals apply the Salini test or an altered form thereof, to establish whether a contended investment constitutes an "investment" under Article 25(1) of the ICSID Convention.[177] Other tribunals, however, have rejected the applicability of the Salini test.[178]

In the *Abaclat* case, the majority decided against employing the Salini test, arguing that the criteria were controversial and that, should the creditors fail to pass the test, it should not serve to restrict ICSID's jurisdiction since the criteria were not originally included in the ICSID Convention.[179] Moreover, the majority reasoned that to block the parties' access to ICSID arbitration after they had previously agreed in their BIT to protect a certain type of investment and to submit to ICSID arbitration would undermine the Convention's aim to "encourage private investment while giving the Parties the tools to further define what kind of investment they want to promote".[180] Accordingly, the majority determined that the only jurisdictional requirement needed to satisfy Article 25 of the ICSID Convention was the creation of value stemming from the investment, which in this case was the purchase of the Argentinian bonds by the Claimants and the right to claim reimbursement from Argentina of the principal and interest on the bonds.[181]

2.3.2.2.1.3 Abaclat: Territorial Nexus

Argentina also objected to ICSID jurisdiction on the basis that even were the tribunal to find that sovereign bonds to constitute protected investments, they failed to meet the territorial nexus requirement contained in Article 1 of the underlying Argentina-Italy BIT.[182] Pursuant to Argentina, the sovereign bonds failed to demonstrate the necessary physical and legal connection to Argentina since (i) they did not produce the transfer of money into the state's territory, (ii) were held outside of the country and (iii) once purchased on the secondary market, cut off any connection between

[175] Id.

[176] Id. See also Martin (2011).

[177] Gaillard (2009), p. 406.

[178] Id.

[179] *Abaclat* Decision on Jurisdiction and Admissibility paragraph 363.

[180] Id paragraph 364.

[181] Id paragraph 366.

[182] Id paragraph 341(ii).

the sovereign bondholders with Argentina rendering their investment claims too remote to be permissible.[183]

This argument failed to persuade the majority, however, as they were of the opinion that the nature of the investment should determine the means by which the place of the investment is determined.[184] The majority determined that in the case of investments of a purely financial nature, different criteria must be applied than in the case of an investment entailing business operations, workers or property. Accordingly, the majority found that in the case of purely financial investments the appropriate criteria "should be where and/or for the benefit of whom the funds are ultimately used, and not the place where the funds were paid out or transferred".[185] As it was evident that the issuance of the bonds generated funds that were ultimately made available to Argentina, the majority found that the bonds satisfied the territorial nexus requirement of an investment made in the territory of Argentina.[186]

2.3.2.2.1.4 *The Abaclat Dissenting Opinion*

The third member of the arbitral tribunal, Professor George Abi-Saab, did not agree with the majority's decision on jurisdiction and instead submitted a dissenting opinion.[187] In his dissent, Professor Abi-Saab addressed Argentina's three objections to ICSID jurisdiction discussed above.[188]

Professor Abi-Saab deemed that the ICSID Convention's silence on mass claims should be settled in favor of Argentina because the drafters of the Convention could not have foreseen such proceedings, and there is no evidence to assume that they would have included mass claims even if they had foreseen them as a possibility.[189] After conducting a detailed analysis of the nature of mass claims and their individual or homogeneous nature, the dissenting arbitrator asserted that given the number of claims totaling 60,000, it would be unjust to compare such proceedings with a multi-party arbitration.[190] Pursuant to Professor Abi-Saab, whilst an arbitral tribunal can handle a small number of separate parties' claims, it would not be capable of individually analyzing the claims of such an extensive number of Claimants.[191]

As with the issue of the admissibility of mass claims, Professor Abi-Saab also dissented with the majority opinion's broad interpretation of the term investment.[192] After considering the jurisprudence as well as the ICSID Convention drafters' notes,

---

[183] Id paragraph 341(ii).

[184] Id paragraph 374. See also Chan (2014), pp. 233–239.

[185] Id paragraph 374.

[186] Id paragraphs 374, 380.

[187] *Abaclat* Dissenting Opinion to Decision on Jurisdiction and Admissibility.

[188] Id.

[189] Id paragraph 165. See also Karamanian (2013), p. 667.

[190] *Abaclat* Dissenting Opinion paragraph 139.

[191] Id paragraph 171.

[192] Id paragraph 46.

he determined that "investment" had an unalterable core meaning which excluded purely financial investments.[193]

Professor Abi-Saab also disagreed with the majority's position on the territorial nexus requirement, arguing that the exchange of funds on the secondary sovereign bond market had no connection with the lump sum issued to Argentina by the underwriters when the bonds were issued.[194]

2.3.2.2.1.5 Abaclat: Case Settlement

The *Abaclat* case never reached a decision on the merits as the parties settled their dispute.[195] The parties requested that the arbitral tribunal record the settlement in the form of a Consent Award resulting in the full termination of the ICSID proceedings.[196] Accordingly, although the *Abaclat* case paved the path for mass claims proceedings at ICSID, it never rendered a decision on the merits of whether Argentina's default on its sovereign bonds constituted a breach of its investment treaty responsibilities.[197]

Furthermore, the settlement of this case is also interesting in light of this book's exploration of the possibility of systematically attempting mediation in the sovereign debt dispute domain. In particular, it is noteworthy that Argentina not only resolved the *Abaclat* dispute outside of the investment arbitration process but that the *Abaclat* settlement occurred at the same time that mediation proceedings produced a U.S. $4.65 billion settlement between Argentina and six major hedge funds that had been pursuing litigation against the Argentine government for 15 years.[198] In fact, news coverage of the settlement between Argentina and the hedge funds noted that "Argentina struck another deal that same week to pay $1.35 billion to a group of Italian investors who were holding defaulted bonds."[199]

2.3.2.2.2 *Ambiente Ufficio and Others v. Argentine Republic*

The *Ambiente* case was the second installment of the three sets of ICSID arbitrations filed by Italian sovereign bondholders against Argentina pursuant to the 1990 Italy-Argentina BIT following Argentina's 2001 default on its sovereign bonds.[200] While

---

[193] Id paragraphs 46, 58.

[194] Id paragraphs 88–119.

[195] Settlement Agreement between the Republic of Argentina and the Associazione per la Tutela degli Investitori in Titoli Argentini.

[196] *Abaclat* Consent Award.

[197] Id. See also: Park and Samples (2017), p. 1033; Kabra (2015), p. 425; Chan (2014).

[198] Stevenson (2016)

[199] Id.

[200] *Ambiente*. See also Blanchard (2014), p. 314; Chan (2014); Strong (2013a).

the *Abaclat* case was still ongoing, 90 Italian investors filed for investment arbitration at ICSID on 26 June 2008.[201]

The tribunal members were Professor Karl-Heinz Böckstiegel (appointed by the bondholders), Dr. Santiago Torres Bernardez (appointed by Argentina) and Judge Bruno Simma as President.[202] In its preliminary award, the majority dismissed Argentina's objections to the tribunal's jurisdiction and admissibility, whilst third arbitrator Dr. Santiago Torres Bernardez issued a dissenting opinion.[203]

2.3.2.2.2.1 Ambiente: Multiple Claimants

As in the *Abaclat* case, Argentina objected to the tribunal's jurisdiction over collective action proceedings.[204] Noting that the ICSID Convention and the applicable BIT were silent on the permissibility of multi-party actions in ICSID arbitration, Argentina argued that the tribunal should dismiss jurisdiction over the proceedings, which it qualified as "an attempt by a great number of unrelated Claimants to jointly arbitrate their claims against a state".[205]

The majority's analysis commenced by differentiating the 90 Claimants in the *Ambiente* case from mass claim proceedings such as the *Abaclat* case involving 60,000 Claimants.[206] The majority pointed out that in the *Ambiente* case, each individual Claimant was participating in the proceedings and that therefore the proceedings could not be characterized as a class action which is distinguished by its representative nature and resulting procedural modifications.[207] Accordingly, the majority characterized the proceedings as a "multi-party" action.[208] Subsequently, the majority determined that multi-party proceedings are compatible with ICSID law, noting several ICSID cases had involved multiple Claimants.[209]

Whereas Argentina had contended that the drafters of the ICSID Convention did not foresee the permissibility of multi-party proceedings, the tribunal found that the notes of the *travaux préparatoires* of the ICSID Convention weakened the Respondent's argument as it demonstrated that the drafters had in fact discussed this possibility but had not reached a conclusion.[210]

Turning to the terms of the underlying Italy-Argentina BIT, the majority adopted the reasoning of the majority in *Abaclat*.[211] Consequently, the *Ambiente* majority

---

[201] *Ambiente.*

[202] Id paragraphs 18–23.

[203] Id.

[204] Id paragraphs 68–69.

[205] Id.

[206] Id paragraphs 115–120.

[207] Id.

[208] Id.

[209] Id paragraphs 135, 146.

[210] Id paragraph 132.

[211] Id paragraph 144.

noted that as the BIT included "mass instruments such as bonds" in its definition of investment, "the authors of the BIT [. . .] were envisaging a high number of potential claimants".[212]

2.3.2.2.2.2 *Ambiente: Investment*

As in the *Abaclat* case, the parties disagreed as to whether the sovereign bonds in question satisfied the requirements of Article 25(1) of the ICSID Convention.[213] Pursuant to the Claimant-creditors, "the overall loan which made funds available to finance Respondent's budgetary needs and which is represented by the bonds issued in respect thereof" constituted the "investment" for the purposes of Article 25 of the ICSID Convention.[214] The Claimants argued that "ample ICSID jurisprudence and legal doctrine" support a broad interpretation of the notion of investment under Article 25 of the ICSID Convention, including financial instruments such as the Argentine sovereign bonds held by the Claimants.[215]

In contrast, Argentina argued that the "investment" in question was separate from Argentina's original bond issuance to the bond underwriters who made a single payment of a global amount to Argentina; since legally, the Claimants themselves hold "security entitlements" which involve no direct relationship with the respondent bond issuer.[216] Further, pursuant to the Respondent, although purchasers of security entitlements in the retail market are referred to as "bond holders" in common parlance, this does not alter the fact that they were not the initial purchasers who contributed to the Argentine treasury.[217] Therefore, Argentina asserted, the investment at issue failed to satisfy the requirements of Article 25 of the ICSID Convention.[218]

Ultimately, the majority of the tribunal agreed with the Claimants' classification of the "investment" grouping bonds and their security entitlements as part of a global transaction, reasoning that to "[t]o seek to split up bonds and security entitlements into different [. . .] operations would ignore the economic realities [. . .] of the bond issuing process".[219] Moreover, the tribunal reasoned that to separate sovereign bonds and security entitlements would render the state's issuance of sovereign bonds useless since the state's funding depends upon the assumption that security entitlements will subsequently be resold on the secondary market.[220]

---

[212] Id paragraph 144.

[213] Id paragraphs 355–414.

[214] Id paragraph 384.

[215] Id paragraphs 389–390.

[216] Id paragraph 359.

[217] Id.

[218] Id paragraph 357.

[219] Id paragraph 425.

[220] Id.

2.3.2.2.2.3 *Ambiente: Territorial Nexus*

Pursuant to the Article 1(1) of the Argentina-Italy BIT, only investments made within the territory of the host state, *i.e.* Argentina, fall within the scope of the BIT's protection.[221] Argentina alleged that the bondholders' investment failed to meet this territorial nexus requirement.[222] To support this allegation, Argentina pointed to the fact that the non-Argentine creditors purchased and registered the security entitlements outside of Argentine territory, held them in a physical location outside of Argentina and that their rights thereunder were governed by non-Argentine law enforceable in foreign jurisdictions.[223]

The Claimants refuted Argentina's claim that the bonds failed to meet the territorial nexus requirement of Article 1(1) of the Argentina-Italy BIT, arguing that the relevant transaction for the purpose of this analysis was the initial bond issuance on the international financial markets, not the ensuing secondary market acquisitions of the bonds.[224] According to the creditors, in determining whether an investment was made within the territory of the host state, the tribunal cannot apply the same reasoning to financial instruments as is applied to physical assets.[225] Instead, the bondholders argued that in analyzing the territorial link for sovereign bonds, the tribunal must trace the ultimate beneficiary of the proceeds raised by the bond issuances, which in this case was clearly the Respondent, Argentina.[226] Moreover, the Claimants refuted the relevance of the bonds' governing law and jurisdiction clauses in determining whether the investment was made within Argentina's territory—pointing to the fact that regardless of these contractual provisions the Claimants were still subject to Argentina's use of its sovereign powers to interfere with the investment.[227]

The majority held that given the non-physical nature of the investment at issue, the physical location of the bonds could not be the determinative factor with respect to the territorial nexus requirement of Article 1(1) of the Argentina-Italy BIT.[228] Rather, the tribunal determined that the decisive factor in establishing the territorial link under the BIT is whether the investment in question contributes to the economic development of the host state,[229] which as discussed above is one of the Salini criteria.[230] Consequently, the majority reasoned that since the "whole bond issuing process, notably including the circulation of security entitlements on the secondary

---

[221] Agreement between Italy and Argentine Republic for the Promotion and Protection of Investment (1990), Article 1.

[222] Id paragraph 374.

[223] Id paragraph 374.

[224] Id paragraph 404.

[225] Id.

[226] Id paragraph 405.

[227] Id paragraph 408. See also Blanchard (2014).

[228] Id paragraph 498.

[229] Id paragraph 499.

[230] See Salini.

market, was devised—and specifically intended by the Respondent itself—to raise money for the budgetary needs of Argentina and thus to further the development of the State" that the investment was made in the territory of Argentina.[231]

2.3.2.2.2.4 Ambiente Dissenting Opinion

The dissenting member of the arbitral tribunal, Dr. Santiago Torres Bernardez, disagreed with the majority's decision upholding the ICSID tribunal's jurisdiction over the *Ambiente* case.[232] In particular, Dr. Bernardez opposed to the majority's reasoning with respect to its findings of jurisdiction and admissibility over the collective proceedings, the security entitlements in Argentine sovereign bonds as "protectable" investments and its interpretation of the territorial nexus requirement.

Although Dr. Bernardez considered that "90 Claimants [. . .] is not unmanageable for the Tribunal", he considered the proceedings to be "defective" because they required the Respondent's consent, which had not been delivered.[233] In his reasoning, the dissenting arbitrator echoed the dissenting opinion of Professor Abi-Saab in the *Abaclat* case, arguing that the silence of the ICSID Convention and the Argentina-Italy BIT on collective proceedings could not be interpreted as implied consent by the Respondent to submit to such multi-party arbitrations.[234]

Dr. Bernardez also disputed the majority's finding that the security entitlements in Argentine sovereign bonds constituted a "protected investment" under the ICSID Convention.[235] The dissenting arbitrator rejected what he viewed as the majority's non-objective analysis of the creditors' security entitlements as part of a global transaction linked to the initial issuance of the sovereign bonds.[236] Accordingly, Dr. Bernardez reasoned that, since the Claimants purchased them "without any intent to perform any economic activity in the host country or in connection with any particular project related to an activity of that kind in that country", they failed to meet the definitional requirements of an investment under Article 25(1) of the ICSID Convention.[237]

Finally, Dr. Bernardez also noted in his dissent that the majority failed to respect the territorial nexus requirement of Article 1(1) of the Argentina-Italy BIT.[238] Observing that the underlying BIT's text expressly stated that the relevant investment must be made "in the territory" of the host state, he stated that the majority could not ignore what was a written recording of the parties "common intention".[239]

[231] Id paragraph 500.

[232] *Ambiente* Dissenting Opinion of Dr. Santiago Torres, paragraph 1.

[233] Id.

[234] Id paragraph 105.

[235] Id paragraph 2(1).

[236] Id paragraphs 164–189.

[237] Id paragraphs 164–189.

[238] Id paragraphs 298–303. See also Blanchard (2014).

[239] Id paragraph 303.

He further rejected what he characterized as the majority's attempt to "bypass" the territoriality requirement of the BIT, despite the fact Article 1(4) of the BIT characterized the term "territory" in a physical/legal manner in contrast to what he deemed to be the "virtual construction" of territory in the majority's decision.[240]

2.3.2.2.2.5 Discontinuance of the Ambiente Proceedings

As in the *Abaclat* case, the *Ambiente* case never reached a decision on the merits.[241] Unlike the *Ambiente* case, however, the parties in the *Abaclat* case did not reach a settlement. Rather, the proceedings were discontinued pursuant to Regulation 14(3)(d) of the ICSID Administrative and Financial Regulations for failure to make necessary payments towards the costs of the proceedings.[242]

2.3.2.2.3 *Giovanni Alemanni and others v. Argentine Republic*

The *Giovanni Alemanni and others v. Argentine Republic* case is the third and final investment arbitration arising out of Argentina's sovereign debt default.[243] Like the preceding *Abaclat* and *Ambiente* cases, the *Alemanni* case was discontinued before the tribunal could make any decision on the merits.[244] Also like the *Abaclat* and *Ambiente* cases, the tribunal's decision on jurisdiction and admissibility in the *Alemanni* arbitration contains many of the same procedural and substantive issues and resembles the tribunals' analyses in those prior cases, but still applies its own unique twist to the analysis of mass/multiparty investment arbitration claims based on sovereign bonds.[245]

The *Alemanni* tribunal, composed of Sir Franklin Berman (President), Professor Karl-Heinz Böckstiegel (appointed by the Claimants) and Mr. J. Christopher Thomas (appointed by Argentina) issued its decision on jurisdiction and admissibility on 17 November 2014.[246] The fact pattern of this case is very similar to the *Abaclat* and *Ambiente* cases discussed above with the main difference being that the *Alemanni* case involved the least number of Claimants at 74.[247]

---

[240] Id paragraph 299.

[241] *Ambiente* Order of Discontinuance of the Proceeding.

[242] Id.

[243] *Alemanni.*

[244] *Alemanni* Order of the Tribunal Discontinuing the Proceeding.

[245] *Alemanni.* See also Maynard (2016), p. 117.

[246] *Alemanni.*

[247] Id 245.

2.3.2.2.3.1 Alemanni: Collective Action

As in the *Abaclat* and *Ambiente* cases, Argentina raised a procedural objection to the arbitration, which it categorized as a "class action".[248] The Respondent argued that its express consent to such proceedings was necessary for the tribunal to have jurisdiction in light of the silence of both the ICSID Convention and the BIT with respect to collective proceedings and that in any event the proceedings would violate due process.[249]

The tribunal stated that it was "not impressed" by these objections.[250] Rather, with respect to the issue of consent, the arbitrators deemed that the relevant question with respect to the state's consent stemming from the interpretation of the BIT is whether the Respondent has "given a consent which is wide enough in scope to cover the proceedings brought (as in this case) by the multiple group of co-Claimants."[251]

To determine this, the tribunal invoked the Vienna Convention on the Law of Treaties Article 31(1) providing for the interpretation of treaties in good faith and "in accordance with the ordinary meaning to be given to the terms of the treaty".[252] In contrast to the *Abaclat* and *Ambiente* tribunals therefore, the *Alemanni* arbitrators concluded that it would be inappropriate to engage in a literal analysis of the BIT's text to interpret "investor" in the singular or plural sense.[253]

In its place, the *Alemanni* tribunal deemed that the correct test is whether the wording of Article 25(1) of the ICSID Convention establishing jurisdiction over any "dispute arising directly out of an investment, between a Contracting State [. . .] and a national of another Contracting State" should be understood as "but only one national" of another Contracting State.[254] Ultimately, the tribunal found that neither the ICSID Convention nor the ICSID Rules supported importing the phrase "but only one" into the text of Article 25(1) of the ICSID Convention.[255]

2.3.2.2.3.2 Alemanni: Investment

As in the previous two cases, the *Alemanni* tribunal debated various substantive objections pertaining to whether the claims arising out of Argentina's sovereign bonds could be considered "investments" under the ICSID Convention and the Argentina-Italy BIT.

---

[248] Id paragraph 47.

[249] Id paragraphs 47–48.

[250] Id paragraph 268.

[251] Id paragraph 269.

[252] Id paragraph 270; Vienna Convention on the Law of Treaties (1969), Article 31(1).

[253] Id paragraph 270.

[254] Id paragraph 270.

[255] Id paragraph 271.

The tribunal dealt swiftly with the central issue as to whether the sovereign bonds constitute an investment within the meaning of the BIT and Article 25 of the ICSID Convention, stating it "is not a [. . .] matter that need detain the Tribunal long", since it agreed with the "comprehensive treatment" of the issue in the *Abaclat* and *Ambiente* decision.[256] The *Alemanni* arbitrators found that there was no "obstacle" in the text of the ICSID Convention barring sovereign bonds and further noted that the drafters of the Convention raised sovereign bonds as an example of the ICSID Convention's potential scope of application during negotiations.[257] As regards the BIT, the tribunal agreed with the conclusions of the *Abaclat* and *Ambiente* decisions finding that the treaty's explicit language or even its implicit reading did not restrict sovereign bonds as an "investment" within the scope of its protection.[258]

2.3.2.2.3.3 Alemanni: Territorial Nexus

As in the previous two ICSID cases, the parties also debated the issue of whether the sovereign bonds, assuming them to be 'investments' within the meaning of the ICSID Convention and the BIT, were 'made within the territory of Argentina' as required by Article 1(1) of the Argentina-Italy BIT.[259] However, the arbitral tribunal deemed that this issue was too closely connected to the parties' substantive rights to be dealt with in the preliminary decision on jurisdiction and therefore postponed the matter to the merits.[260]

2.3.2.2.3.4 Alemanni Concurring Opinion

Interestingly, unlike the *Abaclat* and *Ambiente* decisions, the arbitrator appointed by Argentina in the *Alemanni* tribunal did not dissent from the tribunal's decision.[261] Rather, arbitrator J. Christopher Thomas issued a concurring opinion in which he agreed with the tribunal's finding of jurisdiction on the collective action filed by the Claimants but with different reasoning.[262]

Specifically, Mr. Thomas noted that the bilateral investment treaties of many ICSID member states include consolidation provisions in which multiple parties may apply to a consolidation tribunal for the joinder of separate claims in one proceeding, where they share common questions of fact and/or law.[263] Accordingly, Mr. Thomas concluded that the "very existence of consolidation provisions recognizes that the commonalities between treaty claims may be so strong as to justify their being heard

[256] Id paragraph 296.

[257] Id.

[258] Id.

[259] Id paragraph 297.

[260] Id.

[261] *Alemanni* (n 160).

[262] *Alemanni* Concurring Opinion.

[263] Id paragraph 6.

together" and therefore require "forcibly consolidating separate claims over the objection of one or more disputing parties."[264]

In the present case, the concurring arbitrator considered that the Claimants in the *Alemanni* case had presented the Respondents with a *"fait-accompli"* by having "self-consolidated" their individual claims and presenting them as a single collective claim.[265] Mr. Thomas concluded by underscoring, as stated in the tribunal's decision, the need to verify that there is in fact a single dispute and that due process is afforded to all the parties to the proceeding.[266]

2.3.2.2.3.5 Alemanni: Discontinuance of the Proceeding

On 14 December 2015, the tribunal issued an order discontinuing the proceeding following lack of payment.[267] In its order discontinuing the proceeding, the tribunal recalled the background of the various stages of the proceeding.[268] In particular, the tribunal noted that the Respondent refused to pay its part of the expenses of the proceeding.[269] Ultimately, as the proceeding had been suspended for 6 months for lack of payment, the Acting Secretary General of ICSID requested the tribunal to discontinue the proceeding pursuant to Administrative and Financial Regulation 14(3)(d) of the ICSID Convention.[270]

While recounting the events leading up to the discontinuance of the proceeding, the tribunal referred to the Claimants' letter dated 18 February 2015 criticizing the Respondents' repeated failure to pay its share of the costs of arbitration as a "strategy [...] to abstain from paying its costs of the arbitration, as it had done in the previous two bondholder cases".[271] The tribunal noted that the Claimants' requested that the tribunal consider the Respondent's alleged "strategy" when allocating the burden of the costs of the proceeding.[272]

2.3.2.2.4 Argentine Cases: Conclusion

The decisions on jurisdiction for these three Argentinian sovereign debt cases, *Abaclat*, *Ambiente Ufficio* and *Alemanni* repeatedly held that sovereign bonds qualified as an "investment" pursuant to Article 25(1) of the ICSID Convention,

[264] Id.

[265] Id paragraph 9.

[266] Id paragraph 13.

[267] *Alemanni* Concurring Opinion.

[268] Id paragraph 1.

[269] Id paragraph 8.

[270] Id paragraph 11 and Administrative and Financial Regulation 14(3)(d) of the ICSID Convention.

[271] Id paragraph 8.

[272] Id.

although the reasoning behind this finding differed in each case.[273] In addition, the tribunals also consistently decided that the various claims of the creditors could be combined in a single mass/multiparty ICSID proceeding.[274]

However, doubt lingers on the jurisdictional issue of sovereign bonds qualifying as investments as is evidenced by the dissenting opinions in the decisions above, the numerous academic articles debating the validity of the majority's decisions in these cases and the more recent award in *Poštová banka and Istrokapital v. Greece*.[275]

2.3.2.3 *Poštová banka and Istrokapital v. Greece*

Unlike the preceding three Argentine sovereign debt ICSID cases, on 9 April 2015, the arbitral tribunal in the *Poštová banka and Istrokapital v. Greece* case unanimously decided that the Greek sovereign bonds in question were not a covered investment under the applicable Slovakia-Greece BIT.[276]

The *Poštová* case was filed by Poštová banka, a.s. (Poštová banka), a Slovak bank, and a company filed under Cypriot law, Istrokapital SE (Istrokapital), as Claimants.[277] Poštová banka was the holder of 504 million euros of Greek government bonds and Istrokapital held shares in Poštová banka.[278] As a consequence of Greece's economic downturn following the global financial crisis of 2008, bond rating agencies downgraded Greece's sovereign bonds, significantly reducing their value.[279] This in turn spurred the Claimants to file for arbitration on 3 May 2013 under the Slovakia-Greece and Cyprus-Greece BITs.[280] The tribunal was composed of Colombian national, Eduardo Zuleta (President), U.S. national, John M. Townsend (appointed by the Claimants) and French national, Professor Brigitte Stern (appointed by the Respondent).[281]

2.3.2.3.1 Poštová banka: Dismissal of Istrokapital's Claims

In its claim for jurisdiction, Istrokapital argued that as a shareholder of Poštová banka, it had made an indirect investment in the sovereign bonds protected by the

---

[273] Park and Samples (2017), p. 1033.

[274] Id.

[275] *Abaclat* Dissenting Opinion; *Ambiente* Dissenting Opinion; *Poštová banka,* paragraph 350. See also Peterson (2011); Strong (2013a), pp. 21–31; Newcombe (2011).

[276] *Poštová banka* Award paragraph 350. See also Montanaro (2015); Li (2014); Glinavos (2014), p. 475.

[277] *Poštová banka* Award paragraphs 1–2.

[278] Id.

[279] Id paragraph 46.

[280] Id.

[281] Id.

Cyprus-Greece BIT.[282] However, Greece objected to the tribunal's jurisdiction, arguing that as Istrokapital itself did not directly make an investment under the Cyprus–Greece BIT it could not base its jurisdiction on Poštová banka's ownership of Greek sovereign bonds.[283]

Upon reviewing the case law on shareholders' rights in the underlying company's assets, the tribunal concluded that while "a shareholder of a company incorporated in the host State may assert claims based on measures taken against such company's assets that impair the value of the Claimant's shares," the shareholder does not have "standing to pursue claims directly over the assets of the local company, as it has no legal right to such assets".[284] Accordingly, the tribunal determined that since Istrokapital had failed to establish that it had any rights to Poštová banka's assets protected by the BIT, it must dismiss all of Istrokapital's claims for lack of jurisdiction.[285]

2.3.2.3.2 Poštová banka: Investment

The tribunal first considered whether Poštová banka's sovereign bonds constituted an investment within the meaning of the applicable Slovakia-Greece BIT.[286] It began by differentiating the language of the Slovakia-Greece BIT from the treaty language that led the tribunals of the Argentina cases to conclude that sovereign bonds were investments under the Argentina-Italy BIT.[287] After a detailed comparison and analysis of the two BITs, the tribunal decided that the language of the Slovakia-Greece BIT is not as broad as the language of the Argentina-Italy BIT, which referred to "any right of an economic nature conferred under law or contract".[288] Moreover, the tribunal noted that the Slovakia-Greece BIT does not refer to "sovereign debt, public titles, public securities, public obligations or the like" nor does it contain language suggesting that Slovakia or Greece considered sovereign debt or even public debt or obligations as a protectable investment under the treaty.[289] Further, the tribunal observed that the only reference to bonds in the treaty related to "shares in and stock and debentures of a company and any other form of participation in a company", which the tribunal found to clearly refer only to company-issued bonds or debentures and not to State-issued bonds.[290]

---

[282] Id paragraphs 205–212.

[283] Id.

[284] Id paragraph 245.

[285] Id paragraph 247.

[286] Id paragraph 304.

[287] Id.

[288] Id paragraph 307.

[289] Id paragraph 332.

[290] Id paragraph 333.

Moreover, the tribunal reasoned that, although several treaties include wide-ranging asset-based definitions of investment, they also include descriptive lists of categories that could constitute an investment and that these lists can vary significantly from treaty to treaty.[291] With reference to the Vienna Convention on the Law of Treaties, the tribunal deemed that the good faith interpretation of the Slovakia-Greece BIT required meaningfully considering the list of "investment" examples.[292] Consequently, the tribunal determined that for the Greek sovereign bonds to fall within the protection of the Slovakia-Greece BIT, the "claim to money" must stem from a contractual relationship between the parties as provided in the text of Article 1.1(c) of the BIT covering "loans, claims to money or to any performance under contract having a financial value".[293] However, noting that Poštová banka procured the Greek government bonds on the secondary market via the trading company Clearstream Banking Luxembourg rather from the Greek state directly, the tribunal found that the bonds never produced a contractual relationship between Poštová banka and Greece.[294] Consequently, the tribunal reasoned that Poštová banka's claims could not result from a contract between Poštová banka and Respondent and therefore concluded that Article 1(1)(c) of the Slovakia-Greece BIT failed to cover Greek sovereign bonds within its definition of an 'investment' or to confer subject matter jurisdiction to the tribunal.[295]

2.3.2.3.3 Implications of the Poštová banka Decision

As the tribunal found that the sovereign bonds did not confer investment treaty protection, it dismissed the case without further consideration of the merits.[296] It is notable that this decision is at odds with the preceding case law that treated sovereign debt as an investment entailing dispute resolution access to investment arbitration.[297] To some degree, this different decision is justified by the differences between the applicable investment treaties, as discussed in the *Poštová* decision.[298] Nevertheless, the *Poštová* tribunal's award demonstrates a clear divergence from the *Abaclat*, *Ambiente* and *Alemanni* awards because it refutes the prior tribunals' view that there is a close correlation between the primary and secondary sovereign bond market.[299]

---

[291] Id paragraph 293.

[292] Id paragraphs 289–292; Vienna Convention on the Law of Treaties (1969), Article 31(1).

[293] Id paragraph 316; Agreement Between the Government of the Czech and Slovak Federal Republic and the Government of the Hellenic Republic for the Promotion and Reciprocal Protection of Investments 1991 (Slovakia – Greece BIT); Article 1.1(c).

[294] Id paragraph 347.

[295] Id paragraphs 347–350.

[296] Id paragraph 350.

[297] N 160.

[298] *Poštová banka* Award paragraph 304; Slovakia – Greece BIT. See also Montanaro (2015).

[299] Id paragraph 347; Slovakia – Greece BIT. See also Ortolani (2017); Montanaro (2015).

In light of the divergence amongst the different arbitral tribunals, the case law is not clear as to whether creditors who have purchased sovereign bonds on the secondary market can seek treaty-based protection.[300] Accordingly, the clash between these decisions undermines the viability of investment arbitration as a forum for sovereign debt disputes.[301] Moreover, given the independent nature in which investment arbitral tribunals function, this interpretational conflict is unlikely to be resolved quickly reducing the likelihood that investment arbitration will maintain the forum of choice of sovereign bondholders seeking to protect their interests.[302]

The aim of Sect. 2.3 was to provide an overview of the international investment law framework and the jurisprudence of sovereign debt investment arbitration cases. As has been highlighted in the examination of the case law, although sovereign bonds were initially deemed to qualify as investments for the purpose of Article 25 of the ICSID Convention, the more recent *Poštová* decision has cast doubt on that interpretation as well as the arbitrability of such claims under the investment law framework.

2.4 Sovereign Debt Investment Arbitration: Unknown Outcomes

Adding to the uncertainty of investment arbitration's promise in the sovereign debt dispute context is the fact that the arbitral tribunals in the majority of these cases never proceeded to the phase of rendering a decision on the merits since the cases were settled or otherwise discontinued and the *Poštová* decision was contrary to the case law of the Argentine cases.[303] Therefore, it is not yet clear how successful creditors' compensation claims would be and whether they would face difficulty in the enforcement of arbitral awards in their favor.[304] The following paragraphs in this section consider in turn the questions of bondholder compensation should such cases proceed to the merits in future investment arbitration awards, the extent of success creditors would have in enforcing such awards, and the precedent set by Argentina's history of non-compliance with ICSID arbitral awards.

---

300 Ortolani (2017).

301 Permesly and Craven (2018), pp. 14–19.

302 Id.

303 *Poštová banka* Award; *Abaclat* Consent Award; *Ambiente* Order of Discontinuance.

304 Correa (2018).

2.4.1 Sovereign Debt Investment Arbitration: Unknown Compensation for Bondholders

It is difficult to foresee the level of compensation that sovereign bondholders would be likely to receive were such cases to proceed to the merits as there is insufficient data since the development of the secondary bond market in the mid-1980s.[305] Accordingly, to establish what the tendencies might be, we must borrow from the available international investment case law in international financial disputes on the award of damages.[306] The observable trend indicates that international investment arbitration tribunals have awarded damages corresponding to the quantum of unmet payment obligations under the terms of the contract.[307] In the *Fedax* case, for example, the arbitral tribunal awarded the payment of principal and interest pursuant to the terms of the applicable contract.[308]

However, academics have argued that tribunals must consider differently the compensation scheme for creditors who have acquired their sovereign bonds through the secondary market.[309] Michael Waibel has argued that just compensation for sovereign bonds purchased on the secondary market should correspond to the "generally recognized market value" or the "fair market value".[310] Karen Halverson Cross has also argued that awarding full damages would result in unjust enrichment, writing, "[i]n the sovereign debt context, awarding recovery of the debt's full nominal value would be unlikely to reflect its fair market value at the time of acquisition and thus arguably would provide the investor with a windfall."[311]

The Stockholm Chamber of Commerce investment arbitration tribunal in *Roseinvestco UK Ltd. v. Russian Federation* also adhered to the perspective that full compensation would be excessive.[312] The tribunal refused to grant the full compensation requested by the Claimant, reasoning that Claimant was a company designed for "purchasing shares at such moments of market distress" which had made a speculative investment with "optimistic expectations regarding the future development of the value of the investment."[313]

Accordingly, although purchasers of sovereign debt on the secondary market might have standing to have their claims heard by an investment arbitration tribunal, the return on their investment is likely to be limited in the event the tribunal renders a favorable award on the merits.

---

[305] Waibel (2007), pp. 312–314.

[306] Id.

[307] Menaker and Paliwal (2015).

[308] *Fedax*, subheading C. See also: Menaker and Paliwal (2015)

[309] Waibel (2007), pp. 367–368.

[310] Id 371–372.

[311] Halverson Cross (2014), pp. 165.

[312] *Roseinvestco UK Ltd. v. The Russian Federation*, SCC ARBITRATION V (079/2005), Final Award, 12 September 2010. See also: Waibel (2007); Halverson Cross (2014).

[313] *Roseinvestco* 666, 668, 669–676.

2.4.2 *Sovereign Debt Investment Arbitration: Unknown Level of Enforcement Success*

Resorting to investment arbitration to resolve sovereign debt disputes raises additional uncertainties with regard to the potential ease or difficulty that creditors might face in the enforcement of a favorable award.[314] When a tribunal renders an award, parties can seek recognition and enforcement of the award before national courts.[315] Given that sovereign debt disputes involve state parties, the latter might assert sovereign immunity protection in their domestic jurisdictions to avoid enforcement of the award against state assets.[316] However, there are specific rules about the execution of investment arbitral awards that creditors can employ towards the successful enforcement of a sovereign bond arbitration award.[317]

Starting with Article 54 of the ICSID Convention setting out the ICSID rules of Enforcement and Recognition of Awards, all contracting states must recognize ICSID awards as if they were domestic judgments.[318] In contrast, the New York Convention, which requires that arbitral awards be recognized by national courts, exposes enforcement of said awards to certain exceptions such as, *inter alia*, incapacity of the parties or invalidity of the arbitration agreement.[319] However, where state parties have not ratified the ICSID Convention, or where the dispute has been filed pursuant the ICSID Additional Facility Rules, which offer dispute resolution services for certain disputes that fall outside the scope of the ICSID Convention, the New York Convention would be applicable, therefore once again opening the door to sovereign immunity claims by state parties or other exceptions to enforcement.[320]

Moreover, as exposed by Argentina's non-compliance with ICSID arbitral awards, ICSID's enforcement record reposes on states' voluntary desire to maintain a good reputation in international markets rather than on the fear of imposed sanctions.[321] The legal and financial communities broadly recognize that it is common for contracting states with ICSID to comply voluntarily with unfavorable arbitral awards.[322] States that fail to comply with ICSID awards face the high cost of losing their investment-friendly reputations in the international business community.[323] Moreover, voluntary compliance has been linked to debtor governments'

[314] Lin (2012), pp. 1–22.

[315] Schreuer et al. (2009), pp. 1151–1185; Ding (2016), p. 1137.

[316] Schreuer et al. (2009), pp. 1151–1185; Ding (2016); Bjorklund (2011), p. 211.

[317] Cardosi (2013), p. 10.

[318] ICSID Convention art 54.

[319] Article V of the New York Convention. See also Bjorklund (2009), p. 305.

[320] ICSID Additional Facility Rules (2006). See also Bjorklund (2009).

[321] Lin (2012); Fach Gómez (2011), p. 195; Titi (2014), p. 357.

[322] Ding (2016).

[323] Mistelis (2015); Alexandrov (2009), pp. 326–27.

desire to maintain access to World Bank funding and international credit.[324] Indeed, ICSID's close relationship with the World Bank has generally inspired potential Claimants' trust as stated by academic Michael Waibel, "[p]otential claimants in ICSID perceive this institutional association as an advantage, in that it encourages states to comply with awards voluntarily and more readily than they might otherwise."[325]

However, in recent years Argentina's practice of challenging every adverse award in annulment proceedings has revealed problems with ICSID arbitration's compliance system.[326] Following Argentina's debt crisis in 2001, ICSID tribunals rendered nine final awards against Argentina with an estimated 100 billion U.S. dollars in liability for Argentina.[327] Nevertheless between 2007 and 2013 (approximately 6 years), Argentina failed to recompense these ICSID award creditors and obligated creditors to undertake local enforcement proceedings in the Argentinean court system.[328]

2.4.2.1 Enforcement: Obligation to Comply with ICSID Awards

Under the ICSID Convention, Article 53 imposes a principal obligation on a losing party to abide by and comply with an award.[329] Article 53(1) of the ICSID Convention provides:

> The award shall be binding on the parties and shall not be subject to any appeal or to any other remedy except those provided for in this Convention. Each party shall abide by and comply with the terms of the award except to the extent that enforcement shall have been stayed pursuant to the relevant provisions of this Convention.[330]

This provision establishes that the ICSID award is final and binding on the parties and excludes any external review.[331] Therefore, a party receiving an adverse award must accept and obey the award's terms, without further recourse to domestic enforcement proceedings.[332] Furthermore, Article 53 obligates parties to comply with the award promptly, unless the award contains a grace period.[333] Accordingly, losing parties who fail to pay damages pursuant to the award are not only breaching

[324] Id.

[325] Waibel (2007), pp. 648–650.

[326] Titi (2014), pp. 369–373; Fach Gómez (2011).

[327] Titi (2014), pp. 369–373; Goodman (2007), p. 452.

[328] Hirsch (2016), Law 681; Titi (2014), pp. 369–373; Fach Gómez (2011); Peterson (2011).

[329] ICSID Convention art 53; Schreuer (2009).

[330] ICSID Convention art 53(1).

[331] Id. See also Schreuer et al. (2009), pp. 1096–1114; Tawil (2009), pp. 327, 328.

[332] Id.

[333] Id. See also Schreuer (2009).

their state obligations to an investor but are also violating their international obligations towards other contracting states to the Convention.[334]

Conversely, as stated in Article 53(1), a losing party's duty to comply with an award may be suspended where the post-award ICSID proceedings have been undertaken for interpretation, revision or annulment of the award.[335] To date, requests to suspend enforcement of ICSID awards have only been made in conjunction with annulment proceedings.[336] Under specific conditions, Article 52 of the ICSID Convention permits losing parties to request a stay of the award's enforcement through an annulment application.[337] These grounds are: (i) the arbitral tribunal was not constituted properly; (ii) the tribunal exceeded its powers; (iii) a member of the tribunal engaged in corruption; or the award omits to state the reasons on which it is based.[338] Article 52(5) sets out the authority for *ad hoc* committees to stay the enforcement of an award, but provides no further guidance on when to make the decision other than, "if it considers that the circumstances so require".[339] Accordingly, the committee is free to exercise its discretion.[340]

As stated in Sect. 2.4.2, Article 54(1) of the ICSID Convention sets out Contracting States' obligation to cooperate in the recognition and enforcement of awards.[341] It states:

> Each Contracting State shall recognize an award rendered pursuant to this Convention as binding and enforce the pecuniary obligations imposed by that award within its territories as if it were a final judgment of a court in that State...[342]

Accordingly, as mentioned previously in Sect. 2.3.1, each Contracting State must recognize the finality of ICSID awards and enforce the monetary damages imposed by the award as if it were a domestic final judgment.[343] Consequently, an award creditor can identify contracting states in which the losing state has attachable assets and seek for recognition and enforcement of the award in those states in order to get the award paid.[344] Despite these measures, where the losing state does not possess any enterprises abroad, award creditors are unlikely to obtain compensation.[345]

---

334 Mistelis (2015), p. 142.

335 ICSID Convention art 53(1). See also Schreuer et al. (2009), pp. 1096–1114; Tawil (2009), p. 328.

336 ICSID, 'The ICSID Caseload – Statistics' (Issue 2020-2, 2020); Lin (2012).

337 ICSID Convention art 52. See also Schreuer et al. (2009), pp. 890–1095.

338 ICSID Convention art 52. See also Schreuer et al. (2009), pp. 890–1095.

339 Id.

340 ICSID Convention art 52(2). See also Schreuer et al. (2009); Stevens (2009).

341 ICSID Convention art 54. See also Tawil (2009), p. 328; Schreuer et al. (2009), pp. 1115–1150.

342 Id.

343 ICSID Convention art 54(1); Mistelis (2015), p. 142; Tawil (2009), p. 328; Schreuer et al. (2009), pp. 1115–1150.

344 Schreuer (2009).
ICSID Convention art 53(1).

345 Lin (2012), pp. 1–22; Fach Gómez (2011).

Moreover, a state's own domestic law governs enforcement of ICSID awards pursuant to Article 55 of the ICSID Convention, opening the door for the losing state to assert "sovereign immunity" as a defense from execution.[346] Award creditors might also face difficulty proving to domestic courts that the losing state's assets should not be immune.[347] As of 2015, it was reported that there had been only five known domestic judicial enforcement proceedings for ICSID awards.[348]

2.4.2.2 Alternative Enforcement Recourse for Award Creditors: Diplomatic Protection

An award creditor whose enforcement efforts are frustrated by a recalcitrant losing party may request its home state to provide diplomatic protection against the debtor state pursuant to Article 27(1) of the ICSID Convention.[349] The concept of diplomatic protection, whereby a State adopts the claim of its national against another state in its own name, arises from customary international law.[350] Article 27(1) reads:

> No Contracting State shall give diplomatic protection, or bring an international claim, in respect of a dispute which one of its nationals and another Contracting State shall have consented to submit or shall have submitted to arbitration under this Convention, unless such other Contracting State shall have failed to abide by and comply with the award rendered in such dispute.[351]

Accordingly, the award creditor's home state could employ diplomatic pressure on the losing state to coerce it into carrying out with the compensation under the ICSID tribunal's decision.

In addition, an award creditor's home state may also have recourse to the International Court of Justice (ICJ) pursuant to Article 64 of the ICSID Convention, which states:

> Any dispute arising between Contacting States concerning the interpretation or application of this Convention which is not settled by negotiations shall be referred to the International Court of Justice by the application of any party to such dispute, unless the States concerned agree to another method of settlement.[352]

Accordingly, Article 64 of the ICSID Convention serves to invoke the compulsory jurisdiction of the ICJ which, if juxtaposed with Article 27(1) of the ICSID Convention (Article 27(1) proscribes States from claiming diplomatic protection over

[346] ICSID Convention art 53(1).

[347] Lin (2012), pp. 1–22; Fach Gómez (2011); Goodman (2007), p. 468.

[348] Mistelis (2015), p. 145.

[349] ICSID Convention art 27(1); Schreuer et al. (2009), pp. 414–430.

[350] Schreuer et al. (2009), p. 415.

[351] ICSID Convention art 27(1).

[352] ICSID Convention art 64; Schreuer et al. (2009), pp. 1258–1262.

claims that are already the subject of a pending arbitration), serves as a post-award inter-state enforcement mechanism to ensure compliance with arbitral awards issued under the ICSID Convention.[353] International investment disputes do not have a tendency to be submitted to the ICJ.[354] However, as will be discussed in the next subsection, Argentina's extended practice of non-compliance with ICSID awards suggests that states are hesitant to employ the jurisdiction of the ICJ against other states to enforce the investment treaty rights of their nationals.[355]

2.4.3 *Argentina's Prior Cases of Delayed Compliance with ICSID Awards*

As stated previously, for a period of approximately 6 years Argentina engaged in a practice of delayed compliance with a series of ICSID awards, which raises important questions regarding the certainty with which sovereign debt creditors can expect payment even after receiving a favorable ICSID arbitration award.[356] It is worth observing the particular decisions made by the various ICSID *ad hoc* annulment committees in these non-compliance cases because they reveal the extent to which the ICSID enforcement system may be illusory.[357]

2.4.3.1 *CMS Gas Transmission Company v. Republic of Argentina*

In the *CMS Gas Transmission Company v. Republic of Argentina* Decision on the Argentine Republic's Request for a Continued Stay of Enforcement of the Award (hereinafter, *CMS*) the Claimant, CMS, requested the *ad hoc* committee to reject Argentina's application to suspend enforcement of the ICSID award unless Argentina could provide "adequate assurances" that it would respect the pecuniary obligations under the award, if its annulment request were denied.[358] In support of its request, CMS referred to statements made by some Argentine government officials that Argentina would subject final ICSID Awards "to a novel domestic review

[353] ICSID Convention art 64. See also Desierto (2012), p. 201; Schreuer et al. (2009).

[354] Desierto (2012); Bjorklund (2011).

[355] Kasenetz (2010), p. 709.

[356] Id; Lin (2012).

[357] Id.

[358] *CMS Gas Transmission Company v. the Republic of Argentina*, ICSID Case No. ARB/01/8 Decision on the Argentine Republic's Request for a Continued Stay of Enforcement of the Award, 1 September 2006, paragraph 5. See also von Staden (2011), p. 207; Burke-White (2008), pp. 199–234.

mechanism before the Argentine Supreme Court (or other fora) in open breach of its obligations under the ICSID Convention."[359]

In its analysis, the committee reasoned that "as a general matter a respondent State should be entitled to a stay provided it gives reasonable assurances that the award, if not annulled, will be complied with."[360] The committee also indicated that "if there is doubt" that the state will comply with the ICSID Convention, the committee may require a bank guarantee as a condition for its approval of a stay.[361]

Subsequently the committee asked Argentina to present a written statement demonstrating its intention to comply with the award should it be maintained.[362] In response, Argentina submitted a statement promising CMS that, "in accordance with its obligations under the ICSID Convention, it will recognize the award rendered by the arbitral tribunal as binding and will enforce the pecuniary obligations imposed by that award within its territories, in the event that annulment is not granted".[363]

Satisfied with the strength of this pledge, the committee decided to maintain the stay of the enforcement of the award pending the annulment proceedings.[364] Moreover, the committee did so without requesting further conditions as petitioned by Argentina.[365] Accordingly, pursuant to the *CMS* committee, so long as a state can provide reasonable guarantees of compliance with the award if annulment is nullified, its request for stay of enforcement could be granted.[366] Moreover, the *CMS* Decision indicates that an *ad hoc* committee may impose the additional requirement that the respondent state provide a bank guarantee in the event there is doubt about subsequent compliance with the award.[367]

It is therefore curious that in *CMS*, the committee found that Argentina's "commitment letter" was an adequately reasonable guarantee of Argentina's eventual compliance, given the statements of some Argentinean government officials to the contrary cited by CMS.[368] Furthermore, upon scrutiny of Argentina's written guarantee, it only contains a restatement by Argentina of its enforcement obligations pursuant to Article 54(1) of the ICSID Convention, and nothing that provides further, additional assurances of Argentina's compliance intentions.[369] Ultimately,

[359] *CMS*, paragraph 18. See also von Staden (2011).

[360] *CMS* paragraph 38.

[361] Id.

[362] *CMS* paragraph 47.

[363] Id.

[364] *CMS* paragraph 45–50.

[365] Id.

[366] *CMS*.

[367] *CMS*.

[368] Lin (2012).

[369] *CMS* paragraph 47. See also Lin (2012).

although Argentina succeeded in securing a partial annulment of the *CMS* award,[370] it resisted compliance with enforcement of the award for a further 8 years until Argentina settled the case along with four other outstanding investment treaty arbitration claims in 2015.[371]

2.4.3.2 *Azurix Corp. v. Argentine Republic*

In the *Azurix Corp. v. Argentine Republic* Decision on the Argentine Republic's Request for a Continued Stay of Enforcement of the Award (hereinafter, *Azurix*), the *ad hoc* committee departed from the more "prudent" decision of the *CMS* committee, considering that in general, a stay should be ordered unless there are *"very exceptional circumstances"* requiring the committee to take a contrary decision.[372]

Accordingly, the *Azurix* committee deemed a written commitment from Argentina to be unnecessary.[373] Instead, the *ad hoc* committee considered the fact that Argentina is bound by its international obligations under Article 54 of the ICSID Convention to be the primary guarantee for the *Azurix* award.[374] In addition to this, the *Azurix* committee considered Argentina's domestic legal system to be additional security of its commitment to respect the award as it is in conformity with the ICSID Convention.[375]

Moreover, the *Azurix* committee felt that requiring a security should be limited only to exceptional cases, otherwise it would undermine "the important confidence-balancing function for state parties served by the annulment procedure".[376] In addition, the *ad hoc* committee considered that requiring a security would undermine states' confidence in the transparency of the ICSID system by "introducing the suggestion of discrimination between states" since security is ordinarily only sought against developing countries.[377] Nevertheless, the committee noted that a security requirement could be imposed where a defendant state condemns its ICSID obligations or otherwise expresses an intention not to obey its duties under the award.[378] Consequently, the *ad hoc* committee found that since Argentina did not indicate that it planned to disregard the *Azurix* award or otherwise avoid its ICSID obligations, it

---

[370] CMS Gas Transmission Company v. the Republic of Argentina, ICSID Case No. ARB/01/8 Decision of the ad hoc Committee on the Application for Annulment of the Argentine Republic, 25 September 2007.

[371] Smith Freehills (2013).

[372] *Azurix Corp. v. Argentine Republic*, ICSID Case No. ARB/01/12 Decision on the Argentine Republic's Request for a Continued Stay of Enforcement of the Award, 28 December 2007, paragraph 22. See also Frutos-Peterson (2008), pp. 155–163.

[373] *Azurix*.

[374] Id paragraph 38.

[375] Id.

[376] Id paragraph 31.

[377] Id paragraph 32.

[378] Id paragraph 40.

decided to continue the stay of the enforcement of the award without imposing further conditions.[379]

Once again, the *Azurix* Decision creates uncertainty for creditors relying on the ICSID system to collect damages in sovereign debt disputes. Even where a state seeks to annul the award and therefore to stay enforcement proceedings, the *Azurix* Decision holds that a state's general legal framework and international legal obligations can be substituted as adequate assurance instead of a specific, additional financial security.[380]

2.4.3.3 *Enron Corporation Ponderosa Assets, L.P. v. Argentine Republic*

In the *Decision on the Argentine Republic's Request for a Continued Stay of Enforcement of the Award in Enron Corporation Ponderosa Assects, L.P. v. Argentine Republic* (hereinafter, *Enron*), Enron argued that there was a "substantial risk" that Argentina would not respect its obligations under the award if its annulment petition failed.[381] Enron also claimed that Argentina would also redirect its assets to undermine efforts to satisfy the award, referring to the fact that Argentina had failed to pay the *CMS* award 9 months following the decision of non-annulment.[382] Moreover, Enron asserted that the likelihood of enforcement of ICSID awards pursuant to Article 54 was greatly dubious, following a recent decision by the Argentine Supreme Court concluding that Argentine courts may review and vacate ICSID awards.[383] Argentina responded to this assertion by arguing that it had not failed to comply with the *CMS* award because in its view, (i) Article 53 of the ICSID Convention does not obligate Argentina to pay voluntarily; (ii) Article 54 of the ICSID Convention provides that award creditors must meet the same formal requirements that any person seeking to enforce a final judgement in a local court must follow; and (iii) CMS refused to follow the local Argentine procedure.[384]

In its decision, the *Enron* committee first decided that a request for stay of enforcement of an ICSID award should generally be granted under Article 52(5), unless there are "very exceptional circumstances" justifying a contrary decision.[385] Further, the committee deemed that it must "consider all of the circumstances of the case as a whole, and that a number of circumstances cumulatively may lead to a

[379] Id paragraph 43.

[380] Id.

[381] *Enron Corporation Ponderosa Assets, L.P. v. Argentine Republic*, ICSID Case No. ARB/01/3 Decision on the Argentine Republic's Request for a Continued Stay of Enforcement of the Award, 7 October 2008, paragraph 14; See also Frutos-Peterson (2008), pp. 164–174.

[382] *Enron* paragraph 14.

[383] Id.

[384] Id paragraph 15.

[385] Id paragraph 43.

particular conclusion, even if none of those circumstances alone would have necessarily done so."[386]

Thereafter, the committee turned to the question of provision of securities. The *Enron* committee first established that, since the Convention does not contain a requirement that the provision of a security be a condition for the grant of a stay of enforcement of an ICSID award, it refutes that an award creditor has a "counterbalancing right" to security in every case of continuation of a stay.[387] Instead, the *ad hoc* committee deemed that the decision to require a security should be disconnected from the award creditor's hardship where there is no "established serious risk of non-compliance with the award by the award debtor in the future, or other reason militating in favor of a condition of security."[388] Moreover, the committee reasoned that since Article 52(5) expressly provides that an award creditor's rights are conditioned on the discretion of an *ad hoc* committee to grant a stay of enforcement of the award, eventual adjournment of the award creditor's right to payment cannot therefore be considered to constitute prejudice *per se*.[389] In addition, the committee noted that an automatic guarantee condition would place the award creditor in a better position than in the absence of annulment proceedings since an award creditor would not otherwise have access to such a security.[390] Nevertheless, the *Enron* committee conceded that in exceptional circumstances "sufficient prejudice to the award creditor beyond mere delay" may justify the provision of security as a required condition for the stay of enforcement of the award pending annulment proceedings.[391]

With respect to the interdependence between Article 53(1) (providing that ICSID awards are final and binding) and Article 54 (providing that award execution shall be governed by the local laws of the state in which execution is sought) of the ICSID Convention, the *Enron* committee gave an initial interpretation.[392] Specifically, the committee determined that a state's failure to comply with an award pursuant to Article 53(1) constitutes a breach of the ICSID Convention and that it would be "inconsistent with the purpose of the ICSID Convention if an award creditor has to bring proceedings pursuant to national law enforcement mechanisms under Article 54(1) as a pre-condition for compliance with the award."[393] Accordingly, the committee found that—in the event the annulment failed—Argentina had an obligation under the U.S.-Argentina BIT, "to carry out without delay the provisions of the Award without the need for enforcement action by the Claimants..."[394]

[386] Id paragraph 46.

[387] Id paragraph 44.

[388] Id.

[389] Id.

[390] Id.

[391] Id.

[392] Id paragraph 68.

[393] Id.

[394] Id paragraph 82.

Once again, the *Enron* decision does not eliminate ICSID award creditors' collection risk. Although the committee rejected Argentina's flawed interpretation of an interconnected application of Articles 53 and 54 of the Convention conditioning Argentina's compliance upon the award creditors' successful appeals to Argentina's domestic course system, the *ad hoc* committee nevertheless required Argentina to merely "reconsider its position" as a precondition for a stay of enforcement.[395] In other words, for the *Enron* committee, simply reassessing its position on the nature of its payment obligation under Article 53 of the Convention, without any further guarantee, provided sufficient assurance of Argentina's compliance with the award.[396]

2.4.3.4 *Vivendi Universal S.A. v. Argentina*

The *Vivendi Universal S.A. v. Argentina* decision (hereinafter, *Vivendi*) once again showcased evidence that Argentina could delay compliance with adverse ICSID awards.[397] Vivendi argued that Argentina's recourse to the annulment proceeding was another tactic to avoid fulfilling its obligations under the ICSID award in Vivendi's favor.[398] In response, Argentina counter argued that the provision of a guarantee or an escrow account would have a "cascading" negative impact on its domestic economy since it would establish a precedent for the forty pending ICSID arbitration cases filed against the country, possibly amounting to billions of dollars.[399] Argentina also argued that it otherwise had a good record in terms of compliance with its international obligations under the ICSID Convention.[400]

Unlike the *Azurix* and *Enron* decisions, the *Vivendi* committee held that continuation of the stay should only be permitted when required by exceptional circumstances pursuant to Article 52(5).[401] Moreover, the *Vivendi* committee confirmed the inherently binding character of an ICSID award, which forms the fundamental principle upon which the ICSID system is based, and noted that no further conditions or actions are required for enforcement after the end of a stay. Additionally, the committee overruled the belief that "any organ of the host State can extend an administrative certification function to exercise any possible control over the enforcement process of pecuniary obligations under a finally binding ICSID

---

[395] Id.

[396] Id.

[397] *Compañía de Aguas del Aconquija S.A. and Vivendi Universal S.A. v. Argentine Republic*, ICSID Case No. ARB/97/3 Decision on the Argentine Republic's Request for a Continued Stay of Enforcement of the Award, 4 November 2008. See also Lin (2012).

[398] *Compañía de Aguas* paragraphs 12–16.

[399] Id paragraph 28.

[400] Id paragraph 29.

[401] Id paragraph 33.

award."[402] Indeed, the committee deemed that judicial intervention by the host state "would render the awards simply a piece of paper deprived from any legal value and dependent on the will of state organs" thereby undermining the purpose of the Convention.[403]

Persuaded however by Argentina's argument that the country would be faced by crippling financial burdens and "unquestionably irreparable harm" should the forty other pending ICSID tribunals additionally require a guarantee to secure Argentina's compliance with the forthcoming awards, the *Vivendi* committee decided to continue the stay of enforcement but subject to certain conditions.[404] Notably, the committee referred to Argentina's previous assurances of post-annulment compliance to be "no longer sufficient to grant an unconditional stay of enforcement" and therefore required Argentina to commit to pay in full the pecuniary amount imposed by the award within 30 days—provided the award is not annulled—or otherwise be obligated to provide a bank guarantee according to specific terms.[405] Failure to provide the bank guarantee would result in the *Vivendi* committee automatically terminating the stay of enforcement.[406]

Accordingly, although the *Vivendi* committee reasserted a debtor state's duty to comply unconditionally with its obligations under the ICSID Convention and ordered that a bank guarantee would otherwise be a necessary condition for a stay of enforcement within the absence of payment within a certain period of time, it still stopped short of requiring such a guarantee as a pre-condition for stay of enforcement of an ICSID award.[407]

2.4.3.5 *Sempra Energy International v. Argentina*

In *Sempra Energy International v. Argentina* (hereinafter, *Sempra*) the actual likelihood of Argentina's compliance with the award was the focal point and led to more stringent conditions for a decision in favor of the stay of the award.[408]

According to Argentina's point of view, the critical question was whether the necessary administrative arrangements and internal legal procedures had been put in place should the ICSID award be enforced.[409] Argentina also argued that whether it

402 Id paragraph 36.

403 Id.

404 Id paragraph 40.

405 Id paragraph 45.

406 Id.

407 *Compañía de Aguas* (n 397).

408 *Sempra Energy International v. Argentine Republic*, ICSID Case No. ARB/02/16 Decision on the Argentine Republic's Request for a Continued Stay of Enforcement of the Award, 5 March 2009. See also Lin (2012).

409 *Sempra* paragraphs 33–34.

had taken the necessary steps to give effect to Article 54 would also be an important factor in deciding whether it would comply with an ICSID award.[410]

The *ad hoc* committee remarked that a stay of enforcement is an exceptional measure and that there is no presumption in favor of granting a stay.[411] The committee also noted that pursuant to Article 52(4), it is authorized to stay enforcement of the award only "if it considers that the circumstances so require."[412] The committee also reconfirmed the independent applications of Articles 53 and 54 of the ICSID Convention.[413] The committee noted that the language of Article 53-(1) contains no language supporting the suggestion that compliance is dependent upon an award creditor first seeking enforcement pursuant to Article 54.[414] Instead, the *Sempra* committee reconfirmed that the automatic obligation to comply with an award pursuant to Article 53 and that Article 54 obliges all the parties to the ICSID Convention to "recognize an award rendered pursuant to this Convention as binding and enforce the pecuniary obligations imposed by that award within its territories as if it were a final judgment of a court in that State."[415] Accordingly, an ICSID award, including its monetary obligations, shall be enforced "as if it were a final judgment of a court in the State" and that "there would simply be no rationale for a requirement that an award creditor seeking payment should first subject itself to any form of local enforcement procedure."[416]

Additionally, the committee esteemed that Argentina's "repeated and uncompromising affirmation" that it was not unconditionally bound to "abide by and comply with" an ICSID award, unless the award creditor applied for an enforcement procedure through Argentina's domestic judicial system demonstrated that Argentina had no intention to comply with Article 53 unless *Sempra* first sought enforcement under Article 54.[417] The *Sempra* committee deemed a party's intention to comply with Article 53 to be an important consideration in determining whether to approve a request for a stay.[418] Furthermore, the *Sempra* committee also deemed it critical that Argentina "give some tangible demonstration of its preparedness to comply, unconditionally and in good faith, with its obligations under Article 53 of the Convention" and that "appropriate assurances" could not be sufficiently provided by the provision of a "comfort letter" as had been decided by the *CMS* and *Vivendi* committees.[419]

---

[410] Id.

[411] Id paragraph 27.

[412] Id.

[413] Id paragraphs 37–39.

[414] Id paragraph 37.

[415] Id paragraph 39.

[416] Id paragraphs 39 and 42.

[417] Id paragraph 53.

[418] Id.

[419] Id paragraph 109.

However, the *Sempra* committee deemed it unnecessary for Argentina to provide the award creditor with security for the entire amount of the award and instead ordered Argentina to provide a smaller amount in escrow as a condition for the stay of enforcement pending annulment proceedings.[420] Supporting its reasoning, the committee considered that "the primary purpose of [posting security] is not to guarantee payment but to provide appropriate assurances that compliance will take place in the future if, and to the extent that, Argentina's application for annulment is denied."[421]

Accordingly, compared to the *CMS, Azurix, Enron and Vivendi* decisions, *Sempra* went further in requiring a monetary security as a condition for the committee to grand a stay remedy.[422] At the same time, the decision highlighted just how unreliable Argentina had proved itself to be when it came to paying out its pecuniary obligations pursuant to an ICSID award.[423] Despite Argentina's obligation as a contracting state to the ICSID Convention to follow the decisions of the *ad hoc* committees, the subsequent developments have failed to support that expectation: the *Enron* committee's invitation to Argentina to reconsider its position was left disregarded, the *Vivendi* committee's proposal to Argentina to issue a commitment letter was ignored and the deadline set by the *Sempra* committee to issue U.S.$ 75 million in an escrow account elapsed unheeded.[424]

2.4.3.6 Did Argentina Fail to Comply with ICSID Awards?

Although it is self-evident that Argentina's requests to stay enforcement of the above-mentioned ICSID awards served to delay enforcement thereof, there is also the question of whether Argentina's conduct amounted to a failure of compliance with said awards. The answer to this question hinges on the interpretation of Articles 53 and 54 of the ICSID Convention and whether they are to be construed separately or jointly.[425] If a combined reading of Articles 53 and 54 of the ICSID Convention is recognized, then Argentina did not have an obligation to immediately pay the awards since such payment would have been subject to local judicial enforcement procedures.[426] Alternatively, if a joint reading of Articles 53 and 54 of the ICSID Convention is rejected, then Argentina's delayed payment of the awards constitutes non-compliance with the awards, particularly if it could have been determined that Argentina acted in bad faith.[427]

---

[420] Id paragraph 112.

[421] Id paragraph 110.

[422] Id paragraph 112.

[423] Id paragraph 53.

[424] Lin (2012).

[425] Titi (2014), p. 371.

[426] Id pp. 372–373.

[427] Id p. 373.

2.4.3.7 Summarizing Argentina's Prior Cases of Delaying Enforcement of ICSID Awards

Overall, the precedents set by Argentina's requests to stay enforcement as described in the *CMS*, *Azurix*, *Enron*, *Vivendi* and *Sempra* cases above underscore the risk that award creditors face in utilizing the ICSID arbitral system to resolve their disputes in the sovereign debt context.[428] Although these cases were specific to Argentina, they set an example that could be followed by other reticent debtor governments seeking to avoid the pecuniary obligations of an adverse ICSID award in favor of their bond creditors. As described above, the question of whether Articles 53 and 54 of the ICSID convention should be interpreted separately or jointly was not resolved definitively, leaving future indebted sovereigns to employ the same arguments in requesting to delay enforcement of adverse arbitral awards.[429] The delay in enforcement undermines the value of resorting to investment arbitration since in the end creditors reached settlement agreements with Argentina anyway.

2.5 Cost of Sovereign Debt Investment Arbitrations

As demonstrated during the aftermath of the Argentine economic crisis and default, which sparked decades of litigation, the behavior of holdout creditors makes sovereign debt restructuring slower, more difficult and uncertain by complicating the renegotiation process.[430] In fact, holdout creditors inflict additional financial damage on States in the middle of an economic crisis by having to repay individual creditors significantly greater sums than those agreed upon with cooperating creditors in restructuring negotiations. [431] Moreover, litigation instigated by holdout creditors is very costly for these debtor countries, siphoning away financial and political resources away from other important policy issues.[432]

More importantly, creditor litigation leads to market exclusion for debtor economies as they are unable to issue new bonds on the market and therefore unable to garner much-needed financing.[433] It has been noted that between the years 2000 and 2010, no single government facing a creditor lawsuit in the United Kingdom or the United States placed a sovereign bond in these jurisdictions.[434] Argentina for example was one of the most active emerging markets issuing bonds in the

[428] See Sects. 2.4.3.1–2.4.3.5 above.

[429] Titi (2014), p. 373.

[430] Schumacher et al. (2021); Tamura (2004), pp. 101–127; Hébert and Schreger (2017), pp. 3119–3145.

[431] Id.

[432] Id.

[433] Buchheit and Gulati (2017), pp. 224, 230.

[434] Panizza et al. (2009), pp. 655–656.

1990s.[435] However, following the Argentine default of 2001, it did not issue a single sovereign bond in international markets for 13 years.[436] Contrariwise, the private sector reentered into the foreign bond market regularly starting in late 2003 as soon as the economic conditions had improved.[437] The Argentina case study suggests that sovereign debt litigation undermines access to the sovereign bond market but does not impact corporations' market access.[438] The behavior of litigious hedge funds was also observed obstructing market access for other governments as well, such as in Costa Rica, Panama and Peru.[439]

At the same time, given that sovereign debt default is generally the result of economic crisis and therefore a period of economic hardship and austerity measures for debtor populations, the costs of sovereign debt litigation raises important public policy concerns.[440] One could question the legitimacy of redirecting government funds towards litigation costs with holdout creditors at a time when debtor governments are restricting public services and imposing higher taxes.[441] Moreover, when such litigation lasts decades, as was the case for Argentina, involving a series of investment arbitration cases, as described above, in which the tribunals never made any decisions on the merits all the while preventing debtor governments from accessing bond markets as described above, it is questionable as to whether the outcomes justify the costs.

2.6 Conclusion

This chapter provided an overview of the historical and legal framework of the sovereign financing system as well as an in-depth review of the Argentine and Greek debt crises of the early 2000's and their debt renegotiation efforts. As described in this chapter, the absence of an international bankruptcy mechanism for sovereign debt along with the steady decline in sovereign immunity has undermined the debt renegotiation process and has incentivized sovereign bond creditors to refrain from voluntary participation. Instead, such non-participating creditors have employed legal strategies to recover their full investments. Speculative hedge funds that seek out distressed debt in particular, have especially sought a markedly aggressive litigation strategy of filing arbitration proceedings pursuant to investment treaties.

---

[435] Buera and Nicolini (2019), pp. 14–17; Chabot Santarosa (2017), pp. 9–37.

[436] Id.

[437] Id.

[438] Schumacher et al. (2021); Tamura (2004), pp. 101–112; Hébert and Schreger (2017), pp. 3119–3145.

[439] Id.

[440] Brutti (2020), pp. 1819–1854; Kamenis (2014).

[441] Id.

This chapter detailed the jurisprudence of a series of ICSID arbitration cases filed by sovereign bond creditors. As underscored by the case law, it remains still uncertain whether sovereign bonds qualify as investments for the purpose of Article 25 of the ICSID Convention and therefore the arbitrability of such claims under the investment law framework. Furthermore, as these cases never reached a decision on the merits, it is unclear what impact they could have, nor the likelihood of enforcement or the level of compensation. The fact that Argentina settled with its sovereign bond creditors after years of litigation combined with the uncertainty of arbitrating such claims under the Investor-State Dispute Settlement (ISDS) system begs the question: why not consider mediation from the outset? Accordingly, Chap. 3 will dedicate itself to a deeper understanding of the mediation process.

Sources

International Conventions and Rules

Agreement Between the Government of the Czech and Slovak Federal Republic and the Government of the Hellenic Republic for the Promotion and Reciprocal Protection of Investments 1991 (Slovakia – Greece BIT)
Arbitration Rules of the Arbitration Institute of the Stockholm Chamber of Commerce (2017)
Convention on the Settlement of Investment Disputes between States and Nationals of Other States (ICSID Convention), 18 March 1965, 575 UNTS 159
Council Decision 2000/427/EC of 19 June 2000 in accordance with Article 122(2) of the Treaty on the adoption by Greece of the single currency on 1 January 2001 [2000] Official Journal L 167 of 7 July 2000
Permanent Court of Arbitration Arbitration Rules (2012)
Rules of Arbitration of the International Chamber of Commerce (2021)
Treaty establishing the European Stability Mechanism (ESM, 2012)
Treaty on European Union, Protocol on the Convergence Criteria Referred to in Article 109j of the Treaty Establishing the European Community (Maastricht Treaty, 1992)
UNCITRAL Arbitration Rules (2013)
Vienna Convention on the Law of Treaties (1969)

Domestic Rules and Legislation

Argentine Law No. 26547, art. 1, Dec. 9, 2009, B.O. 31798
United Kingdom State Immunity Act of 1978

References

Articles

Bjorklund AK (2011) Sovereign immunity as a barrier to the enforcement of investor-state arbitral awards: the re-politicization of international investment disputes. Am Rev Int Arbitr 21(1–4): 211

Blackman JI, Mukhi R (2007) The evolution of modern sovereign debt litigation: vultures, alter egos, and other legal fauna. Law Contemp Probl 73:53

Blanchard S (2014) Ambiente Ufficio S.p.A. and others v. Argentine Republic, ICSID Case No. ARB/08/9 (formerly Giordano Alpi and others v. Argentine Republic), Decision on Jurisdiction and Admissibility, 2 February 2013 (Bruno Simma and Karl-Heinz Böckstiegel) and Dissent Santiago Torres Bernárdez, 2 May 2013. J World Invest Trade 15:314

Bratton WW (2004) Pari passu and a distressed Sovereign's rational choices. Emory Law J 53:823

Brutti DJ (2020) Sovereign debt crises and and vulture hedge funds: issues and policy solutions. Boston Coll Law Rev 61(5):1819–1854

Buchheit LC, Gulati M (2017) Restructuring Sovereign debt after NML v. Argentina. Cap Mark Law J 12:224–230

Buera F, Nicolini JP (2019) The monetary and fiscal history of Argentina, 1960–2017. University of Chicago, Becker Friedman Institute for Economics Working Paper, pp 14–17

Burke-White WW (2008) The Argentine financial crisis: state liability under BITs and the legitimacy of the ICSID system. Asian J WTO Int Health Law Policy 3(1):199–234

Butenskey J (2017) Tango or Sirtaki? The Argentine and Greek dance with Sovereignty and a multilateral Sovereign debt restructuring framework. Boston Univ Int Law J 35:157

Cardosi JM (2013) Precluding the treasure hunt: how the World Bank Group can help investors circumnavigate sovereign immunity obstacles to ICSID Award Execution. Pepperdine Law Rev 41(1):1

Chabot B, Santarosa V (2017) Don't cry for Argentina (or other sovereign borrowers): lessons from a previous era of sovereign debt contract enforcement. Cap Mark Law J 12(1):9–37

Chan K-W (2014) The relationship between international investment arbitration and sovereign debt restructuring. Contemp Asia Arbitr J 7(1):229

Cibils A, Vuolo RL (2007) At debt's door: what can we learn from Argentina's recent debt crisis and Restructuring? Seattle J Soc Justice 5:755

Dale G, El-Enany N (2013) The limits of social Europe: EU law and the ordoliberal Agenda. Ger Law J 14:613

Desierto D (2012) The International Court of Justice in the settlement of international investment disputes. J Disp Prev Resol 1(1):201

Ding J (2016) Enforcement in international investment and trade law: history, assessment, and proposed solutions. Georget J Int Law 47:1137

Euler D (2013) Breaking the bond: vulture funds and investment arbitration. ASA Bull 31(3):558

Fisch J, Gentile CM (2004) Vultures or vanguards? The role of litigation in sovereign debt restructuring. Emory Law J 53:1043

Foster GK (2008) Collecting from sovereigns: the current legal framework for enforcing arbitral awards and court judgments against states and their instrumentalities, and some proposals for its reform. Ariz J Int Comp Law 25:665

Frutos-Peterson C (2008) Azurix Corp. v. Argentine Republic (ICSID Case No. ARB/01/12) Annulment Proceeding Decision on the Argentine Republic's Request for a Continued Stay of Enforcement of the Award. ICSID Rev 23(1):155–163

Georgakopoulos N (2012) Lessons from greco-multilateralism for creditors. Conn J Int Law 28:21

Glinavos I (2014) Haircut undone? The Greek drama and prospects for investment arbitration. J Int Disput Settl 5(3):475

Gómez KF (2011) Latin America and ICSID: David vs Goliath. Law Bus Rev Am 17:195

Goodman CL (2007) Uncharted waters: financial crisis and enforcement of ICSID awards in Argentina. Univ Penn J Int Econ Law 28(2):449
Gutierrez M (2013) Case comment, flying too close to the sun: how an EMU expulsion provision will prevent the European sovereign debt crisis from becoming a modern day Greek tragedy. Hous J Int Law 35:431
Hébert B, Schreger J (2017) The costs of sovereign default: evidence from Argentina. Am Econ Rev 107(10):3119–3145
Hirsch M (2016) Explaining compliance and non-compliance with ICSID awards: the Argentine case study and a multiple theoretical approach. J Int Econ Law 19(3):681
Hofmann C (2013) A legal analysis of the Euro zone crisis. Fordham J Corp Fin Law 18:519
Housos K (2015) Austerity and human rights law: towards a rights based approach to austerity policy, a case study of Greece. Fordham Int Law J 39:425
Iversen A (2019) Vulture fund legislation. Bank Financ Serv Policy Rep 38(5):57
Joiner J (2015) Past due: an introduction to sovereign debt, the ongoing dispute between NML capital and Argentina, and possible ramifications of the dispute's outcome. Law Bus Rev Am 21:85
Kabra R (2015) Has Abaclat v Argentina Left the ICSID with a 'Mass'ive Problem? Arbitr Int 331(3):425
Kamenis SD (2014) Vulture funds and the sovereign debt market: lessons from Argentina and Greece. Hellenic Foundation for European and Foreign Policy (ELIAMEP) 13
Karamanian SL (2013) Introductory Note to Abaclat & Others v. Argentine Republic: Decision on Jurisdiction and Admissibility (ICSID). Int Leg Mater 52(3):667
Kasenetz ED (2010) Desperate times call for desperate measures: the aftermath of Argentina's state of necessity and the current fight in the ICSID. Geo Wash Int Law Rev 41:709
Lakhani A (2015) David versus Goliath and multilateral diplomatic negotiations in the 21st century: how the Greek debt crisis negotiations marked the revenge of Goliath. Cardozo J Int Comp Law 24:97
Lapavitsas C, Kaltenbrunner A, Lindo D et al (2011) Breaking up? A radical route out of the Eurozone crisis. Research on Money and Finance:33
Li Y (2014) Policy implication of Poštová Tribunal's jurisdiction over sovereign bonds: bankruptcy cram-down and ICSID arbitration. Negot Disput Resol e-J. https://papers.ssrn.com/sol3/papers.cfm?abstract_id=2402643
Lin T-y (2012) Systemic reflections on Argentina's non-compliance with ICSID arbitral awards: a new role of the annulment committee at enforcement? Contemp Asia Arbitr J 5(1):1–22
Linares JC (2005) After the Argentine crisis: can the IMF prevent corruption in its lending? A model approach. Rich J Global Law Bus 5:13
Macias L (2012) Case comment, the Greek debt crisis: the weaknesses of an economic and monetary union. Duq Bus Law J 14:251
Maynard S (2016) A New Framework for the Analysis of Multi-Party Claims: Giovanni Alemanni and Others v The Argentine Republic ICSID Case No. ARB/07/8, Decision on Jurisdiction and Admissibility, 17 November 2014 (Sir Franklin Berman, Karl-Heinz Böckstiegel, J. Christopher Thomas). J World Invest Trade 17(1):117
Montanaro F (2015) Postova Banka SA and Istrokapital SE v Hellenic Republic: sovereign bonds and the puzzling definition of 'investment' in International Investment Law. ICSID Rev 3(3): 549
Olivares-Caminal R (2011) The pari passu interpretation in the Elliott Case: a brilliant strategy but an awful (mid-long term) outcome? Hofstra Law Rev 40:39
Ortolani P (2017) Are bondholders investors? Sovereign debt and investment arbitration after Poštová. Leiden J Int Law 30:383
Paddock JV (2002) Case comment, IMF policy and the Argentine crisis. Univ Miami Inter-Am Law Rev 34:155
Panizza U, Sturzenegger F, Zettelmeyer J (2009) The economics and law of sovereign debt and default. J Econ Lit 47(3):651, 655–651, 656

Park SK, Samples TR (2017) Tribunalizing sovereign debt: Argentina's experience with investor-state dispute settlement. Van J Transnatl Law 50:1033
Permesly J, Craven M (2018) Where are we now? Investment treaty arbitration, sovereign debt, and mass claims in the post-abaclat era. Transnatl Dispute Manag 15(1):1, 14–1, 19
Peterson LE (2011) Majority opinion in ICSID bondholders claim has broader lessons for defaulting sovereigns, fractured tribunals, shareholder groupings, and would-be claimants needing help getting ICSID claims registered. Invest Arbitr Rep 4
Power PJ (1996) Sovereign debt: the rise of the secondary market and its implications for future restructurings. Fordham Law Rev 64:2701
Rogoff K, Zettelmeyer J (2002) Bankruptcy procedures for sovereigns: a history of ideas, 1976-2001. Int Monetary Fund Staff Pap 49:470
Samples TR (2014) Rogue trends in sovereign debt: Argentina, vulture funds, and Pari Passu under New York Law. Northwest J Int Law Bus 35:49
Schilling D (2012) NML Capital, Ltd. v. Argentina 2011 WL 524433 (S.D.N.Y. Feb. 15, 2011). N Y Int Law Rev 25:159
Christoph Schreuer (2009) Revising the system of review for investment awards. BIICL. Available at http://www.univie.ac.at/intlaw/wordpress/pdf/99_rev_invest_awards.pdf
Schubert MF (2013) Note, when vultures attack: balancing the right to immunity against reckless sovereigns. Brook Law Rev 78:1097
Schumacher J, Trebesch C, Enderlein H (2021) Sovereign defaults in Court. J Int Econ 131:103388
Smits R (2015) The crisis response in Europe's economic and monetary union: overview of legal developments. Fordham Int Law J 38:1135
Snyder EC (1994) The Menem revolution in Argentina: progress toward a hemispheric free trade area. Texas Int Law J 29:95
Strong SI (2013a) Mass Procedures as a Form of "Regulatory Arbitration" – Abaclat v. Argentine Republic and the International Investment Regime. J Corp Law 38(2):259
Tamura K (2004) The problem of sovereign debt restructuring: holdout problem and exit consents. J Restruct Financ 1(1):101–127
Titi C (2014) Investment arbitration in Latin America: the uncertain veracity of preconceived ideas. Arbitr Int 30(2):357
Tsoukala P (2013) Euro zone crisis management and the new social Europe. Columb J Eur Law 20: 31–32
von Staden A (2011) Towards greater doctrinal clarity in investor-state arbitration: the CMS, Enron, and Sempra Annulment Decisions. Czech Yearb Int Law 2:207
Waibel M (2007) Opening Pandora's box: sovereign bonds in international arbitration. Am J Int Law 101:711
Weidemaier WMC (2014) Sovereign immunity and sovereign debt. Univ Ill Law Rev 67:68
Wright MLJ (2012) Sovereign debt restructuring: problems and prospects. Harv Bus Law Rev 2: 172

Books and Book Chapters

Alexandrov SA (2009) Enforcement of ICSID Awards: Article 53 and 54 of the ICSID Convention. In: Binder C, Kriebaum U, Reinisch A et al (eds) International investment law for the 21st century, essays in Honour of Christoph Schreuer. Oxford University Press
Bjorklund AK (2009) State immunity and the enforcement of investor-state arbitral awards. In: Binder C, Kriebaum U, Reinisch A, Wittich S (eds) International investment law for the 21st century, essays in Honour of Christoph Schreuer. Oxford University Press
Buckley RP, Arner DW (2011) From crisis to crisis. Kluwer Law & Business

Correa TDR (2018) Sovereign bond disputes caseload: basis for legal strategies. In: International investment law arbitration. MPIL research paper series

Gaillard E (2009) Identify or define? Reflections on the evolution of the concept of investment in ICSID practice. In: Binder C, Kriebaum U, Reinisch A et al (eds) International investment law for the 21st century: essays in Honour of Christoph Schreuer. Oxford University Press

Gallagher K (2013) The new vulture culture: sovereign debt restructuring and international investment rules. In: Gallagher K (ed) The clash of globalizations: essays on the political economy of trade and development policy. Anthem Press

Gulati M, Scott RE (2013) The three and a half minute transaction. University of Chicago Press

Halverson Cross K (2014) Sovereign arbitration. In: Lastra RM, Buchheit L (eds) Sovereign debt management, 1st end. Oxford University Press

Martin AT (2011) International mediation: an evolving market. In: Rovine AW (ed) Contemporary issues in international arbitration & mediation: the Fordham Papers (2010). Brill

Maute J (2006) Hyperinflation, currency board, and bust: the case of Argentina. Peter Lang

McLachlan C, Shore L, Weiniger M (2008) International investment arbitration: substantive principles. Oxford University Press

Megginson WL (2018) Privatization, state capitalism, and state ownership of business in the 21st century. Now Publishers

Menaker AJ, Paliwal SG (2015) Remedies – damages. In: Golden J, Lamm C (eds) International financial disputes - arbitration and mediation, 1st edn. Oxford University Press

Mistelis LA (ed) (2015) Concise international arbitration, 2nd edn. Wolters Kluwer

Oliveri EJ (1992) Latin American debt and the politics of international finance. Praeger

Schlemmer EC (2008) Investment, investor, nationality, and shareholders. In: Muchlinski P, Ortino F, Schreuer C (eds) The Oxford handbook of international investment law. Oxford University Press

Schreuer C, Dolzer R (2008) Interpretation and application of investment treaties. In: Principles of international investment law. Oxford University Press

Schreuer C, Malintoppi L, Reinisch A, Sinclair A (2009) The ICSID convention: a commentary. Cambridge University Press

Stevens M (2009) The power of ICSID Ad Hoc Committees to order security when granting a stay of enforcement. In: Doak Bishop R (ed) Enforcement of Arbitral Awards Against Sovereigns. JurisNet

Strong S (2013b) Mass procedures in Abaclat v. Argentine Republic: are they consistent with the international investment regime? Yearb Int Arbitr 3:261

Sturzenegger F, Zettelmeyer J (2007) Debt defaults and lessons from a decade of crises. MIT Press

Tawil GS (2009) Binding force and enforcement of ICSID awards: untying Articles 53 and 54 of the ICSID convention. In: van den Berg AJ (ed) 50 years of the New York Convention: ICCA International Arbitration Conference, ICCA Congress Series No. 14. Kluwer Law International

Thrasher RD (2021) The emerging role of international investment agreements in sovereign debt restructuring. In: Thrasher RD (ed) Constraining development: the shrinking of policy space in the international trade regime. Anthem Press

Vitale G (1995) Multilateral sovereign debt restructuring: the Paris Club and the London Club. In: Eichengreen B, Portes R (eds) Crisis? What crisis? Orderly workouts for sovereign debtors. Center for Economic Policy Research

Waibel M (2013) Tracing the origins of the UNCTAD principles. In: Bohoslavsky JP, Esposito C, Li Y (eds) Sovereign financing and international law: the UNCTAD principles on responsible sovereign lending and borrowing, 1st edn. Oxford University Press

Yannaca-Small K (ed) (2018) Arbitration under international investment agreements: a guide to the key issues. Oxford University Press

Zettelmeyer J, Trebesch C, Mitu Gulati G (2014) Managing holdouts: the case of the 2012 Greek exchange. In: Lastra RM, Buchheit L (eds) Sovereign debt management. Oxford University Press

Cases

Abaclat and others v. Argentine Republic, ICSID Case No. ARB/07/5 Decision on Jurisdiction and Admissibility, 4 August 2011
Abaclat and others v. Argentine Republic, ICSID Case No. ARB/07/5 Dissenting Opinion to Decision on Jurisdiction and Admissibility, 4 August 2011
Abaclat and others v. Argentine Republic, ICSID Case No. ARB/07/5 Consent Award Under ICSID Arbitration Rule 43(2) 29 December 2016
Allied Bank Intern. v. Banco Credito Agricola, 757 F.2d 516 (1985)
Ambiente Ufficio S.p.A. and others (Case formerly known as Giordano Alpi and others) and Argentine Republic, ICSID Case No. ARB/08/9 Decision on Jurisdiction and Admissibility Dissenting Opinion of Dr. Santiago Torres Bernardez 2 May 2013
Ambiente Ufficio S.p.A. and others (Case formerly known as Giordano Alpi and others) and Argentine Republic, ICSID Case No. ARB/08/9 Order of Discontinuance of the Proceeding 28 May 2015
Ambiente Ufficio S.p.A. and others v. Argentine Republic, ICSID Case No. ARB/08/9, Decision on Jurisdiction and Admissibility, 8 February 2013
Azurix Corp. v. Argentine Republic, ICSID Case No. ARB/01/12 Decision on the Argentine Republic's Request for a Continued Stay of Enforcement of the Award, 28 December 2007
CIBC Bank & Trust Co. v. Banco Cent. Do Brasil, 886 F. Supp. 1105 (S.D.N.Y. 1995)
CMS Gas Transmission Company v. the Republic of Argentina, ICSID Case No. ARB/01/8 Decision on the Argentine Republic's Request for a Continued Stay of Enforcement of the Award, 1 September 2006
CMS Gas Transmission Company v. the Republic of Argentina, ICSID Case No. ARB/01/8 Decision of the ad hoc Committee on the Application for Annulment of the Argentine Republic, 25 September 2007
Compañía de Aguas del Aconquija S.A. and Vivendi Universal S.A. v. Argentine Republic, ICSID Case No. ARB/97/3 Decision on the Argentine Republic's Request for a Continued Stay of Enforcement of the Award, 4 November 2008
Elliott Associates, LP v Republic of Peru [1998] 12 F Supp 2d 328 (SDNY 1998)
Elliott Assocs., L.P., General Docket No. 2000/QR/92, 16 (Court of Appeal of Brussels, 8th Chamber, Sept. 26, 2000)
Enron Corporation Ponderosa Assets, L.P. v. Argentine Republic, ICSID Case No. ARB/01/3 Decision on the Argentine Republic's Request for a Continued Stay of Enforcement of the Award, 7 October 2008
Fedax N.V. v. The Republic of Venezuela, ICSID Case No. ARB/96/3, Decision of the Tribunal on Objections to Jurisdiction, 11 July 1997
Fedax N.V. v. The Republic of Venezuela, ICSID Case No. ARB/96/3, Award, 9 March, 1998, subheading C
Giovanni Alemanni and others and Argentine Republic, ICSID Case No. ARB/07/8 Concurring Opinion of Mr J Christopher Thomas QC 17 November 2014
Giovanni Alemanni and others v. Argentine Republic, ICSID Case No. ARB/07/8 Decision on Jurisdiction and Admissibility, 14 November 2014
Giovanni Alemanni and others v. Argentine Republic, ICSID Case No. ARB/07/8 Order of the Tribunal Discontinuing the Proceeding 14 December 2015
Poštová banka, AS and Istrokapital SE v., ICSID Case No. ARB/13/8 Award of 9 April 2015
Republic of Argentina v. Weltover, Inc 504 U.S. 607 (1992)
Roseinvestco UK Ltd. v. The Russian Federation, SCC ARBITRATION V (079/2005), Final Award, 12 September 2010

Salini Costruttori S.p.A. and Italstrade S.p.A. v. Kingdom of Morocco, ICSID Case No. ARB/00/4 Decision on Jurisdiction, 23 July 2001
Sempra Energy International v. Argentine Republic, ICSID Case No. ARB/02/16 Decision on the Argentine Republic's Request for a Continued Stay of Enforcement of the Award, 5 March 2009
Settlement Agreement between the *Republic of Argentina and the Associazione per la Tutela degli Investitori in Titoli Argentini* dated 21 April 2016

Official Reports

Alogoskoufis G (2012) Greece's Sovereign Debt Crisis: Retrospect and Prospect. Hellenic Observatory Papers on Greece and South East Europe, pp 16–17
Enter the troika: the European Commission, the IMF, the ECB. European Stability Mechanism
European Commission. Second Economic Adjustment Programme for Greece – 4th Review. https://ec.europa.eu/info/sites/default/files/economy-finance/ecfin_presentation_4th_review_2nd_programme_brussels_en_0.pdf
European Commission on Economic and Financial Affairs Occasional Papers No. 123 of Dec. 2012, The Second Economic Adjustment Programme for Greece – First Review (December 2012). http://ec.europa.eu/economy_finance/publications/occasional_paper/2012/pdf/ocp123_summary_en.pdf
European Commission on Economic and Financial Affairs Occasional Papers No. 148 of May 2013, The Second Economic Adjustment Programme for Greece – Second Review (May 2013) http://ec.europa.eu/economy_finance/publications/occasional_paper/2013/pdf/ocp148_summary_en.pdf
European Commission on Economic and Financial Affairs Occasional Papers No. 159 of July 2013, The Second Economic Adjustment Programme for Greece – Third Review (July 2013). http://ec.europa.eu/economy_finance/publications/occasional_paper/2013/pdf/ocp159_summary_en.pdf
European Union Economic and Financial Committee. Collective Action Clauses in the Euro Area. https://europa.eu/efc/efc-sub-committee-eu-sovereign-debt-markets/collective-action-clauses-euro-area_en
Memorandum of Economic Policies of the Government of Argentina. (14 February 2000) International Monetary Fund
Pohl J, Mashigo K, Nohen A (2012) Dispute settlement provisions in international investment agreements: a large sample survey. Organization for Economic Cooperation and Development
Sovereign Borrowing Outlook for OECD Countries: 2021 (2021) Organization for Economic Development
The Role of the IMF in Argentina, 1991–2002 (2003) International Monetary Fund
Ziegler J (2015) Draft progress report on the activities of vulture funds and the impact on human rights. United Nations Human Rights Advisory Committee

Websites and News Articles

A synopsis of the Greek debt crisis (2011) The Denouement. http://knightin.typepad.com/denouement/2011/07/a-synopsis-of-the-greek-debt-crisis.html
Angeletos GM, Azariadis C, Arkolakis C et al (2017) Opinion: Grexit would be catastrophic for Greece. Ekathimerini. https://www.ekathimerini.com/opinion/216374/grexit-would-be-catastrophic-for-greece/

BBC News (2015) Argentina profile – Timeline. http://www.bbc.com/news/world-latin-america-18712378
Chambers A, Spink C (2012) Greece bond restructuring set for Friday. Reuters. https://www.reuters.com/article/U.S.-greece-restructuring-idUKTRE81M1L020120223US
Cibils A (2015) Argentina could show Greece a way out of its crisis. Financial Justice Ireland. http://www.socialeurope.eu/2015/08/argentina-show-greece-way-crisis/
Creighton A (2015) Greece should default on debt, take Argentina's path to recovery. The Australian. https://www.theaustralian.com.au/business/greece-should-default-on-debt-take-argentinas-path-to-recovery/news-story/2d1c18fc4d003ac27f4a04a6fd638f09
Elliot L (2015) Could Greece emulate Argentina's success after it defaulted in 2001? The Guardian. https://www.theguardian.com/world/2015/jul/08/greek-crisis-emulate-argentina-default-success
Gallagher KP, Marx D, Lachman D et al (2011) What lessons can Europe learn from Latin America? Inter-American Dialogue's Latin American Advisor. https://www.aei.org/wp-content/uploads/2011/10/LAA110711.pdf?x91208
Georgiopoulos G, Babington D (2014) Greece emerged from its 'Great Depression' at start of year. Reuters. http://uk.reuters.com/article/ukeurozone-economy-greece-idUKKCN0IY10B20141114
Graham C, Masson PR (2002) The IMF's dilemma in Argentina: time for a new approach to lending? Brookings. http://www.brookings.edu/research/papers/2002/11/globaleconomics-graham
Greece – Overview of economy (n.d.) Nations Encyclopedia. http://www.nationsencyclopedia.com/economies/Europe/Greece-OVERVIEW-OF-ECONOMY.html
Greece repays ECB after tapping fresh bailout funds (2015) EuroNews. https://www.euronews.com/2015/08/20/greece-repays-ecb-after-tapping-fresh-bailout-funds
Greece submits new reform plan to EU and IMF (2015) BBC News. http://www.bbc.com/news/business-33062202
ICSID. Database of bilateral investment treaties. https://icsid.worldbank.org/en/Pages/resources/Bilateral-Investment-Treaties-Database.aspx/
ICSID. The ICSID caseload – statistics (Issue 2020-2, 2020). https://icsid.worldbank.org/sites/default/files/publications/The%20ICSID%20Caseload%20Statistics%20%282020-2%20Edition%29%20ENG.pdf
IMF reaches staff-level agreement with Greece on €30 billion stand-by arrangement (2010) IMF Survey Magazine. http://www.imf.org/external/np/sec/pr/2010/pr10176.htm
Inman P (2015a) Greece warns it is set to default on debt repayment loans. The Guardian. http://www.theguardian.com/world/2015/may/24/greecewarns-it-is-set-to-default-on-debt-repayment-loans
Inman P (2015b) Greek exit would trigger Eurozone collapse, says Alexis Tsipras. The Guardian. http://www.theguardian.com/bU.S.iness/2015/jun/09/greekexit-would trigger-eurozone-collapse-says-alexis-tsipras
Investopedia. Brady bonds. https://www.investopedia.com/terms/b/bradybonds.asp
Krauss C (2000) One-day national strike freezes much of Argentina. The New York Times. http://web.archive.org/web/20140613141320/http://www.nytimes.com/2000/06/10/world/one-day-nationalstrike-freezes-much-of-argentina.html
Krugman P (2015) Argentine lessons for Greece. The New York Times. https://krugman.blogs.nytimes.com/2015/07/09/argentine-lessons-for-greece/
Leivada D (2015) Greek unemployment figures show no sign of decline. Huffington Post. http://www.huffingtonpost.com/entry/greece-unemploymentrate_U.S._55efa2fce4b03784e27714f4
Little A (2012) How 'magic' made Greek debt disappear before it joined the Euro. BBC News. http://www.bbc.com/news/world-europe-16834815
Newcombe A (2011) Mass claims and the distinction between jurisdiction and admissibility. Kluwer Arbitration Blog. http://kluwerarbitrationblog.com/2011/10/25/mass-claims-and-the-distinction-between-jurisdiction-and-admissibility

Press Release (2014) ECB announces operational details of asset backed securities and covered bond purchase programmes. European Central Bank. https://www.ecb.europa.eu/press/pr/date/2014/html/pr141002_1.en.html

Rooney B (2012) Greece: historic restructuring paves way for bailout. CNN Money. http://money.cnn.com/2012/03/09/markets/greece-creditors-default/

Schmidt B (2015) The distressed debt vulture now gobbling up the Cayman Islands. The Independent. https://www.independent.co.uk/news/business/analysis-and-features/distressed-debt-vulture-now-gobbling-cayman-islands-a6729521.html

Shell A (2015) Greek debt crisis: everything you need to know. U.S.A TODAY. http://www.usatoday.com/story/money/markets/2015/06/25/qa-greece-debtcrisis-loan/29284181/

Smith Freehills H (2013) Argentina settles five outstanding investment treaty arbitration claims in historic break with its anti-enforcement stance. Arbitration Notes. https://hsfnotes.com/arbitration/2013/10/14argentina-settles-five-outstanding-investment-treaty-arbitration-claims-in-historic-break-with-its-anti-enforcement-stance/

Sotiris P (2012) Austerity, limited sovereignty and social devastation. Greece and the dark side of European integration. Gesellschaftsanalyse Und Linke Praxis. https://www.zeitschrift-luxemburg.de/austerity-limited-sovereignty-and-social-devastation-greece-and-the-dark-side-of-european-integration/

Stevenson S (2015) Are the Greeks sound negotiators? The Slate. https://slate.com/business/2015/02/greece-debt-negotiations-are-greek-leaders-U.S.ing-sound-negotiating-techniques.html

Stevenson A (2016) How Argentina settled a billion-dollar debt dispute with hedge funds. The New York Times. https://www.nytimes.com/2016/04/25/business/dealbook/how-argentina-settled-a-billion-dollar-debt-dispute-with-hedge-funds.html

Thomas B, Hennessey K, Holtz-Eakin D (2011) Commentary, what caused the financial crisis? Wall Street J. https://www.wsj.com/articles/SB10001424052748704698004576104500524998280

Timeline: the unfolding Eurozone crisis (2012) BBC News. https://www.bbc.com/news/business-13856580

Traynor I (2015) Greece and lenders agree new bailout deal, finance minister says. The Guardian. https://www.theguardian.com/world/2015/aug/11/greece-and-lenders-agree-new-bailout-deal-says-finance-ministry-official

Chapter 3
Mediation

The previous chapter of this thesis detailed the history of sovereign debt disputes and the growth of investment arbitration claims from sovereign bondholders following default by debtor governments. Despite the flurry of ICSID cases following the Argentine and Greek economic crises, none of these cases reached an outcome on the merits therefore leaving many questions unanswered. Indeed, despite the high costs of these arbitration proceedings, the parties failed to resolve their disputes through the arbitral process but instead by other means, including settlement. Given that debtor states and sovereign bond creditors in these cases were capable of reaching settlement agreements to resolve their disputes, it is worthwhile exploring mediation as a more direct mechanism for settling sovereign debt disputes. This chapter is therefore dedicated to gaining a full understanding of mediation.

Accordingly, this chapter is subdivided into nine sections, each dedicated to giving a detailed description of a specific aspect of mediation. Section 3.1, will review some of the past and current definitions of mediation and propose a working definition for the purpose of this thesis. Section 3.2, will distinguish mediation from conciliation, since the terms have often been used interchangeably but do not in fact refer to the same process. Section 3.3 gives an extensive explanation of the different steps of the mediation process. Section 3.4 elucidates the training and various techniques mediators use to assist the parties in reaching a settlement agreement. Section 3.5 defines the array of available mediation styles and indicates according to which criteria the mediator and or the parties can select the appropriate mediation style to resolve their dispute. Section 3.6 sets out the possibility for parties to resort to blended styles of mediation which combine mediation with other dispute resolution mechanisms. Section 3.7 delineates the legal framework surrounding mediation. Section 3.8 describes the newest and most important addition to mediation's legal framework, which is the Convention on International Settlement Agreements Resulting from Mediation, also known as the Singapore Convention. Finally, Sect. 3.9 concludes this subsection of the thesis.

C. M. Sudborough, *Mediating Sovereign Debt Disputes*, EYIEL Monographs - Studies in European and International Economic Law 35,
https://doi.org/10.1007/978-3-031-46787-5_3

3.1 Debate Surrounding the Definition of Mediation

Here I shall discuss the various definitions that have been used to label mediation as well as the confusion between the terms "mediation" and "conciliation". I will conclude by proposing a working definition of mediation for the purpose of this thesis.

Mediation is essentially a form of interest-based negotiation facilitated by a neutral third party in a voluntary, informal and flexible process in which the parties remain in control over the outcome.[1] However, there are hundreds of differing published definitions of mediation.[2] The likely reason for this is that mediation has independently developed in different parts of the world and in different sectors taking into account the specific contexts relevant to the particular circumstances.[3] Unfortunately, this has created great confusion as to what is "proper mediation" and has fostered a debate as to what the "universal" definition of mediation should be.[4]

Some definitions refer to mediation as simply being a form of negotiation facilitated by a third party. For example, the United States-based for-profit dispute resolution organization, JAMS, formerly known as Judicial Arbitration and Mediation Services, Inc. defines mediation as follows:

> Mediation is a process wherein the parties meet with a mutually selected impartial and neutral person who assists them in the negotiation of their differences.[5]

Other definitions, go a step further indicating that the third party mediator will not have any decision-making capacity. For example, the newly adopted Singapore Mediation Convention provides the following definition,

> "Mediation" means a process, irrespective of the expression used or the basis upon which the process is carried out, whereby parties attempt to reach an amicable settlement of their dispute with the assistance of a third person or persons ("the mediator") lacking the authority to impose a solution upon the parties to the dispute.[6]

This definition is echoed in the Mediation Guidance Notes that accompany the ICC Mediation Rules:

> [M]ediation is a flexible settlement technique, conducted privately and confidentially, in which a mediator acts as a neutral facilitator to help the parties try to arrive at a negotiated settlement of their dispute. The parties have control over both the decision to settle and the terms of any settlement agreement.[7]

---

[1] Menkel-Meadow et al. (2020), pp. 85–87.

[2] Leathes (2011).

[3] Id.

[4] Id.

[5] 'What Is Mediation? What Happens In A Mediation?' (Jamsadr.com).

[6] United Nations Convention on International Settlement Agreements Resulting from Mediation, 12 September 2020, art 2, paragraph 3.

[7] 2014 International Chamber of Commerce (ICC) Mediation Guidance Notes, paragraph 1.

The definition provided in the Guide on Investment Mediation of the Energy Charter Conference (ECT), provides further detail by specifying the types of interests that the mediation process takes into consideration in the endeavor to reach a settlement agreement, including business interests, risk assessments, policy considerations as well as legal positions:

> Mediation is a process in which a neutral third party, a mediator, meets with the disputing parties and actively assists them in reaching a settlement based on their business interests and risk assessments or policy considerations and not only their legal positions.[8]

Given that the Guide on Investment Mediation of the ECT is specifically designed to addressed mediation proceedings in the context of investor-state disputes, and since the focus of this thesis is sovereign debt disputes, which may be treated as falling in the ISDS domain, the author of this thesis suggests to adopt the definition of mediation of the ECT as cited above. Moreover, this definition specifically mentions that mediation permits the parties to reach a settlement based not only on their legal positions but also on their *policy* considerations, which corresponds to the specific characteristics of states as parties to mediation proceedings. As can be observed in the aforementioned definition of mediation, a mediator has the responsibility of assisting the parties to come to an amicable accord of their own design based on the parties' interests. Accordingly, the mediation process is quite distinct from a judicial or arbitral process because the focus is not on establishing who is "right" in the eyes of the applicable law, but rather on negotiating a practical agreement that best fulfils the parties' various interests for a mutually beneficial outcome.[9]

3.2 Distinction Between Mediation and Conciliation

Mediation is often associated with conciliation as part of the various non-binding forms of dispute resolution and the terms are frequently interchanged.[10] However, it is a mistake to employ conciliation and mediation as synonyms because the two mechanisms are not by any means identical.[11]

Conciliators are empowered to issue reports with settlement recommendations.[12] This means that conciliators employ a more formal and evaluative process focused on the parties' legal rights that is akin to a non-binding arbitration. By contrast, mediation is more informal and less institutionalized than conciliation, placing the emphasis on open communication between the parties.[13] The mediator usually takes

---

[8] Energy Charter Conference, 'Guide on Investment Mediation' (Energy Charter Conference, 2016), paragraph 1.

[9] Moore (2014), pp. 19–20.

[10] Stipanowich (2015), p. 1191; Strong (2014), p. 28; Diathessopoulos (2012); Shane (1995), p. 31.

[11] Nitschke (2019), p. 121; Alexander (2009), p. 932.

[12] Nitschke (2019).

[13] Joubin-Bret and Knörich (2010), pp. 1–9.

a facilitative approach that operates as a form of assisted negotiation in which the mediator refrains from suggesting terms of settlement but rather focuses on identifying ways in which the parties can build an agreement that satisfies their interests.[14]

Until recently, procedural rules and guidelines did not always accord an independent definition to mediation but rather grouped mediation along with conciliation and other "amicable dispute resolution" techniques as being synonymous.[15] For example, the now-outdated UNCITRAL Model Law on Commercial Conciliation (2002) used the terms "conciliation" and "mediation" interchangeably:[16]

> For the purposes of this Law, "conciliation" means a process, whether referred to by the expression conciliation, mediation or an expression of similar import, whereby parties request a third person or persons ("the conciliator") to assist them in their attempt to reach an amicable settlement of their dispute arising out of or relating to a contractual or other legal relationship. The conciliator does not have the authority to impose upon the parties a solution to the dispute.[17]

Moreover, although the recently updated UNCITRAL Model Law on International Commercial Mediation and International Settlement Agreements Resulting from Mediation (2018) expressly stated that it was replacing the term "conciliation" with "mediation", the new Model Law still defines mediation as being a process that can be referred to as conciliation or any similar amicable settlement technique:

> For the purposes of this Law, "mediation" means a process, whether referred to by the expression mediation, conciliation or an expression of similar import, whereby parties request a third person or persons ("the mediator") to assist them in their attempt to reach an amicable settlement of their dispute [. . .].[18]

Wishing to sidestep the confusion over terminology, the International Chamber of Commerce's Amicable Dispute Resolution (ADR) Rules which were in force from 2001 to 2013, expressly provided the parties with the freedom to choose the settlement mechanism applicable to their dispute.[19] The preamble did, nevertheless, state that where the parties fail to agree upon the settlement technique, mediation would be settlement technique used:

> The International Chamber of Commerce ("ICC") sets out these amicable dispute resolution rules, entitled the ICC ADR Rules (the "Rules"), which permit the parties to agree upon whatever settlement technique they believe to be appropriate to help them settle their dispute. In the absence of an agreement of the parties on a settlement technique, mediation shall be the settlement technique used under the Rules.[20]

---

[14] Id.

[15] Stipanowich (2015), p. 1191.

[16] UNCITRAL Model Law on Commercial Conciliation (2002).

[17] Id Article 1(3).

[18] UNCITRAL Model Law on International Commercial Mediation and International Settlement Agreements Resulting from Mediation (2018), paragraph 3.

[19] International Chamber of Commerce's Amicable Dispute Resolution (ADR) Rules (2001) (ICC ADR Rules), Article 5(1).

[20] Id preamble.

The problem with this amalgamation of the conciliation and mediation labels and interchangeable use of the terms is that, according to practitioners, conciliation and mediation are actually two different methods of dispute resolution, involving different experiences for the disputing parties and possibly resulting in very different outcomes.[21] This was stated quite clearly by lawyer and mediator, Michael B. Shane, in his 1995 article "Differences Between Mediation & Conciliation" in Dispute Resolution Journal:

> I have come to believe there may be some confusion about the meaning of the terms mediation and conciliation. In the conciliation process, the conciliator is called upon by the parties to make a non-binding recommendation or finding that often concerns the factual or the legal issues in dispute, as well as what the conciliator considers to be the appropriate resolution of the dispute. [...] For purposes of this article, mediation will be defined as a process wherein the mediator is not mandated by the parties to make a finding or decision nor to recommend, jointly, to the parties. Finally, arbitration involves a binding, fact-finding resolution by a neutral third party. With these working definitions, it is clear then that the process moves from a negotiation model (in mediation) to a litigation model (in arbitration), with conciliation falling somewhere in the middle.[22]

Accordingly, pursuant to the growing consensus, the role of the third party neutral in mediation is to facilitate the parties' negotiations towards the creation of their own settlement terms whereas the role of the conciliator is to make findings based on the parties' factual and legal arguments and to make non-binding recommendations for the terms of a settlement agreement.[23] Thus, in the spectrum between negotiation and litigation, mediation is closer to the former whereas conciliation is closer to the latter.

This distinction becomes clearer when one compares the World Bank's descriptions of the proceedings for conciliation in the ICSID Rules of Procedure for Conciliation Proceedings (ICSID Conciliation Rules) and mediation.[24] According to the World Bank's overview of the Conciliation Commission process, the goal of the conciliation process is to "clarify the issues in dispute between the parties" with the aim of reaching an agreement on "mutually acceptable terms".[25] Accordingly, pursuant to the ICSID Conciliation Rules, the "Conciliation Commission" may "request documents, hear witnesses, make site visits and issue recommendations to assist the parties" in resolving their dispute.[26] Moreover, the parties are expected to "cooperate in good faith" and "seriously consider" the Conciliation Commission's recommendations.[27] Based on this description of the conciliation process, it is

---

[21] Shane (1995), p. 31.

[22] Shane (1995).

[23] Fawehinmi and Zlatanska (2016), pp. 146–152.

[24] Schreuer et al. (2009), pp. 431–453; ICSID, 'Overview of Conciliation under the ICSID Convention' (Icsid.worldbank.org) https://icsid.worldbank.org/en/Pages/process/ICSID-Convention-Conciliation.aspx, accessed 15 October 2021.

[25] Id.

[26] Id.

[27] ICSID Conciliation Rules (2006), Rules 22 and 23; Schreuer et al. (2009).

evident that the focus is on making findings on the parties' factual and legal claims and orienting the disputing parties towards particular settlement terms.[28] In contrast, the World Bank describes the mediation process as third party assisted negotiations, in which the mediator acts as a facilitator by "helping each party to identify its interests, overcome barriers to settlement, and develop possible settlement options with the parties" in an entirely voluntary process.[29]

Manifestly, therefore, the difference between conciliation and mediation, at least according to the World Bank, lies in the allocation of responsibility for the outcome of the proceedings.[30] Whereas conciliation emphasizes the role of the conciliator as having the burden of finding the terms of settlement for the parties, mediation defines the role of the mediator as an "enabler" in which the parties remain responsible for designing the terms for the resolution of their dispute.[31]

This distinction is important because the parties' experiences in conciliation proceedings is markedly different than in mediation proceedings.[32] In the former, given the conciliator's investigative and evaluative role, the parties are relatively passive in the process of coming to an agreement, and are instead expected to respond to the conciliator's requests to provide information.[33] By contrast, in the mediation process it is imperative that the parties actively participate with the mediator's assistance, to design a mutually beneficial settlement agreement.[34] According to Frauke Nitschke, Senior Counsel at ICSID, conciliation employs a more formal and evaluative process focused on the parties' legal rights that is akin to a non-binding arbitration.[35] By contrast, mediation is more informal and less institutionalized than conciliation, placing the emphasis on open communication between the parties.[36] The mediator refrains from suggesting terms of settlement but rather focuses on identifying ways in which the parties can build an agreement that satisfies their interests.[37]

Arguably, these important differences between the conciliator and mediator's roles and the parties' experiences in the different processes explains the different success rates for these two dispute resolution mechanisms. Notably, the reported success rate of ICSID conciliations is only around 22% of cases filed, with 86% of cases reporting a failure of the parties to reach an agreement.[38] In contrast,

---

[28] Fawehinmi and Zlatanska (2016), pp. 146–152; Shane (1995).

[29] ICSID, 'Investor-State Mediation' (Icsid.worldbank.org).

[30] ICSID, 'Investor-State Mediation' (2021); ICSID, 'Overview of Conciliation under the ICSID Convention' (2021).

[31] Id.

[32] Shane (1995).

[33] Id.

[34] Id.

[35] Nitschke (2019).

[36] Joubin-Bret and Knörich (2010); Shane (1995).

[37] Id.

[38] ICSID, 'The ICSID Caseload – Statistics' [2020-2], 15.

organizations administering mediation proceedings indicate a settlement rate that ranges from 70 to 89% of mediation cases.[39] However, it is true that investment conciliation proceedings and international commercial mediation proceedings are not entirely comparable, given the difference between disputes arising out of investment treaties and commercial contracts. Nevertheless, in both types of disputes, one can hypothesize that parties are less reticent to agree to settlement terms of their own design than on terms recommended by a third party.[40]

3.3 Mediation Proceedings

To gain a deeper understanding of the mediation process, it is necessary to become familiar with the proceedings in actual practice. In this subsection, I shall explain the various stages of mediation proceedings from the agreement to mediate to the termination of the mediation proceedings.

Mediation, as explained above, is an informal and dynamic process and therefore there is no rigid sequence of steps that must be followed in every mediation nor is it obligatory that every mediation involve the same procedure.[41] Even where the parties conduct mediation proceedings pursuant to specific procedural rules established by an administrative body, these rules tend to structure the process leading up to the mediation and the administrative aspects surrounding the mediation but still provide the maximum flexibility to the parties during the mediation itself.[42] Actually, successful mediators must adapt to the parties' needs and the particular dynamics of their dispute in structuring the proceedings.[43] Moreover, the mediation process is fluid and therefore one phase may commence without terminating a prior segment in the mediation procedure.[44] Even where a particular stage has been completed the communication of new information or other change in circumstances might require that a particular step in the mediation be reopened.[45] Nevertheless, despite the fact that mediations may operate inconsistently, a description of the different phases of a mediation should provide useful insight towards understanding the mediation process.

---

[39] Martin (2011), p. 405.

[40] Shane (1995).

[41] Moore (2014), pp. 19–20.

[42] International Bar Association (IBA) Rules for Investor-State Mediation Article 8(1); 2014 International Chamber of Commerce (ICC) Mediation Rules Article 7(1).

[43] Dilloff (2010), p. 63.

[44] Abramson (2004).

[45] Id.

3.3.1 Initiation of the Mediation Process

As stated previously, one of the key characteristics of mediation is that it is a voluntary process. The term "voluntary" with respect to mediation refers to the fact that the parties cannot be compelled to reach an agreement during the mediation and also, with the exception of court-ordered mediation, that parties cannot be compelled to participate in mediation against their free will.[46] Even with the exception of court-ordered mediations, this implies that a judge may order the parties in a particular case to attempt mediation by engaging in a minimum number of meetings with a mediator, but the parties may still exercise their free will as to whether they wish to pursue to the mediation past the minimum requirement and whether to reach an agreement within that process.[47]

Accordingly for non-court-ordered mediations, and as a voluntary process, every mediation must be the result of an agreement to mediate by the parties.[48] This can occur in two different ways. Firstly, the parties might have a pre-existing mediation clause in the underlying contract of their dispute.[49] Alternatively the parties might subsequently agree to mediate once a dispute has arisen in the absence of such a pre-existing agreement.[50]

A particularly effective means of ensuring that the parties commence mediation proceedings is to have a pre-existing agreement to mediate that would obligate the parties to participate at least until the first meeting with the mediator.[51] Such a clause could deny the parties the right to file for judicial or arbitral proceedings until the first mediation meeting has taken place or at least require that mediation proceedings be initiated in parallel to arbitration proceedings.[52] For example, Clause C of the ICC Mediation Rules creates an obligation to refer a dispute to mediation under the ICC Mediation Rules whilst permitting parallel arbitration proceedings if required, whereas Clause D states that the parties may not commence arbitration proceedings, if necessary, until an agreed period has elapsed following the filing of the request for mediation.[53] The advantage of such a compulsory, prior mediation agreement is that it forces the parties to at least attempt mediation, which in turn gives the parties the greatest chance of reaching settlement.[54] However, the mediation clause could also

---

[46]UNCITRAL Model Law on International Commercial Mediation (n 18) art 1(3); 2008 EU Mediation Directive Article 3(a); 2003 Uniform Mediation Act Section 2(1). For a critical view of the characterization of mediation as being voluntary, see Greenberg (2015), p. 11.

[47]Anderson (2010), p. 479.

[48]Moore (2014), pp. 19–20.

[49]Abramson (2004).

[50]Id.

[51]2014 International Chamber of Commerce (ICC) Mediation Rules, Mediation Clauses C and D; ICC Mediation Guidance Notes.

[52]2016 Trans Pacific Partnership, Article 9.19.

[53]2014 ICC Mediation Rules Mediation Clauses C and D; ICC Mediation Guidance Notes.

[54]Tümpel and Sudborough (2011), p. 269.

provide for non-compulsory mediation in which the parties would be invited to consider mediation prior to filing for judicial or arbitral proceedings but not be obligated to do so.[55] Even where no mediation clause exists, the parties could nevertheless enter into a subsequent agreement to mediate.[56] However, in such a case there is no guarantee that they will reach such an agreement. Therefore, the party seeking to propose mediation to the other party would probably benefit from filing the request for mediation through an institution that could help persuade the other party to accept the proposal by explaining the mediation process and ensuring that it is a neutral, productive and time and cost efficient process.[57]

Once the agreement to mediate is established, there are various administrative aspects prior to the commencement of mediation proceedings, including the choice of procedural rules, selection of the mediator, place of the mediation proceedings and the allocation of costs and payment procedures.[58]

In any dispute resolution proceedings, including mediation, the parties have the choice whether to conduct the proceeding *ad hoc* or under the administration of an institutional body.[59] In *ad hoc* proceedings, the parties will have to determine all aspects themselves, such as the governing rules, the selection of the mediator, the division of costs etc.[60] Although this approach might save on the costs of fees to an administering institution, the parties are likely to spend a considerable amount of time seeking to resolve unexpected hurdles without any guarantee that they will manage to do so, particularly once the dispute has arisen.[61] Nevertheless, parties may still involve the limited assistance of an administering institution at some point during the proceedings even where they prefer to conduct the proceedings *ad hoc*, for example as an appointing authority for the mediator.[62]

Where parties choose the assistance of an institutional body to assist with the administrative aspects of the mediation, the administering institution will be responsible for either obtaining the agreement of the parties on the various procedural issues that might arise or in making a decision in the absence of an agreement to ensure that the proceedings are conducted as efficiently as possible.[63] Accordingly, although the costs of such proceedings will include fees to be paid to the administering body, that institutional body will in turn have the responsibility to ensure that the overall costs of the proceedings remain low, for example by scrutinizing any

[55] 2014 ICC Mediation Rules, Mediation Clause B.

[56] 2012 IBA Investor-State Mediation Rules art 1(a); 2014 ICC Mediation Rules article 3.

[57] Tümpel and Sudborough (2011), p. 270.

[58] 2012 IBA Investor-State Mediation Rules (n 42); 2014 ICC Mediation Rules (n 51); Tümpel and Sudborough (2011), p. 270.

[59] McIlwrath and Savage (2010), pp. 64–67.

[60] Id.

[61] Id.

[62] 2015 International Chamber of Commerce (ICC) Rules for the Appointment of Experts and Neutrals.

[63] Folberg et al. (2016), pp. 335–338.

expenses the mediator seeks to have reimbursed and by making decisions necessary to expedite the process, as might be the case where the parties are unable to agree on the place of the mediation meetings or seek to replace the mediator.[64] Several institutions have published rules for conducting mediation proceedings. I shall address this later [section dedicated to mediating sovereign debt disputes].

Additionally, the parties need to select a mediator. Where the mediation proceedings are being conducted according to the procedural rules of an administering institution, usually the parties are free either to jointly nominate the mediator or to jointly select the mediator from an existing panel of mediators that have been preselected by the administering institution.[65] Alternatively, the administering institution will appoint the mediator pursuant to the applicable criteria of the case and any applicable criteria communicated by the parties.[66] Where the parties are conducting the proceedings *ad hoc* and are unable to jointly agree on the nomination of the mediator, they may seek the appointment of the mediator from an institution as well.[67] We shall examine the issue of mediator qualifications in a subsequent section of this thesis.[68]

Moreover, the parties must agree on the date(s), place and, if necessary, the language of the mediation proceedings.[69] Generally, the parties are free to agree on each of these issues based on what best meets their needs.[70] Where the parties fail to agree on these issues, they may seek the assistance of the administering institution, should there be one, or the appointed mediator.[71]

3.3.2 Pre-Mediation Submissions and Pre-Mediation Conference

Pre-mediation submissions, which are generally brief summaries of the dispute and the parties' claims addressed to the mediator before the start of the mediation sessions, are not required systematically in mediation proceedings.[72] Where mediators do invite the parties to make such submissions, they may do so for various reasons and therefore the type of information requested varies greatly as well.[73] For example, a mediator may simply request information about the parties, their legal

[64] 2014 ICC Mediation Rules Appendix Article 3.

[65] Leoveanu and Erac (2019), p. 86.

[66] Id.

[67] Id.

[68] See Chap. 4.

[69] McIlwrath and Savage (2010), pp. 187–188.

[70] Id.

[71] Id.

[72] Lande (2002), pp. 129–131.

[73] Abramson (2004), p. 75.

representatives, if any, and a description of the history and subject of their dispute to become familiar with the case in advance of their first mediation meeting.[74] Another mediator might wish to engage the parties in the problem-solving process in advance of the first meeting by asking the parties to suggest new ideas that could serve as a basis for their settlement discussions.[75]

Similarly, pre-mediation conferences, meetings that are held before the start of the mediation sessions dedicated at informing the mediator and all the parties of the issues to put on the agenda for the proceedings, are also not standard practice.[76] Should a mediator call for such a meeting, it will likely be brief and limited in scope.[77] The purpose of such a meeting is similar to the purpose of pre-mediation submissions: to get to know the parties and the issues that will be discussed during the mediation.[78] Perhaps the mediator will want to make sure that all the necessary parties for securing a settlement will be at the meeting or to ensure that any preliminary procedural issues that could hinder the parties from making progress in the mediation are resolved.[79]

3.3.3 Mediation Session

As stated above, the mediation process does not involve a rigid series of steps but is rather a flexible, flowing process that must respond to the circumstances.[80] Nevertheless, one can generally identify eight phases in every mediation session: (i) the mediator's opening statement, (ii) parties' opening statements, (iii) identification of issues, interests and impediments, (iv) formulation of the agenda; (v) working through any impediments to settlement, (vi) generating options for settlement, (vii) assessing and selecting options for settlement and (viii) conclusion.[81] Further, not all of these phases necessarily occur during joint or plenary session as the parties or the mediator may request private discussions, called "caucuses".[82] I shall now provide a brief description of each of these phases:

---

[74]Id 76.

[75]Id.

[76]Warnlof (n.d.).

[77]Ratliff (2018).

[78]Id.

[79]Id.

[80]Lande (2002), pp. 129–131.

[81]Abramson (2004), p. 74.

[82]Strasser and Randolph (2005), pp. 84–85.

3.3.3.1 Mediator's Opening Statement

The mediator's opening statement generally marks the start of the mediation and serves to set the tone of the mediation with the aim of encouraging a relaxed and collaborative atmosphere.[83] Except in rare circumstances, this phase takes place during joint session with the parties.[84] It is at this point that the mediator introduces him/herself to the parties if s/he has not already had the occasion to do so and to introduce the parties and any legal representatives to the mediation process.[85]

The mediator will seek to ensure that the parties clearly understand the purpose of the mediation process and to ensure that the parties understand that they are going to be engaging in a collaborative problem-solving process.[86] The mediator tends to explain that the parties may request private caucuses with him or her and informs the parties that he or she will not divulge to the other party any information given to the mediator in confidence.[87] In addition, the mediator will reassure the parties that what is said during the mediation will remain confidential and cannot be used against the parties in any subsequent proceedings unless it could have been discovered outside of the mediation.[88] Finally, the mediator normally establishes any ground rules with the parties about how they will communicate with each other, including whether they will address each other formally or by their first names, not interrupting each other, using threats or insults. [89] The mediator will also offer to answer the parties' questions.[90]

3.3.3.2 Parties' Opening Statements

The purpose of this phase is commonly twofold: to allow the parties to "vent" and to gather relevant information.[91] Venting in mediation gives the parties a safe place to release their pen-up emotions: such as frustration, anger, sadness etc.[92] This is a widespread practice in mediation as it is recognized as being a necessary prior step to getting the parties to work together collaboratively towards resolving their dispute.[93]

---

[83] Garcia (2011), p. 210.

[84] Moore (2014), pp. 307–308.

[85] Id. pp. 309–310.

[86] Id.

[87] Ratliff (2018).

[88] Id.

[89] Id.

[90] Moore (2014), p. 322.

[91] De Girolamo (2020), pp. 103–115.

[92] Id.

[93] Id.

More importantly, valuable information may be hidden in the expression of the parties' emotions that may be key towards crafting a settlement agreement.[94]

In addition, this phase also allows the mediator and the parties to gather information necessary for developing a full picture: What are the parties' interests? What are the issues? What are the impediments to settlement?[95]

Unless communication between the parties has broken down so much that the parties cannot be in the same room at the same time, this phase also occurs generally in joint session.[96] Although, venting and information gathering will likely occur at other phases of the mediation besides the parties' opening statements which may or may not be in joint session or in caucus with the mediator.[97]

3.3.3.3 Identifying Issues, Interests and Impediments

In this phase, the mediator helps the parties to identify the issues to be resolved, the parties' specific underlying interests and the impediments, which prevented the parties from reaching agreement during direct negotiations.[98] The parties and the mediators will then use this information to formulate the agenda for the mediation meeting(s).[99]

3.3.3.3.1 Formulating the Agenda

Once the parties have revealed sufficient information, the mediator can work with the parties to put together the agenda for the mediation.[100] Normally, a mediator constructs the agenda according to the list of issues for resolution.[101] Predictably, coupled with each issue is the hurdle preventing that issue from settlement.[102]

Mediators have different approaches to creating the agenda.[103] For example some may choose to only disclose one issue for discussion at a time, whereas others establish the full agenda openly.[104] Moreover, some mediators might invite the parties to work with the mediator in articulating the agenda.[105] In terms of the way

---

[94] Picard and Siltanen (2013), p. 33.

[95] Moore (2014), p. 327.

[96] Abramson (2004), p. 77.

[97] Id.

[98] Moore (2014), p. 123; Abramson (2004), p. 78.

[99] Moore (2014), p. 340; Abramson (2004), p. 78.

[100] Sammut and Bauer (2020), pp. 163–167.

[101] Id.

[102] Id.

[103] Moore (2014), p. 351; Abramson (2004), p. 78.

[104] Pepperdine University Strauss Institute for Dispute Resolution (2009), pp. 3:5–3:8.

[105] Id.

the issues are ordered, mediators might have different suggestions for the parties such as: progressing from easiest to most difficult issue; starting with the issue of greatest importance and ending with the issues of least importance; selecting an all-encompassing principle for selecting the issues to be discussed or asking the parties' to propose other means of grouping issues together.[106]

3.3.3.3.2 Working Through Any Impediments to Settlement

The focus of this stage of the mediation is to discuss how the parties can overcome any impasse they have.[107] For the mediator, this might require caucusing with the parties in order to ask probing questions and assisting the parties to analyse their interests and positions in order to make any necessary decisions. [108]

3.3.3.3.3 Generating Options for Settlement

The purpose of this stage is critical as it allows the parties to generate creative settlement options that might not be possible in court or arbitration proceedings.[109] To do so, the mediator guides the parties through various methods of creating value in the parties' negotiations.[110] This is often called "expanding the pie" by negotiators.[111] Typically, parties will be focused on competing to claim as much value as possible in the negotiation.[112] Therefore, the mediator will have to help the parties to first concentrate on expanding the value by inventing options, using their creativity and taking some risks before deciding on the feasibility and desirability of those options.[113]

Mediators employ various techniques to assist the parties towards generating options for settlement.[114] The best-known method is brainstorming.[115] When brainstorming, participants are free to generate a sweeping range of ideas without constraint as parties are under express instruction not to criticize any ideas until the decision-making phase.[116]

---

[106] Id.

[107] Paula Young, 'Overcoming Impasse in Mediation: A Short Literature Review' (July 2003) Mediate.com.

[108] Id.

[109] Abramson (2004), pp. 86–89.

[110] Id. p. 79.

[111] Fisher et al. (1997), pp. 61–65.

[112] Id.

[113] Id.

[114] Boulle et al. (2008), pp. 217–219.

[115] Id.

[116] Id.

3.3.3.3.4 Assessing and Selecting Options for Settlement

At this juncture of the mediation the mediator summons the parties to evaluate the list of settlement options.[117] In doing so, the parties will need to consider the various alternatives against recognized standards of fairness and agreed-upon objective criteria to determine which outcome best meets their interests.[118]

This is frequently the most challenging interval in the mediation as the parties must commit to final and possibly painful decisions.[119] Therefore, the mediator may engage various techniques to facilitate this round in the parties' negotiations.[120] To begin, the mediator might assist the parties in developing and implementing a settlement formula consisting of agreed-upon criteria for filtering through the various settlement options.[121] In this way the parties can identify the most appealing options, and with the mediator's help, further improve them to develop a top list of settlement possibilities.[122] Next, the mediator will likely help the parties in designing measured concessions that could gradually lead the parties to converge upon an agreement.[123] Another method the mediator might use is to propose that a party devises a bold and attractive packaged proposal that will induce the other party to seize the opportunity to enter into a final agreement.[124]

3.3.3.3.5 Conclusion of the Mediation Session(s)

The purpose of this segment of the proceedings is to bring closure; either the mediator helps the parties to reach a final agreement or to work out any remaining details regarding the substance or implementation of their agreement or where the parties are still at an impasse the mediator will discuss with the parties their various options.[125]

In either scenario, the mediator will generally summarize the progress made by the parties in the mediation as well as any subsequent tasks to be completed.[126] Even where the parties failed to resolve all issues in the mediation, they probably were able to clarify those unresolved issues and to reach partial agreement, which clarifies or helps to develop the path towards resolution of their dispute.[127]

---

[117] Abramson (2004), pp. 80, 87.

[118] Id. p. 80.

[119] Beer et al. (2012), pp. 68–70.

[120] Id.

[121] Abramson (2004), p. 80.

[122] Riskin (2003), pp. 34–46.

[123] Id.

[124] Id.

[125] Beer et al. (2012), pp. 75–77.

[126] Id.

[127] Abramson (2004), p. 81.

3.3.3.4 Post-Mediation Session

Occasionally, after the conclusion of the mediation proceedings the parties might request or accept the mediator's offer to supervise the finalization and implementation of their agreement.[128] This could involve helping the parties or their counsel in drafting the terms of the settlement agreement or to oversee the execution of key terms in the parties' agreement such as important payments or delivery of assets often by making conference calls, sending letters and emails.[129]

3.4 Mediator's Techniques

In this part, I shall provide some background on the skills that mediators develop through training that allows them to engage during the mediation process.

3.4.1 Guiding the Parties from an Adversarial Approach to Joint Problem-Solving Process

When negotiating, parties are often mired in inefficient, confrontational strategies.[130] Typically, parties will state their positions and then participate in what has been coined by negotiation practitioners and academics as the "dance" of offers and counter-offers wherein each party struggles to stay as close as possible to his or her originally stated position often resulting in a package of less than ideal compromises.[131]

One of the mediator's main objectives in mediation is to guide the parties away from an adversarial approach in their negotiations and towards a joint problem-solving mind-set.[132] To do so, the mediator will often invite the parties to take a break in the exchange of offers and counter-offers to consider jointly constructing a creative solution in which the parties' step away from their stated positions and focus instead on their broader interests.[133] Alternatively, the mediator might make some proposals based on the parties' broader interests in order to reorient the negotiation towards a problem-solving approach.[134]

---

[128] Id.

[129] Id 82.

[130] Pepperdine University Strauss Institute 1:1–1:7.

[131] Pepperdine University Strauss Institute 4:1–4:12; Fisher et al. (1997), p. 32.

[132] Abramson (2004), p. 82.

[133] Id.

[134] Id.

3.4.2 *Promoting and Improving Communication Between the Parties*

Throughout the mediation, the mediator uses various techniques to improve communication, including some of the subsequently listed techniques such as questioning techniques, listening techniques, managing emotions, reframing issues and statements.[135]

More generally, the mediator will strive to encourage the participants to communicate openly.[136] The mediator will do so by demonstrating verbally and physically his or her interest in what the speaker is saying.[137] The mediator will also develop a safe space for free speech, by reminding the parties of the confidentiality of the proceedings and the need to respect each other by not interrupting each other, or engaging in threatening or insulting language.[138]

3.4.3 *Questioning Techniques*

To improve communication and elicit information in the mediation, mediators ask many carefully phrased questions throughout the mediation.[139] Under all circumstances, the mediator must maintain his or her appearance of impartiality, and will therefore frame (and react to said) questions neutrally.[140] Depending on the particular circumstances, the mediator must select the appropriate form of question, whether it be an open-ended or a closed question, a clarifying question or a leading question.[141]

The most frequently used question types used by mediators are open-ended questions and clarifying questions.[142] Open-ended questions are the most extensively used form of questions in mediation because they invite expansive, unconstrained answers typically provided in the form of a narrative.[143] The mediator's purpose in posing such a question is to extract as much information as possible by bringing to light previously unrevealed information.[144] For example, the mediator may pose an open-ended question such as "What happened?", "What are your

---

[135] Moore (2014), pp. 251–260.

[136] Cloke (2001), pp. 55–86.

[137] Thomas Repicky, 'How to Talk and Listen Effectively in Mediation' (July 2011) Mediate.com.

[138] Moore (2014), p. 302.

[139] O'Sullivan (2018), pp. 5–14.

[140] Id.

[141] Id.

[142] Moore (2014), p. 261.

[143] Id.

[144] Id pp. 261–264.

concerns?", "How has this affected you?" Mediators also heavily employ clarifying questions, in which the mediator asks a direct question that seeks further explanation of information that has been presented.[145] For example, "Can you explain further what happened?" or "What do you mean, when you say...?"

Although sometimes necessary, mediators will refrain from overusing closed questions and leading questions.[146] Closed questions anticipate a specific answer, generally either "yes" or "no" or other very short replies, and the information they provide is relatively limited.[147] Mediators will employ closed questions when it is necessary to confirm a particular point relevant to the mediation.[148] Examples of closed questions that a mediator might ask are, "How long have you been employed by...?", "Do you agree to...?" Leading questions suggest the answer to the party being questioned and generally seek agreement with the question.[149] For example, "Is it not true that...?", "It is correct that..., isn't it?" Trainers dissuade mediators from using such questions because they discourage complete, unrestricted answers and could make the responding party uncomfortable and defensive.[150]

3.4.4 Listening Techniques

To improve communication and the exchange of information between the participants to the mediation, the mediator may use both passive and active listening techniques.[151] Mediators' astute use of these techniques can entice the different sides to engage in frank and open discussion.[152]

Passive listening techniques involve expressing nonverbal and verbal indications of the mediator's interest in what his or her interlocutor is saying.[153] For instance, the mediator might use unspoken indicators through body language, such as nodding his or her head, making eye contact, leaning forward, smiling, or even staying silent to encourage the speaker to continue talking etc.[154] The mediator might also use simple vocal prompts like "oh", "mmm-hm", "interesting", "I see", "really", "sure", "go on", etc.[155]

---

[145] Abramson (2004), p. 83.
[146] Lehman and Page (2007).
[147] Id.
[148] Id.
[149] O'Sullivan (2018), pp. 5–14.
[150] Id.
[151] Abramson (2004), p. 83.
[152] Id.
[153] Bogdanoski (2009), pp. 206–207.
[154] Id.
[155] Id.

Mediators are also trained to use active listening techniques in which the listener carefully restates or paraphrases the sender's message in his or her own words and acknowledges the speaker's feelings and emotional reactions.[156] Active listening does not imply that the mediator agrees with the speaker's positions and ideas.[157] Rather, by engaging in reflective responding, the mediator explicitly demonstrates to that party that she or he is being heard and understood, which encourages the party to speak more fully about his or her feelings, priorities and frames of reference.[158] Consequently, the mediator can better understand the party's negotiation position as well as the underlying factors and interests that support that position, allowing the mediator to help the party reconcile that position with his or her underlying preferences, interests and priorities.[159]

Reflective responding is critical to active listening, but to be successful it requires that the mediator respect the following guidelines: (i) focus more on listening rather than on speaking, (ii) respond to the speaker's feelings, beliefs and positions rather than abstract ideas, (iii) allow the speaker to frame the conversation process by refraining from leading the speaker and instead following him or her into areas that the listener thinks that should be explored, (iv) seek only to clarify the speaker's statements but abstain from questioning or suggesting what he or she should be thinking or feeling, and (v) recognize any sentiments that the speaker has expressed.[160]

3.4.5 Managing Emotions

In mediation, it is recognized that dealing with the emotional dimension of a dispute can be an essential prerequisite for resolving the overall conflict.[161] If the emotional aspect is neglected, it will often prevent the parties from engaging in constructive problem solving.[162] Therefore, mediators are prepared to welcome parties who express feelings of anger, frustration, sadness, fear etc. during the mediation.[163] Moreover, mediators are skilled at detecting the emotional obstacle in the dispute as it is not always apparent.[164] Accordingly, mediators are coached to be perceptive to subtle cues that can be found in the parties' tone of voice, facial expressions and

[156] Cohen (2014), pp. 158–159.

[157] Id.

[158] Id.

[159] Moore (2014), p. 254.

[160] Id pp. 254–256.

[161] Irvine and Farrington (2016), pp. 211–239.

[162] Id.

[163] Jameson et al. (2009), p. 170–173.

[164] Id.

body language.[165] Moreover, mediators have learned various strategies that they can implement to help the parties overcome the emotional hurdle to reaching agreement.[166]

Typically, the mediator will seek to diffuse the emotion by giving the emotionally charged party the opportunity to vent his or her feelings and thus obtain psychological and physical release from having been heard.[167] However, the mediator will generally establish some ground rules to limit escalation of the conflict or further damage of the parties' relationship, such as forbidding direct personal attacks and suggesting that the party focus on expressing his or her own feelings and understandings rather than making accusatory remarks.[168]

In addition, the mediator might seek to analyse and identify the underlying significance of the emotional display to determine whether it is a negotiation tactic or actually genuine.[169] Once having done so the mediator can then devise the means to remove the cause or to mitigate it.[170]

In extreme cases, the mediator might resort to the extreme measure of cutting off communications between the parties and requiring them to communicate only through the mediator.[171] The mediator might do this by separating the parties into separate rooms and then shuttling between them.[172]

3.4.6 *Framing and Reframing Statements and Issues*

People facing the same dispute often make sense of it differently due to their different backgrounds, experiences, expectations and needs.[173] Framing is the process by which people categorize these different analyses of the circumstances.[174] In mediation, how a party frames a particular issue or problem strongly reflects their goals, expectations and preferences.[175] As frames are malleable, mediators can use them to shift the conversation towards a common frame that promotes agreement.[176]

---

165 Id.

166 Moore (2014), pp. 164–169; Abramson (2004), p. 84.

167 Kelly and Kaminski (2016), pp. 56–59.

168 Id.

169 Moore (2014), pp. 164–169.

170 Id.

171 Abramson (2004), pp. 85.

172 Id.

173 Lewicki et al. (2015), pp. 198–202.

174 Id.

175 Rule (2018).

176 Id.

Mediators often use the technique of framing and reframing when the issues are being defined.[177] It is typical for disputants to define issues in such a way that is biased in their own favor, similar to how lawyers draft court submissions.[178] In order to facilitate the settlement process, the mediator will remove each side's incendiary language and reframe the issues more broadly while still encapsulating the parties' vital interests so as to bring the parties towards a common frame while also boosting the number of settlement options.[179]

Moreover, mediators frequently reframe parties' hostile, accusatory or otherwise biased statements in more neutral terms in order to prevent escalation of the conflict.[180]

3.4.7 Brainstorming

Brainstorming is the most prominent technique amongst the various methods that mediators employ to assist the parties in generating alternative and creative solutions to their dispute.[181] In brainstorming, an issue is framed by the mediator and the participants who work to create as many possible solutions to the problem as possible while the mediator or someone else records the various suggestions.[182]

The mediator instructs the parties to react freely to the problematic without constraint suggesting all ideas that come to mind without censorship and without evaluating any proposals to encourage creativity.[183] No one shall be held accountable for ideas put forth during the brainstorming process and the proposals will only be assessed after the brainstorming process is terminated.[184]

3.4.8 Decision-Making Methods

To structure the process of inventing and deciding amongst settlement options, mediators can use different sequencing and design mechanisms.[185] The bottom-up, top-down and single text negotiating approaches are described here.[186]

---

[177] Livingood (2002), pp. 42–49.

[178] Id.

[179] Beer et al. (2012), p. 47.

[180] Id.

[181] Golann (2011), pp. 22–26; Moore (2014), pp. 402–404.

[182] Id.

[183] Limbury (2019).

[184] Id.

[185] Moore (2014), pp. 413–420.

[186] Id.

In the bottom-up approach, the mediator helps the parties to subdivide the issues into smaller blocks that are easier to manage.[187] The parties then generate and decide upon settlement options for each sub-issue sequentially, moving towards resolution of the full dispute.[188] In the top-down method, the mediator assists the parties to construct guiding principles that will be used to construct and evaluate their settlement options.[189]

In the single-text negotiating strategy, the mediator summons the parties to discuss the issues and their interests which the mediator then centralizes into a single document.[190] This draft might be written on a flip-chart for example.[191] The idea is to change the parties' mind-set from criticizing and reacting to the other side's proposals and instead to work together towards providing and improving proposals that meet everyone's interests.[192] This technique is often employed in multiparty mediations.[193]

3.4.9 *Managing Power-Imbalances*

Power in mediation refers to the ability to get what you want from the other party.[194] There are different kinds of negotiation power relating to a party's financial resources, available information, organizational status, relationships, gender, etc.[195]

A long running debate amongst mediators is whether they should be responsible for the fairness of the content of the resulting settlement agreements.[196] On the one hand, a mediator's ethical duty to remain neutral and impartial forbids the mediator from advocating for a weaker party in the mediation.[197] On the other hand, the mediator also has a moral obligation to help the parties reach a relatively just, satisfactory and robust agreement.[198]

Practical experience and academic research indicate that when negotiators have relatively balanced power relationships, they negotiate more fruitfully.[199] Unbalanced bargaining power between the disputants can significantly affect the resulting

---

[187] Abramson (2004), pp. 86–89.

[188] Id.

[189] Id.

[190] Smith (2005).

[191] Moore (2014), pp. 413–420.

[192] Smith (2005).

[193] Abramson (2004), pp. 86–89.

[194] Moore (2014), p. 260; Abramson (2004), p. 89.

[195] Id.

[196] Agusti-Panareda (2004), p. 25.

[197] Voyles (n.d.).

[198] Id.

[199] Lewicki et al. (2015), p. 256–261.

substance of the parties' agreement in mediation.[200] Consequently, mediators often seek to minimize the negative effects of unequal power between the parties in the mediation.[201]

When working with disputants in a relatively symmetrical power relationship, mediators will seek to enhance the parties' cognizance of equal power in their relationship and minimize the use of intimidating behavior or otherwise manipulative use of power.[202] Conversely, where there is a wider discrepancy in the power balance, mediators promote greater equality by ensuring equal access to data, instructing and supporting the parties on executing a successful negotiation strategy, helping them to brainstorm about gathering the necessary financial resources necessary, referring parties to professional or expert advice, urging the parties to make realistic offers or necessary concessions.[203]

3.4.10 Overcoming Impasse

There are myriad reasons why parties might reach a stalemate during the mediation process.[204] The academic literature on mediation has various approaches to categorizing the causes for impasse, ranging from three to ten different classifications, but often including some version of the following five groupings: "relationship", "data", "value", "interest", and "structural".[205]

Relationship deadlocks arise when parties are profoundly distraught with each other, are bound by misconceptions about each other or have very dysfunctional communications.[206] Data conflicts arise when relevant information is lacking, false or misleading or when the parties do not agree on the interpretation or even the importance of the relevant data.[207] Value-related impasse is possibly the hardest to resolve because it stems from people's core beliefs and moral principles.[208] Interest-based conflict result when what the parties "want" is at odds—either because they want the same thing that cannot be shared or split in different amounts or because they want different things that the other side is not willing to give, for example.[209] Structural deadlock is the hardest to identify and can overlap with other causes of

[200] Id.

[201] Abramson (2004), p. 89.

[202] Voyles (n.d.).

[203] Id.

[204] Fisher et al. (1997); Moore (2014), p. 295; Abramson (2004), p. 105.

[205] Abramson (2004), p. 105.

[206] Lewicki et al. (2015), p. 521.

[207] Id.

[208] Abramson (2004), p. 107.

[209] Id 106.

impasse such as relationship.[210] The two most common sources are deadlocks due to unequal bargaining power or conflicts between the clients' and their attorneys' objectives.[211] Other more subtle structural conflicts arise from one side lacking sufficient settlement authority, lack of a deadline, time constraints or other technical/practical limitations that have a disproportionate impact on the parties and asymmetrical control of conflict resolution resources.[212]

Each type of impasse will require a tailored approach from the mediator to help the parties overcome the deadlock.[213] From a general standpoint however, the mediator will help the parties to overcome such impasses by first assisting them to identify what the impediments to settlement are and then to design a strategy to overcome the particular impasse.[214] Mediators will ask probing questions in order to expose why the negotiation has reached gridlock.[215] Once identified, mediators will work with the parties to devise a suitable strategy for breaking the deadlock.[216]

The most common obstacle to settlement stems from the parties being equally confident about their alternatives if the dispute does not settle in the mediation, or what is referred to as their "BATNA" (Best Alternative to a Negotiated Agreement).[217] In the mediation context, this means what is the likelihood of each party getting a favorable outcome in litigation or arbitration.[218] Of course, both parties cannot be correct.[219] A party's perception of its BATNA influences his or her behavior in mediation and in particular his or her desire to reach settlement.[220] Accordingly, it is important for the mediator to ensure that both sides have a realistic assessment of their alternatives to settlement.[221] To do so, the mediator may use diverse methods in private caucus with each side or in joint session that are aimed at testing the parties' assumptions, understanding of the law and evaluation of litigation costs.[222]

[210] Schweinsberg et al. (2021), pp. 1436–1439.

[211] Id.

[212] Id.

[213] Moore (2014), p. 295; Abramson (2004), pp. 105–108.

[214] Id.

[215] O'Sullivan (2018), pp. 179–185.

[216] Moore (2014), p. 295; Abramson (2004), pp. 105–108.

[217] Fisher et al. (1997), p. 53.

[218] Id.

[219] Moore (2014), pp. 428–429; Abramson (2004), pp. 250–252.

[220] Lewicki et al. (2015), pp. 51–52.

[221] Id. pp. 51, 54–56.

[222] Spangler (2003).

3.4.11 *Closing the Final Gap*

Despite diverse attempts at finding a creation solution, the mediator may still be faced with parties who have failed to converge on a settlement.[223] Often, in such a case, the parties have reached their "bottom lines" and the only option appears to be the non-ideal method of "splitting the difference".[224] When faced with such a final gap, mediators can use various techniques to help the parties converge and reach a deal.[225] These techniques include the "mediator's proposal", an evaluation of the merits of the legal case or settlement proposals, packaging of various trades ("log-rolling") or a scheme designed to induce each side to surpass their "bottom lines".[226]

The "mediator's proposal" refers to a settlement deal formulated by the mediator based on the mediator's understanding of the dispute, the advancement of the parties in the mediation, and an evaluation of what is a just outcome that is adequate for each side.[227] Generally, the mediator presents this proposal to each disputant confidentially and if accepted by all, then the mediator informs the parties that the dispute has been settled.[228] Should one party reject the proposal, the mediator simply informs the parties that the proposal has been rejected without revealing whether any side had accepted the deal, and thus not revealing that any particular party was willing to make further concessions.[229] Such a gap-sealing technique may be suitable for money gaps but less so for more complex settlement terms.[230] Moreover, the mediator's proposal is a very risky technique for a mediator to employ because it can undermine the mediation dynamics by shifting the problem-solving responsibility to the mediator, hardening the positional stance of the parties for or against the proposal's terms as well as undermining the mediator's neutrality in the eyes of the parties.[231] Therefore, if used, mediators are advised to do so only towards the very end of the mediation process and with caution.[232]

Another technique that the mediator might employ is to evaluate the legal merits of the case or settlement proposals.[233] Such a technique might be necessary for breaking a final impasse but bears the same risks as the mediator's proposal, particularly with respect to the perception of the mediator's neutrality in the eyes of the parties.[234] Moreover, the parties might be concerned about how confidential

[223] Golann (2009), p. 12.

[224] Id.

[225] Id.

[226] Moore (2014), pp. 397–400; Golann (2009), pp. 12–14; Abramson (2004), pp. 91–93.

[227] Hochman (2012).

[228] Id.

[229] Id.

[230] Abramson (2004), pp. 91–93.

[231] Id.

[232] Id.

[233] Moore (2014), pp. 54–57; Abramson (2004), pp. 136–139.

[234] Id.

information shared with the mediator has influenced the mediator's evaluation and thus the use of such techniques might encourage parties to withhold useful information from the mediator during the mediation process.[235] Accordingly, mediators are advised again to refrain from using such a method until the end of the mediation and only with the parties' explicit consent.[236]

Mediators might also employ the technique of "logrolling" which is the process of packaging trades based on the parties' differing priorities for the various issues in conflict in order to help the parties overcome final impediment to settlement.[237] Using this method, the mediator must negotiate with the parties to package their concessions in such a way as to ensure that each party achieves a greatly favored outcome on an issue of high priority.[238] However, this implies that the parties do in fact have dissimilar preferences on different issues that permit each side to get its most favored outcome on a high-priority issue.[239]

The mediator's toolbox also includes various other mechanisms for engaging parties to utilize their "bottom lines".[240] The bottom line refers to the point at which a negotiator will make no further concessions in order to reach settlement.[241] These various mechanisms include final-offer arbitration, hypothetical testing, confidential disclosure of bottom lines, confidential disclosure of settlement numbers and the safety deposit box.[242] Each technique has unique dynamics, but all involve obtaining confidential disclosure of the parties' bottom lines to the mediator who then either informs the parties that there is still bargaining room or who designs an outcome based on this information.[243]

3.5 Different Styles of Mediation

As mediation has developed professionally and academically over the past several decades, various styles (or "schools" as some would label them) of mediation have been established.[244] Mediators who adhere to a particular mediation style share a similar philosophy, goals and approach in the delivery of their dispute resolution services.[245] The increasingly refined approaches and different styles of mediation

---

235 Id.

236 Love (1997), pp. 940, 945.

237 Lewicki et al. (2015), pp. 89–90.

238 Id.

239 Id.

240 Moore (2014), p. 428.

241 Fisher et al. (1997), p. 53.

242 Abramson (2004), p. 250.

243 Id.

244 Alexander (2008b), p. 97.

245 Id.

one finds in mediation practice include facilitative mediation, evaluative mediation, deal making mediation, deal mending mediation, transformative mediation, settlement mediation, expert advisory mediation, wise counsel mediation and tradition-based mediation.[246] However, it is important to observe that although these schools of mediation can be distinguished academically, in practice mediators rarely engage in an entirely pure form of mediation.[247] Rather, most mediators' practice is ultimately a blend of various styles, despite their particular orientation towards a particular style, depending on the context of the dispute, the extent of conflict escalation, the types of issues in dispute, the number of issues that are in fact contested and the extent to which the parties perceive that their issues, needs and interests are negotiable or not.[248] This section will provide an overall view of the main variations of mediation styles. First, a system for categorizing this mediation styles will be discussed and then the six main variations will be summarized succinctly.

3.5.1 Categorizing the Different Mediation Styles

Scholars have different approaches for categorizing these various "flavors" of mediation. One particularly detailed approach focuses on two overarching variables which are (i) the type of discourse in the mediation and (ii) whether the mediator's intervention is problem-based or process-based.[249] These two predominant variables are then further broken down according to more detailed sub-classifications.[250] The second and broader approach focuses on three possible orientations and type of assistance provided by the mediator in the mediation process: (i) procedural, (ii) relationship or (iii) substantive.[251]

For the purpose of accuracy, let us examine the first, more detailed approach to categorizing the various schools of thought and practice in mediation using the two principal variables (i) discourse and (ii) problem-based or process-based mediator intervention.[252]

With respect to the first variable that we can label "discourse", there are three sub-classifications, as follows. (a) distributive bargaining; (b) integrative negotiation and (c) dialogue.[253] The objectives of each classification as well as the sought-after result differ. In the first sub-category, distributive or "positional" bargaining, the

[246] Id.

[247] Golann (2000), pp. 50–54.

[248] Id.

[249] Riskin (2003), pp. 29–50.

[250] Id.

[251] Id.

[252] Alexander (2008b), pp. 97.

[253] Id.

assumption is that the parties' must reach an agreement on the distribution of finite resources in a zero-sum game.[254] Therefore, the parties' discourse focuses on their stated positions (legal or otherwise) and a back-and-forth process of linear concession making in which the goal is to reach a compromise on mutually-acceptable settlement terms.[255] In the second type of discourse, integrative negotiation, the parties' focus on their underlying interests, needs, motivations, and concerns that are hidden behind their stated positions.[256] By engaging in such an integrative discourse, the parties aim to move away from a battle over finite resources to create a settlement agreement that more broadly resolves the parties' conflict.[257] Unlike the first two classifications, dialogue-based discourse does not focus on achieving any particular outcome but rather on nurturing constructive, respectful communication between the disputants.[258] By establishing such positive and beneficial dialogue, the purpose of the discourse-based approach is to improve the parties' relationship and thus their capacity to resolve conflicts by themselves.[259]

Now we shall turn to the second of the two variables by which mediation styles can be categorized, which we shall label "intervention".[260] This variable organizes the various types of mediation practice according to the predominant orientation of the mediator's intervention, in relation to either the problem or the process.[261] Mediators who are problem-oriented intervene primarily on the subject matter and the merits of the dispute by providing technical, legal or general information, advising the parties on their options should they choose not or fail to mediate as well as evaluating or suggesting settlement options and terms.[262] Contrary to problem-oriented mediators, process-oriented mediators focus on the mediation's structure and dynamics. Accordingly, process-oriented mediators will engage in configuring the mediation agenda, arranging the parties' seating arrangements and organizing joint and separate sessions while also focusing on how the parties communicate and interact with each other.[263]

Having defined the variables and sub-categories for understanding the different styles of mediation, let us now turn to defining these refined approaches to mediation practice.

[254] Riskin (2003), pp. 7–51.

[255] Id.

[256] Alexander (2008b), pp. 97.

[257] Id.

[258] Lewicki et al. (2015), pp. 77–78.

[259] Id.

[260] Riskin (2003), pp. 1–53.

[261] Id.

[262] Id.

[263] Alexander (2008a).

3.5.2 *Expert Advisory Mediation*

In expert advisory mediation, the goal is to obtain quick settlement and justice.[264] Accordingly, the need for a swift and typically legally or technically oriented resolution necessitates that the discourse adopt a predominantly distributive bargaining approach and a very high level of mediator intervention with respect to the problem.[265] Therefore, expert advisory mediators tend to be senior lawyers or professionals chosen for their particular expertise regarding the substantive aspects of the dispute and their level of seniority, rather than their mediation process-specific skills.[266]

Expert advisory mediators provide disputants with technical and legal guidance, counsel on the merits of the case, possible settlement terms and probable consequences if the dispute proceeds to arbitration or adjudication.[267] By keeping the discourse based on the parties' positions and legal rights, the problem can be defined in a narrow, legally-oriented manner that excludes broader issues from clouding the agenda.[268] Consequently, the parties are frequently accompanied by their legal counsel in such mediations and the resulting settlements tend to mirror the possible outcomes of court proceedings.[269]

It is often difficult to distinguish expert advisory mediation from other alternative dispute resolution methods such as conciliation or neutral evaluation.[270] Parties and mediators may opt for expert advisory mediation where the parties lack technical expertise regarding the substance of the dispute, are under a court order to participate in mandatory mediation or seek an expedited resolution of their conflict.[271] This style of mediation is less adapted for disputes where the parties' relationship is a priority and where it is important for the parties' to develop their own ability to resolve conflict.[272]

Moreover, critics of this school of mediation disparage the fact that the mediator is disproportionately responsible for the outcome and solicits relatively little participation from the parties in the process.[273] They also decry expert advisory mediation's focus on the parties' positions and legal rights to the detriment of the parties' long-term interests and their relationships.[274] These drawbacks, detractors argue, may lead to dissatisfaction with the resulting settlement or failure to discover

[264] Welsh (2001), pp. 787–861.

[265] Id.

[266] Id.

[267] Alexander (2008a).

[268] Id.

[269] Id.

[270] Welsh (2001), pp. 787–861.

[271] Id.

[272] Roberts (2007), pp. 197–201.

[273] Id.

[274] Id.

opportunities for settlement.[275] Faultfinders also point out that by providing their expert opinion, mediators may actually be encouraging parties to withhold information that they believe would be damaging to their case, impair the perception of mediator impartiality and expose themselves to lawsuits for the unauthorized practice of law.[276]

3.5.3 Settlement Mediation

Like expert advisory mediation, settlement mediation's goal is to provide a swift and just settlement.[277] However, settlement mediation assigns more importance to the parties' self-sufficiency in the dispute resolution process than is the case in expert advisory mediation.[278] Consequently, while positional bargaining characterizes the discourse variable in settlement mediation as it does in expert advisory mediation, the prevailing intervention variable is process-oriented rather than problem-oriented.[279]

In settlement mediation, the mediator acts like a trainer coaching the parties in the bargaining process.[280] However, the more zealous settlement mediators might also engage in more strong-arm tactics to drive the parties into making concessions.[281] Moreover, although settlement mediators are supposed to be oriented towards the process variable, parties often select their mediators also on the basis of their technical or legal knowledge because they feel reassured knowing that they can be confident in the mediator's understanding of the technical aspects of the dispute.[282] In turn, settlement mediators commonly provide a combination of process and problem-oriented services.[283]

In practice, settlement mediators regularly separate the parties soon after the mediation has been convened, favoring a "shuttle mediation" approach of going back and forth between the parties to communicate offers, counteroffers, concessions and draft agreements before finally reuniting the parties in a joint session towards the end of the process.[284] This practice emphasizes the mediator's focus on the process dimension of the dispute resolution process in settlement mediation.[285]

---

[275] Golann and Aaron (2010), pp. 330–331.

[276] Id.

[277] Spencer and Brogan (2006), pp. 100–102.

[278] Id.

[279] Alexander (2008a).

[280] Welsh (2001), pp. 787–861.

[281] Id.

[282] Alexander (2008b), p. 97.

[283] Id.

[284] Hoffman (2011), pp. 264–270.

[285] Id.

Settlement mediation is most suitable for disputes where the parties are in conflict over a single-issue in which there is a "fixed pie", or no means of expanding the value to be gained by the parties or the range of possible outcomes.[286] Furthermore, settlement mediation is more appropriate for disputes in which the parties care more about the outcome than their relationship or who will have no future relationship after the mediation.[287] Accordingly, parties might even send their legal representatives to settlement mediation rather than participate personally in the process.[288] Conversely, settlement mediation is risky for weaker, less experienced negotiators who are disadvantaged by the common use of bargaining tricks, threats and bluffs.[289] Moreover, by neglecting the parties' needs and interests, settlement mediation fails to identify creative problem-solving and win-win settlement opportunities for all the parties.[290]

3.5.4 Facilitative Mediation

As in settlement mediation, facilitative mediators seek to create the most favorable negotiation environment and coach the parties in their negotiations.[291] However, in facilitative mediation the emphasis is on integrative, interest-based negotiation rather than on the positional bargaining that is the focus of settlement mediation.[292] In this type of mediation, mediators urge the disputants to disclose their needs and interests and to recognize the other party's viewpoint as well.[293] The aim of the facilitative mediation process is to foster the parties' self-determination.[294] Therefore, facilitative mediators mainly limit themselves to the process rather than the merits of the dispute, and are selected by the parties based on their facilitation and communication skills rather than on their substantive expertise.[295]

Facilitative mediation is fitting for disputes involving (i) multiple and especially non-legal issues, (ii) parties seeking to maintain their relationships, (iii) the need for creative and/or long-term solutions as well as impasse.[296] On the other hand, even though mediation is a confidential process, by encouraging the disclosure of information through the facilitative process, detractors argue that mediators may be

---

286 Welsh (2001), pp. 787–861.

287 Id.

288 Id.

289 Alexander (2008a).

290 Id.

291 Stitt (2004), pp. 1–6.

292 Id.

293 Id.

294 Nolan-Haley (2005), pp. 278–284.

295 Alexander (2008a).

296 Id.

putting a disclosing party at a disadvantage in subsequent arbitration or adjudication proceedings should the mediation fail to result in a settlement agreement.[297] According to critics, once parties disclose sensitive information it may alter the balance of power between the parties and the non-disclosing party may then obtain the information independently from the mediation in order to use it against the disclosing party in subsequent proceedings.[298] In addition, critics complain that facilitative mediation requires the parties to invest a greater amount of time than in settlement styles focused on positional bargaining.[299]

3.5.5 *Wise Counsel Mediation*

In wise counsel mediation, the mediator targets his or her services to both an evaluation of the merits of the case (the problem) as well as well as the parties' broader interests (process).[300] Accordingly, wise counsel mediation resembles expert advisory mediation but with the integrative negotiation focus of the facilitative model.[301] Therefore, although the mediators provide advice on the merits, this form of mediation still requires a greater investment of time that allows the mediator to also probe below the surface to identify the parties underlying interests.[302] Nevertheless, although focused on the integrative negotiation model, wise counsel mediators do not limit themselves to the process and instead weigh in on the substantive aspects of the dispute.[303] Consequently, parties tend to seek wise counsel mediators who have both a certain level of high standing in the community as well as facilitation and communication skills.[304]

Wise counsel mediation is thus recommended for disputes involving (i) several issues and/or multiple parties needing substantive guidance on how to solve their conflict as well as (ii) an imbalance of negotiating power between the parties.[305] Additionally, wise counsel mediation allows parties to assign the moral burden for the outcome to a third party.[306] Contrariwise, wise counsel mediation fails to teach the parties the facilitative process skills necessary to carry out their agreement once the mediation concludes as the mediator maintains disproportionate responsibility in

[297] Riskin (2003), pp. 7–51.

[298] Id.

[299] Id.

[300] Lohvinenko et al. (2021), p. 55.

[301] Id.

[302] Id.

[303] Riskin (2003), pp. 1–53.

[304] Alexander (2008a).

[305] Hardy and Rundle (2010), p. 60.

[306] Id.

this range.[307] Moreover, wise counsel mediators may struggle to maintain the perception of impartiality after expressing their views and opinions on the merits.[308]

3.5.6 *Tradition-Based Mediation*

In some ways, tradition-based mediation is similar to wise counsel mediation.[309] As in wise counsel mediation, the mediator's focus is on the problem and mediators are selected for their respected status and good judgment in the community.[310] However, unlike wise counsel mediation tradition-based mediation is oriented to the restoration of justice and stability to the group or community rather than the parties.[311] Therefore, tradition-based mediators consider the members of the community as stakeholders in the conflict and therefore free to witness or even participate in the mediation.[312] Accordingly, confidentiality is less important in this form of mediation than in others, especially since mediators encourage open conversation—sometimes involving symbolic rituals—that restore the group's relationships through understanding.[313]

Tradition-based mediation is perhaps one of the most ancient forms of mediation, having roots in many traditional, kinship-based communities in Australia, New Zealand, Asia and the Pacific.[314] In such societies, the welfare of the community is more important than individual interests.[315] Similarly, tradition-based mediation also lends itself to conflict resolution in religious communities where a religious elder acts as mediator.[316] More generally, well-defined groups with strong social, cultural, religious or political norms seeking to resolve their conflicts within the group in a reliable fashion are likely to find tradition-based mediation helpful.[317] However, where there is concern about the values imposed by the dominant culture on minorities within the group, this form of mediation does not afford much flexibility for self-determination.[318]

307 Alexander (2008a).

308 Id.

309 Hardy and Rundle (2010), pp. 61–62.

310 Id.

311 Chia et al. (2004), pp. 451–452.

312 Id.

313 Id.

314 Barnes (2007), p. 72.

315 Id.

316 Bercovitch and Kadayifci-Orellana (2009), pp. 183–204.

317 Id.

318 Alexander (2008a).

3.5.7 *Transformative Mediation*

Transformative mediation concentrates on altering the relationships between the parties and on healing and restoration.[319] In this type of mediation, parties seek mediators with process and communication know-how as well as psychology and behavioral science expertise.[320] The transformative mediator must create a space where the disputants can express their feelings, needs and interests and also recognize and acknowledge those of the other parties.[321]

Therapeutic mediation falls in the same category as transformative mediation.[322] Therapeutic mediation involves the use of techniques found in therapy and is thus process oriented, aiming to create a transformative dialogue towards reconciliation.[323] The best-known type of therapeutic mediation is narrative mediation, inspired by narrative therapy.[324] In narrative mediation, the goal is to provide a safe environment for the parties to analyze their conflicting stories that shape their perceptions of the world and then to help them create a new, shared narrative of their reality.[325] To do so, mediators can employ the option-generative and problem-solving techniques of facilitative mediation as well.[326]

Parties might find transformative mediation helpful where a dispute is actually a recurring manifestation of an underlying conflict that the parties are prepared to address first and where there are significant conflicts about the parties' relationship and differing values and principles.[327] However, parties should be prepared to spend more time in transformative mediation than in other forms of mediation.[328] Moreover, where the mediator lacks sufficient skills, extraneous issues might derail the mediation and the process may not provide adequate protection for weaker parties.[329]

---

[319] Baruch Bush and Folger (2004), pp. 41–84.

[320] Id.

[321] Id.

[322] Gora (2008).

[323] Id.

[324] Winslade and Monk (2000), XII.

[325] Id. pp. 57–93.

[326] Id.

[327] Alexander (2008a).

[328] Id.

[329] Winslade et al. (1998), pp. 21–41.

3.6 Blended Mediation Practices

In addition to the different styles of mediation mentioned above, there are occasions when neutrals have "switched hats" during the course of proceedings between mediator and arbitrator and vice-versa.[330] Depending on the order of the methods used, these blended mediation practices are known as Med-Arb, Arb-Med and even Arb-Med-Arb.[331]

Med-arb refers to a voluntary dispute resolution process in which the mediator switches to the role of arbitrator capable of rendering a binding award in the event the mediation proceedings fail to fully resolve the dispute.[332] Although cultural factors and an interest in efficiency might motivate the use of med-arb, it also raises concerns in light of the mediator's previous *ex parte* communications with the parties during mediation caucuses.[333]

Like med-arb, arb-med is also a consensual dispute resolution process but in which the arbitrator switches to the role of mediator at some point during the arbitration proceedings.[334] Should mediation resolve the dispute, the parties may choose to transform the settlement agreement into an arbitration award by consent.[335] However, should the mediation fail to resolve the dispute, the mediator's transition back to the role of arbitrator could raise the same concerns as med-arb described above.[336]

Although such blended practices have not yet gained widespread popularity, the flexibility of such processes particularly in the sovereign debt dispute context might be of interest and worth exploring further.[337]

3.7 Legal Framework for Mediation

Mediation does not exist in a vacuum, but within the context of a legal framework.[338] In this section, I shall attempt to shed light on the "law of mediation" or "mediation law", which refers to the legal rules, jurisprudence and legal standards within which mediation operates.[339] When referring to the scope of mediation law, I

---

330 Moore (2014), pp. 10–11.

331 Id.

332 Stipanowich (2021).

333 Coe (2010), pp. 46–47.

334 Stipanowich (2021).

335 Id.

336 Coe (2010), pp. 46–47.

337 Id.

338 Alexander (2010), pp. 2439–2656.

339 Id.

am including any law that directly or indirectly controls some aspect of the mediation process.[340]

The fact that this thesis does not focus on any particular jurisdiction complicates the exercise of setting out the legal framework for mediation. Therefore it is necessary to discuss mediation law as it stands generally around the world today, despite the enormous variation that exists in the different legal systems in each country.

To comprehend mediation law, it is helpful to categorize mediation laws based on their purpose.[341] Accordingly, mediation laws can be classified as follows: (i) "triggering" laws that help initiate the mediation process, (ii) procedural laws for managing the mediation process, (iii) standard-setting laws for ensuring the quality of the services provided by mediators and (iv) "protection" laws that benefit mediators and consumers by setting out their rights and defending the integrity of the mediation process.[342] To have a more complete understanding of the legal backdrop within which mediation operates, it is also important to understand interface laws controlling the interaction between mediation and other legal proceedings, default vs mandatory mediation laws and mediation laws' scope or target audience (either general, sector-specific or integrated).[343] Having established a means of categorizing the different types of mediation laws based on their purpose, the following subsections of this chapter will address each category of mediation law in turn.

3.7.1 Triggering Laws

The purpose of triggering laws is to promote the start of the mediation process.[344] These laws help commence mediation in numerous ways from mandatory information sessions about mediation,[345] requiring lawyers to consult their clients to consider the use of mediation,[346] referrals to mediation with or without the consent of all of the parties and preventing parties from filing a claim in court unless they have first attempted mediation.[347]

---

[340] Id.

[341] Robyn (2002), pp. 172–180.

[342] Id.

[343] Id.

[344] European Commission for the Efficiency of Justice (2019), pp. 19–23.

[345] French Civil Procedure Code Article 255; Family Law Act 1996 (UK) Part III; German Law on Marriage and the Civil Procedure Code; European Directive on Mediation Article 5.

[346] McAdoo and Welsh (2005), pp. 407–408; Minnesota General Rules of Practice Article 114; UK Pre-action Protocols 4.7 and the Civil Procedure Rules.

[347] French Civil Procedure Code Article 131-1; German Code of Civil Procedure S. 278 V 2; Austrian Federal Court Rules (Amendment) 1991 N° 461 r 4(1); U.S. Florida Statutes S. 44.102(2) (a) 2008 Title V, Ch. 44.

Not all of these laws exist in every jurisdiction and in others several might coexist.[348] For example, the European Directive on Mediation states in Article 1(1) that its goal is 'to facilitate access to alternative dispute resolution' and then sets out in Article 5 various means for encouraging the start of mediation proceedings that member-states might adopt.[349] These include inviting the parties to information sessions on mediation in court as well as making mediation compulsory or subject to sanctions before or after court proceedings have commenced.[350]

Although less direct triggering mechanisms than information sessions or referrals, financial incentives also seek to encourage parties to engage in mediation.[351] In England, Australia and in the United States parties might be subject to cost sanctions for unreasonably refusing to participate in mediation or alternatively they might benefit from subsidies and legal aid for the mediation process.[352] In an even bolder move, lawyers in Slovenia benefit from a 50% increase in their fees for mediated settlements.[353] Underlying this decision by the Slovenian Bar Association was the desire to encourage lawyers to use mediation and promote settlement in mediation.[354]

3.7.2 *Procedural Laws*

The purpose of procedural laws is to oversee the various features and phases of the mediation process, including commencement and termination of the mediation, codes of conduct as well as the selection and appointment of mediators.[355]

For example, the UNCITRAL Model Law on International Commercial Mediation and International Settlement Agreements Resulting from Mediation (2018) sets out provisions for the commencement of mediation proceedings, the number and appointment of mediators, the conduct of the mediation proceedings, communications between the mediator and the parties, information disclosure, and termination of the proceedings.[356]

Moreover, dispute resolution organizations, bar associations and other professional bodies have also often elicited provisions governing mediation procedure.[357]

---

348 Alexander (2010), p. 2488.

349 European Directive on Mediation (n 345).

350 Id.

351 Alexander (2010), p. 2502.

352 Id.

353 Galič (2003), pp. 71–76.

354 Id.

355 Alexander (2010), p. 2502.

356 UNCITRAL Model Law on International Commercial Mediation.

357 2020 World Intellectual Property Organization (WIPO) Mediation Rules; 2014 ICC Mediation Rules; 2012 IBA Investor-State Mediation Rules.

For example, the International Bar Association's Rules for Investor-State Mediation cover the commencement, conduct, termination and costs and fees of mediation proceedings, the role of and the independence and impartiality of the mediator and the mediator's designation as well as his or her resignation or replacement and that of his or her co-mediator(s) where applicable.[358] Although these institutional rules are not legislative forms regulating mediation practice, this procedural rules nevertheless legally bind parties that have incorporated them into their contracts.[359]

3.7.3 Standard-Setting Laws

Regulations focused on mediator's qualifications and certifications refer to standard-setting mediation laws.[360] They tend to operate like rules overseeing professions such as the legal and medical fields by prohibiting anyone to practice as a mediator without having first demonstrated acquisition of specified minimum standards.[361]

For instance, depending on the jurisdiction, to practice as a mediator one must generally have attended a certain minimum number of hours of training with an approved body and passed a certification exam with a recognized certification body.[362] Moreover, for specialized fields such as family or medical mediation there might be additional, stricter requirements and standards to fulfill.[363]

Mediation standard-setting provisions also seek to encourage high standards of practice in mediation for the benefit of mediation providers and users.[364] Accordingly, under such a regulatory system, a mediator who does not meet the minimum standard may still provide mediation services but will not benefit from an accreditation attesting to the assured quality of his or her services.[365] This is the standard-setting approach developed by the International Mediation Institute, whose accreditation process seeks to ensure a global level of high minimum professional standards for mediators.[366]

---

[358] 2012 IBA Investor-State Mediation Rules.

[359] WIPO Mediation Rules; 2014 ICC Mediation Rules; IBA Rules for Investor-State Mediation; Alexander (2010), p. 2502.

[360] Id. p. 2514.

[361] Id.

[362] Id.

[363] Australian Family Law Act 1975 (Cth); Australian Family Law Regulations 1984 (Cth); French Law of 26 May 2004 Relating to Family Mediation; French Decree No. 2003-1166 of 2 December 2003; Austrian Marriage Law; Austrian Childrens Law Reform; Alexander (2010), p. 2514.

[364] Alexander (2010), p. 2021.

[365] Id.

[366] 2021 International Mediation Institute (IMI) Code of Professional Conduct.

Similarly, regulations setting out mediation standards might also be advisory in nature.[367] Examples include the American Bar Association Section on Dispute Resolution's Model Standards of Conduct for Mediators and the European Directive on Mediation's Code of Conduct.[368] Furthermore, there is often either a convergence of multiple, different mediation standards in place within a particular jurisdiction.[369] Accordingly, it is then up to dispute resolution providers and industry groups concerned by mediation to self-regulate by developing their own accreditation and quality requirements.[370]

3.7.4 *Beneficial Laws*

Where mediators have met the minimum standards needed to mediate based on the applicable regulatory framework, they can benefit from laws that set out their rights, known as beneficial laws.[371] Mediators who fail to meet the standard-setting criteria do not benefit from these protective rules.[372]

Beneficial mediation laws aim to benefit the mediator and the parties in the mediation process by defending its integrity.[373] Typically, such rules cover confidential information, without prejudice privilege, legal professional privilege covering communications between a lawyer and his or her client, in jurisdictions where it is recognized, mediation privilege covering all communications between the mediator and the parties during the mediation proceedings, enforceability of mediated settlements and the operation of limitation periods.[374] Beneficial laws are also found in the European Directive on Mediation Articles 6, 7 and 8 as well as the UNCITRAL Model Law on Conciliation Articles 10, 13, 14 and optional Article X, covering the enforceability of mediated settlements, admissibility of evidence and limitation periods.[375]

---

[367] Id. p. 2524.

[368] 2005 American Arbitration Association (ABA) Model Standards of Conduct for Mediators; 2004 European Code of Conduct for Mediators.

[369] Alexander (2010), p. 2524.

[370] 'Quality Assurance' International Mediation Institute. https://imimediation.org/about/quality-assurance/, accessed 15 October 2021.

[371] Alexander (2010), p. 2537.

[372] Id.

[373] Laflin (2014), pp. 499–516.

[374] 2003 Uniform Mediation Act s. 4.

[375] 2008 European Mediation Directive; UNCITRAL Model Law on International Commercial Mediation.

3.7.5 "Interface" Laws

As opposed to mediation laws that concentrate on procedural aspects, there are specific mediation laws that govern the interface between mediation and other proceedings.[376] These interface laws manage the interaction between mediation proceedings and other dispute resolution proceedings such as arbitration and litigation, govern the admissibility of mediation-derived information used as evidence in subsequent proceedings, decide the enforceability of mediation settlement agreements and establish limitation periods during which legal claims may not be made during ongoing mediation proceedings.[377]

Beneficial laws also regulate many of the aforementioned mediation characteristics as stated previously in the previous section. Since the rights and protections concerned by beneficial laws also impact facets of subsequent arbitral and judicial proceedings, such as discovery and admissible evidence, the overlap is inevitable.[378]

The European Directive on Mediation contains interface laws regarding the distinction between judicial settlement and judicial mediation (Article 3), enforceability of mediated settlements (Article 6), admissibility of evidence (Article 7) and limitation periods (Article 8).[379] The UNCITRAL Model Law on International Commercial Mediation also sets various articles with interface regulations such as the admissibility of evidence (Article 10), mediators as arbitrators (Article 12), enforceability of agreements to mediate and mediated settlements (Articles 13 and 14) and limitation periods (optional Article X).[380]

The distinction between procedure-oriented mediation law and interface mediation law allows us to identify which topics are better governed under legislative norms and which are better dealt with by self-regulation or private, contractual approaches.[381] Generally, legislation is better suited for interface matters because legislation encourages consistency and certainty for such circumstances.[382] On the other hand self-regulation and private, contractual approaches are more appropriate for concerns relating to the mediation process itself as they permit the party a greater amount of party autonomy to tailor the mediation process to their needs.[383]

---

[376] Alexander (2010), p. 2561.

[377] Id.

[378] Id.

[379] 2008 European Mediation Directive.

[380] UNCITRAL Model Law on International Commercial Mediation.

[381] Alexander (2010), p. 2574.

[382] Alexander (2008a), p. 1–8.

[383] Id.

3.7.6 *Default vs. Mandatory Laws*

The law of mediation can be further classified according to whether the relevant norms operate as default or mandatory regulations.[384] Default rules only apply where the parties have not expressly agreed for other provisions to apply whereas mandatory rules always apply regardless of any contrary agreement by the parties.[385]

Both the U.S. Uniform Mediation Act and the UNCITRAL Model Law on International Commercial Mediation contain instances of laws that only apply should there be an absence of an agreement by the parties for a different provision.[386] The Uniform Mediation Act covers the admissibility of information from a mediation to be used as evidence in all proceedings and allows parties to even opt out of privilege.[387] In addition, the UNCITRAL Model Law on Conciliation also contains default provisions allowing the parties to opt-out of certain regulations and thus maximize on the short amount of time together on the ground.[388]

Contrary to default rules, mandatory mediation laws always apply even where the parties have, by agreement, provided otherwise by "opting-out".[389] For example, the UNCITRAL Model Law on International Commercial Mediation's Article 6-(3) functions as a mandatory rule preserving the principle of fair treatment in mediation which is applicable to all mediations falling within its scope.[390]

3.7.7 *Scope of Mediation Law: General, Sector-specific and integrated*

Lastly, one can structure mediation law based on whether it targets a general audience, a specific sector or integrated.[391]

3.7.7.1 General Mediation Law

General mediation laws cover all proceedings and mediators in a particular jurisdiction regardless of the type of mediation practice (civil, criminal, family etc.).[392]

[384] Eidenmüller (2002), p. 15.

[385] Id.

[386] 2003 Uniform Mediation Act; UNCITRAL Model Law on International Commercial Mediation.

[387] 2003 Uniform Mediation Act s. 4(c).

[388] UNCITRAL Model Law on International Commercial Mediation art 2 and 6(3).

[389] Eidenmüller (2002), p. 15.

[390] UNCITRAL Model Law on International Commercial Mediation art 6(3).

[391] Robyn (2002), p. 175.

[392] Alexander (2010), p. 2597.

Currently, there is no country that has a national general mediation law that extends to all areas of and aspects of mediation practice, however there appears to be a trend moving in that direction as there are several countries that have passed national mediation legislation covering civil matters.[393]

Other examples of mediation legislation with general application are the 2001 Uniform Mediation Act (UMA) and the 2008 European Directive on Mediation (EU Mediation Directive).[394] The UMA was drafted by the National Conference of Commissioners of Uniform State Laws and officially recognized by the American Bar Association, a precursor step to adoption by the various U.S. States.[395] The UMA's most important legal contribution is the creation of a broad "mediation privilege" ensuring the confidentiality of all mediation-connected communications.[396] The UMA's scope covers most mediations except collective bargaining, peer mediations and judicial settlements.[397] One of the EU Mediation Directive's main goals is for Member States to recognize and enforce mediated settlements of other Member States as they would court judgments so as promote the use of mediation.[398] Although the EU Mediation Directive applies to cross-border civil and commercial mediations, recital 8 in the preamble to the Directive explicitly provides that Member States may also apply similar stipulations to domestic mediation proceedings.[399]

3.7.7.2 Sector-Specific Mediation Law

Sector-specific mediation laws pertain to mediation in a particular context such as a certain industry, court-connected mediation program or under a defined area of law.[400] On the national level, such legislation for example could cover compulsory mediation prior to foreclosure on farms or mediation related to the medical field.[401] On the cross-border level, an example of sector-specific mediation law is the European Directive on Insurance Mediation, although this is now no longer in force.[402]

---

[393] Alexander (2008a).

[394] 2003 Uniform Mediation Act; 2008 European Mediation Directive.

[395] 2003 Uniform Mediation Act; Alexander (2010), p. 2611.

[396] Uniform Mediation Act and Official Comments (2003), pp. 47–48.

[397] Id.

[398] Nolan-Haley (2012).

[399] European Mediation Directive.

[400] Alexander (2010), p. 2611.

[401] Id pp. 2611–2622.

[402] 2002 European Directive on Insurance Mediation.

3.7.7.3 Integrated Mediation Law

Like sector-specific mediation laws, integrated mediation laws focus on a particular area. However, unlike sector-specific law, integrated mediation law does not stand alone but is integrated into legislation concentrating on a specific subject.[403] For example, the U.S. Californian Code of Evidence includes stipulations on mediation as does the 1990 U.S. Individuals with Disabilities Education Act (DEA) governing the funding of education for students with disabilities.[404] Similarly, several jurisdictions have civil procedure regulations that have integrated rules on court-referred mediation.[405]

Interestingly, this variation between general, sector-specific and integrated mediation law demonstrates the different legal philosophies between the civil and common law traditions.[406] Whereas civil law jurisdictions tend to enact more general mediation laws in light of their centralized, paternalistic approach, common law jurisdictions tend to enact more sector-specific and integrated mediation laws as part of their desire to remain decentralized and adaptable.[407]

3.8 Singapore Convention on Mediation

In this section, I shall describe the recently adopted Singapore Convention on Mediation ("Singapore Convention"), also known as the United Nations Convention on International Settlement Agreements Resulting from Mediation.[408] The Convention provides for the recognition and enforcement of mediated settlement agreements resolving international commercial disputes, similar to the framework established by the 1958 New York Convention for the recognition and enforcement of arbitral awards.[409]

3.8.1 Purpose of the Singapore Convention

The United Nationals Commission on International Trade Law (UNCITRAL) approved the multilateral treaty on 26 June 2018 and was open for signature as of

[403] Alexander (2010), p. 2622.
[404] 1990 U.S. Individuals with Disabilities Education Act (IDEA).
[405] Californian Code of Civil Procedure; IDEA.
[406] Lundmark (2012), pp. 294–339.
[407] Alexander (2010), p. 2646.
[408] Singapore Convention.
[409] Schnabel (2019).

August 2019.[410] The Singapore Convention entered into force in September 2020, and as of September 2021 has 54 countries as signatories.[411]

The Singapore Convention's purpose is to facilitate the enforcement of international commercial settlement agreements resulting from mediation.[412] Prior to the convention, if parties to an international dispute settled their case in mediation there was no procedure for the direct enforcement of that agreement.[413] That meant that the parties would be required to enforce the settlement agreement as if it were any other contract: namely, by filing a complaint for the enforcement of the contract (in this case the settlement agreement) in the courts of the counter-party's country and obtaining a favorable verdict before seeking to enforce that judgment.[414]

Considering that one of the main reasons for engaging in mediation proceedings is to avoid lengthy and complex litigation, many companies cited the prospect of having to engage in such lawsuits to carry out the enforcement of the settlement agreement as weighing against their willingness to use mediation.[415] Therefore, the Singapore Convention attempts to allow a party wishing to enforce a settlement agreement to skip the litigation step and to enforce the agreement directly.[416]

3.8.2 Scope of the Singapore Convention

The Singapore Convention's scope is limited to international commercial disputes that have been settled in mediation.[417] This means that either: (i) at least two parties to the dispute must operate in different countries; or (ii) that the country in which the countries conduct business is different from the country where the settlement agreement is to be performed; or (iii) that the country in which the parties conduct business is different from the country that is most closely linked to the settlement agreement.[418]

Moreover, the scope of the convention also excludes settlement agreements that are subject to other international conventions such as the Hague Convention and the New York Convention.[419] Examples of such settlement agreements would include those that have been settled during the course of a court proceeding, those that have

---

[410] United Nations Treaty Collection.

[411] Id.

[412] Singapore Convention.

[413] Chua (2019), pp. 573–577.

[414] Id.

[415] Schnabel (2019).

[416] Singapore Convention art 4.

[417] Id art 1.

[418] Id art 1, paragraph 1.

[419] Id art 1, paragraph 3.

already been approved by a court or those that have been recorded or are otherwise enforceable as an arbitral award.[420]

3.8.3 *Singapore Convention Enforcement Mechanisms*

The Singapore Convention does not specify a particular mode of enforcement.[421] Instead, the convention stipulates that the settlement agreement will be enforced according to the rules of procedure of the signatory country.[422] This ensures that signatory countries maintain maximum flexibility in the enforcement of mediated settlement agreements.[423]

There are some minimum requirements for enforcement, however, for a party wishing to enforce a settlement agreement under the convention.[424] The first requirement is that the party seeking enforcement must provide the signed settlement agreement to the competent authority.[425] The second requirement is that the party seeking enforcement must provide proof that the parties negotiated the settlement agreement through mediation.[426] Proof can be provided by various means including; the mediator's signature on the settlement agreement, a document signed by the mediator confirming that the mediation took place, a confirmation by the institution administering the mediation or any other proof that is suitable to the competent authority.[427]

3.8.3.1 Enforcement Exceptions Under the Convention

The Singapore Convention also provides several bases for signatory States to choose not to enforce the mediated settlement agreement.[428] These exceptions include, *inter alia*, incapacity of a party, performance of the settlement agreement is not permissible pursuant to the applicable law or contrary to the public policy of the State in which enforcement is sought, subsequent modification of the settlement agreement, unclear or incomprehensible obligations in the settlement agreement, "serious breach" of the mediator of mediation standards or failure to disclose facts or

---

[420] Id.

[421] Singapore Convention; Schnabel (2019).

[422] Singapore Convention art 3, paragraph 1.

[423] Abramson (2019).

[424] Singapore Convention art 4.

[425] Id art 4, paragraph 1(a).

[426] Id art 4, paragraph 1(b).

[427] Id.

[428] Id art 5.

circumstances undermining the mediator's impartiality or independence.[429] These grounds for refusal to enforce a settlement agreement under the Convention can be classified into four major categories: (i) contract-like defenses (Article 5(1)(a)–(d)), mediator-misconduct defenses (Article 5(1)(e)–(f)), subject matter not capable of mediated settlement (Article 5(2)(b)) and public policy (Article 5(2)(a)).[430]

It appears that Article V of The Convention on the Recognition and Enforcement of Foreign Arbitral Awards (also known as the "The New York Convention"), which applies to the recognition and enforcement of foreign arbitral awards and the referral by a court to arbitration, served as the inspiration for the exceptions to the enforcement of mediated settlements under the Singapore Convention.[431] For example, Articles 5(1)(a)–(c) are similar to Article V(1)(a) and (e) of the New York Convention, which covers a party's inability to enter into an arbitration agreement or other invalidity of the arbitration agreement, as well as when an arbitral award has not yet become binding on the parties or has been set aside or suspended.[432] In addition, Article 5(2) of the Singapore Convention emulates Article V(2) of the New York Convention, which provides an exception to enforcement if the "*subject matter of the difference is not capable of settlement by arbitration under the law of* [the country where recognition and enforcement is sought]" and where recognition or enforcement "*would be contrary to the public policy of that country*".[433]

Contrariwise, there are no comparable articles in the New York Convention to Article 5(1)(d)–(f) of the Singapore Convention because these provisions are specifically tailored to the mediation context.[434] For example, since mediation settlements mirror contracts in that they are based on the parties' consent and mutual agreement, it stands that where the claim for relief is contrary to the terms of the settlement agreement, Article 5(1)(d) of the Singapore Convention could provide grounds for refusal.[435] Additional provisions specific to the mediation process are Article 5(1)(e) and (f) of the Convention.[436] These articles provide grounds for non-enforcement of a mediated settlement where the mediator has engaged in a serious breach of mediation standards or failed to disclose circumstances without which the party would not have agreed to the settlement terms.[437] Given the unique circumstances of the mediator's role, which includes private, separate caucuses with

---

[429] Id art 5; Abramson (2019).

[430] Chua (2019), pp. 113–138.

[431] Convention on the Recognition and Enforcement of Foreign Arbitral Awards, 10 June 1958, 330 UNTS 38 (1959) (New York Convention); Singapore Convention art 5; Chua (2019), pp. 113–138.

[432] New York Convention; Singapore Convention art 5.

[433] Id.

[434] New York Convention; Singapore Convention art 5; Chua (2019), pp. 113–138.

[435] Id.

[436] Convention on the Recognition and Enforcement of Foreign Arbitral Awards, 10 June 1958, 330 UNTS 38 (1959), Article 5.

[437] New York Convention; Singapore Convention.

individual parties, the confidentiality of the proceedings, the voluntary nature of the parties' participation and the limited number of procedural rules governing the mediation process, the drafters of the Singapore Convention included safeguards against exceptional misconduct by the mediator without which the "party would not have entered into the settlement agreement".[438]

3.8.3.2 "Seat" of Mediation Under the Convention

Whilst examining the Singapore Convention's exceptions to enforcement of mediated settlement agreements, the difference between the "seat", or place, of international arbitration proceedings and mediation proceedings must also be discussed. The seat of arbitration refers to the parties' selected location as the legal place of arbitration.[439] This location determines the procedural framework of the arbitration, including its enforcement.[440] However, the seat of the arbitration proceedings must be distinguished from the place of the arbitration hearings, because whereas the former is a essentially a legal construct, the latter is a physical, geographical choice.[441] For example, the arbitral laws of a particular country may be chosen as the seat of the proceedings but the arbitral hearings may take place in a different country without anyone involved ever traveling to the country that serves as the seat of the arbitration.[442] Generally, parties are free to agree on the seat of arbitration.[443] In the context of investor-state arbitration, and under the ICSID Convention in particular, the parties' choice to select the place of arbitration is limited to those States who are parties to the New York Convention.[444]

With regard to the enforcement of non-ICSID arbitral awards, the national courts of the seat of arbitration can determine whether relief can be sought under its terms.[445] The New York Convention provides that the arbitration law of the country of the place of arbitration determines the scope of review of non-ICSID awards and the degree of scrutiny exercised in the review process.[446] Accordingly, the standard of judicial review of non-ICSID awards may vary considerably.[447] In contrast, the annulment process for ICSID arbitral awards is self-contained as a party seeking the annulment of an ICSID Award must make an application to the Secretary General of

[438] Singapore Convention.
[439] Brekoulakis et al. (2016), pp. 278–286.
[440] Id.
[441] Coutelier (2011).
[442] Id.
[443] Id.
[444] 2006 ICSID Additional Facility Rules, Article 19.
[445] New York Convention art V.
[446] Id.
[447] Schreuer (2011), pp. 222–224.

ICSID who may then grant an *ad hoc* committee with the authority to annul an award on any of the grounds provided in Article 52(1) of the ICSID Convention.[448]

Under the Singapore Convention, mediated settlement agreements have no "nationality" as there is no seat of mediation.[449] The UNCITRAL Working Group II responsible for the drafting of the Singapore Convention specifically considered and rejected the concept of a seat of mediation.[450] In rejecting the creation of a place of mediation under the Singapore Convention, there is no jurisdiction that is given greater legal importance amongst the various jurisdictions that may be impacted by the settlement agreement.[451] Moreover, by not tying mediation proceedings to the law of a seat, the Singapore Convention emancipates mediated settlements from the legal constraints of any given place of mediation.[452] However, as to the question of which country's substantial law would apply to the judicial review of any refusal to enforce a mediated settlement, the Singapore Convention provides no direction in its articles.[453] Presumably, the enforcing authority or the court seized with the matter would apply the applicable conflict-of-law rules at the place of enforcement and consider the parties' choice of law in the settlement agreement, if applicable.[454]

3.8.4 Application of the Singapore Convention to Investment Disputes

The Singapore Convention arguably makes mediation a more attractive dispute resolution tool by making international mediated settlements directly enforceable in State parties that ratify the Convention instead of relying on a mediated settlement agreement as a contract to be enforced in a local court.[455] This is potentially also the case for investor-state disputes as well. The text and the *travaux préparatoires* of the Singapore Convention encourage the interpretation that the Singapore Convention applies provided the dispute is "commercial".[456]

Conversely, Article 8 of the Singapore Convention provides signatory States two possible reservations to its application.[457] In particular, Article 8(a) provides States

---

[448] Caron (2012), pp. 173–199.

[449] Chong (2019).

[450] United Nations Commission on International Trade Law, 'Report of Working Group II (Arbitration and Conciliation) on the work of its sixty-third session (Vienna, 7–11 September 2015)' A/CN.9/861, paragraph 35.

[451] Id.

[452] Chong (2019).

[453] Id.

[454] Id.

[455] Tan (2020).

[456] Id.

[457] Singapore Convention.

the opportunity exclude themselves from application of the Singapore Convention in respect of their investor-state disputes thereby excluding investors from the guarantee of enforcement of mediated settlement agreements.[458] However, the existence of Article 8 also indicates that States and government entities are not automatically excluded from the Singapore Convention suggesting that the Singapore Convention's purpose is to include and facilitate the enforcement of investor-state dispute mediated settlements.[459] Furthermore, as of January 2021, it is noteworthy that only three States, namely Saudi Arabia, Belarus and Iran, out of the 59 States that have signed or ratified the Singapore Convention have made reservations under Article 8 thereof.[460] Consequently, one may deduce from this trend that States are so far committed to supporting the Singapore Convention's provisions and purpose including a commitment to enforce mediated settlement agreements even where the State was a party to the underlying dispute.[461] This leads to the question of whether investor-state disputes should be mediated, and sovereign disputes in particular.

3.9 Conclusion

This chapter was dedicated to providing a through understanding of mediation, starting with a review of its various definitions and distinguishing it from conciliation to describing the various phases of the process, techniques and styles used by mediators and the possibility of combining mediation with other dispute resolution mechanisms such as arbitration. In this chapter, we also examined the legal framework surrounding mediation and described the United Nations Convention on International Settlement Agreements Resulting from Mediation ("Singapore Convention") and its potential application to investment disputes.

As discussed in this chapter, mediation is a particularly flexible process capable of adapting to the parties' needs and the circumstances surrounding the dispute. The tremendous malleability of the mediation process suggests that it could also be put to use for disputes between indebted states and their creditors. It is therefore

---

[458] Id.

[459] United Nations Commission on International Trade Law Working Group II (Dispute Settlement) Sixty-fifth session, Vienna, 12–23 September 2016, Settlement of commercial disputes: International commercial conciliation: preparation of an instrument on enforcement of international commercial settlement agreements resulting from conciliation, Note by the Secretariat https://undocs.org/en/A/CN.9/WG.II/WP.198, paragraph 24; United Nations Commission on International Trade Law Forty-ninth session New York, 27 June–15 July 2016, Report of Working Group II (Arbitration and Conciliation) on the work of its sixty-fourth session, A/CN.9/867, paragraph 11; Tan (2020).

[460] United Nations Treaty Collection, 'Chapter XXII Commercial Arbitration and Mediation: 4; Singapore Convention'.

[461] Tan (2020).

worthwhile to examine how this process could be adapted for resolving sovereign debt disputes in the investor-state context.

Sources

International Conventions and Rules

Convention on the Settlement of Investment Disputes between States and Nationals of Other States (ICSID) Conciliation Rules (2006).
Convention on the Settlement of Investment Disputes between States and Nationals of Other States (ICSID) ICSID Additional Facility Rules (2006).
Convention on the Recognition and Enforcement of Foreign Arbitral Awards, 10 June 1958, 330 UNTS 38 (1959) (New York Convention).
Energy Charter Conference, 'Guide on Investment Mediation'.
EU Mediation Directive (2008).
European Code of Conduct for Mediators (2004).
International Bar Association (IBA) Rules for Investor-State Mediation.
International Mediation Institute (IMI) Code of Professional Conduct (2021).
International Chamber of Commerce's Amicable Dispute Resolution (ADR) Rules (2001) (ICC ADR Rules).
International Chamber of Commerce (ICC) Mediation Guidance Notes (2014).
International Chamber of Commerce (ICC) Rules for the Appointment of Experts and Neutrals (2015).
Trans Pacific Partnership (2016).
Uniform Mediation Act (2003).
UNCITRAL Model Law on Commercial Conciliation (2002).
UNCITRAL Model Law on International Commercial Mediation and International Settlement Agreements Resulting from Mediation (2018).
United Nations Convention on International Settlement Agreements Resulting from Mediation, 12 September 2020.

Domestic Rules and Legislation

American Arbitration Association (ABA) Model Standards of Conduct for Mediators (2005).
Austrian Childrens Law Reform (Kindschaftsrechts-Änderungsgesetz 2001, BGBl I 135/2000.
Australian Family Law Act 1975 (Cth).
Australian Family Law Regulations 1984 (Cth).
Austrian Federal Court Rules (Amendment) 1991 N° 461.

Austrian Marriage Law Reform (Eherechts-Änderungsgesetz 1999 BGBl I 125/1999).
French Decree No. 2003-1166 of 2 December 2003 (Décret portant creation du diplôme d'Etat de médiateur familial).
French Law of 26 May 2004 Relating to Family Mediation.
German Law on Marriage and Civil Procedure Code (Familienrechts-Änderungsgesetzes 2009 – Fam-RÄG 2009).
Family Law Act 1996 (UK).
French Civil Procedure Code (Code de procedure civile, C pr civ).
Minnesota General Rules of Practice, Article 114.
UK Pre-action Protocols 4.7 and the Civil Procedure Rules.
U.S. Florida Statutes S. 44.102(2)(a) 2008, Title V, Ch. 44.

References

Articles

Agusti-Panareda J (2004) Power imbalances in mediation: questioning some common assumptions. Disp Resol J 59(2):24
Alexander N (2008a) Mediation and the art of regulation. Queensland Univ Technol Law Just J 8(1):1
Alexander N (2008b) The mediation metamodel: understanding practice. Confl Resol Q 26:92
Anderson DQ (2010) Mandatory mediation: an oxymoron? Examining the feasibility of implementing a court-mandated mediation program. Cardozo J Confl Resol 11(2):479
Bercovitch J, Kadayifci-Orellana SA (2009) Religion and mediation: the role of faith-based actors in international conflict resolution. Int Negot 14:175
Bogdanoski T (2009) The Importance and challenge of active listening in mediation. Aust Disp Resol J 20(4):201
Caron DD (2012) Framing the work of ICSID annulment committees. World Arbitr Med Rev 6:173
Chia H-B, Lee-Partridge J, Chong C-L (2004) Traditional mediation practices: are we throwing the baby out with the bath water? Confl Resol Q 21(4):451
Chua E (2019) Enforcement of international mediated settlements without the Singapore Convention on Mediation. Singap Acad Law J 31:572
Cohen JR (2014) Open-minded listening. Charlotte Law Rev 5(1):139
Coutelier LE (2011) Annulment and Court Intervention in International Commercial Arbitration. Research Paper. https://ssrn.com/abstract=1957278 or https://doi.org/10.2139/ssrn.1957278
Diathessopoulos MD (2012) The alternative forms of dispute settlement and the essential difference between these and arbitration. https://ssrn.com/abstract=2026606 or https://doi.org/10.2139/ssrn.2026606
Dilloff NJ (2010) Tips for successful mediation. Maryland Bar J 43(4):62
Eidenmüller H (2002) A legal framework for national and international mediation proceedings. J Int Disp Resol Beilage 12
Fawehinmi F, Zlatanska E (2016) Mediation and conciliation: in pursuit of clarity. Int J Arbitr Med Disp Manag 82:146
Galič A (2003) Alternative dispute resolution in Slovenia. ADR Bull 6(4):71
Garcia A (2011) The role of interactional competence in mediation. Confl Resol Q 28(2):205

Golann D (2000) Variations in mediation: how–and why–legal mediators change styles in the course of a case. J Disp Resol 2000(1):41
Golann D (2011) Beyond brainstorming: the special barriers to interest-based mediation, and techniques to overcome them. Disp Resol Mag 18(1):22
Greenberg EE (2015) When "yes" may actually mean "no": rethinking informed consent to ADR processes. N Y Disp Resol Lawyer 8:1
Hoffman DA (2011) Mediation and the art of shuttle diplomacy. Negot J 27:263
Jameson JK, Bodtker AM, Porch DM et al (2009) Exploring the role of emotion in conflict transformation. Confl Resol Q 27(2):167
Kelly EJ, Kaminski N (2016) Importance of emotional intelligence in negotiation and mediation. Int Comp Jurisprud 2(1):55
Laflin ME (2014) Preserving the integrity of mediation through the adoption of ethical rules for Lawyer-Mediators. Notre Dame J Law Ethics Public Policy 14(1):479
Lande J (2002) Using dispute system design methods to promote good-faith participation in court-connected mediation programs. UCLA Law Rev 50:129–131
Livingood JM (2002) Reframing and its uses. Disp Resol J 57(4):42
Lohvinenko M, Starynskyi M, Rudenko L et al (2021) Models of mediation: theoretical and legal analysis. Confl Resol Q 39(1):51
Love LP (1997) Top ten reasons why mediators should not evaluate. Fla State Law Rev 24:937
McAdoo B, Welsh NA (2005) Look before you leap and keep on looking: lessons from the institutionalization of court-connected mediation. Nevada Law J 5:399
Nolan-Haley J (2005) Self-determination in international mediation: some preliminary reflections. Cardozo J Confl Resol 7:277
Picard C, Siltanen J (2013) Exploring the significance of emotion for mediation practice. Confl Resol Q 31:31
Riskin LL (2003) Decision-making in mediation: the new old grid and the new new grid system. Notre Dame Law Rev 79(1):3
Roberts KM (2007) Mediating the evaluative-facilitative debate: why both parties are wrong and a proposal for settlement. Loy Univ Chi Law J 39(1):187
Robyn C (2002) Trends in mediation legislation: "all for one and one for all" or "one at all"? Univ West Aust Law Rev 30:172
Schnabel T (2019) The Singapore Convention on Mediation: a framework for the cross border recognition and enforcement of mediated settlements. Pepp Disp Resol Law J 19:1
Schweinsberg M, Thau S, Pillutla MM (2021) Negotiation impasses: types, causes and resolutions. J Manag 47(6):1430
Shane MB (1995) The difference between mediation and conciliation. Disp Resol J 50(3):31
Stipanowich TJ (2015) The international evolution of mediation: a call for dialogue and deliberation. Vic Univ Wellingt Law Rev 46(4):1191
Stipanowich TJ (2021) Arbitration, mediation and mixed modes: seeking workable solutions and common ground on med-arb, arb-med and settlement-oriented activities by arbitrators. Harv Negot Law Rev 26(Spring):265
Strong S (2014) Use and perception of international commercial mediation and conciliation: a preliminary report on issues relating to the proposed UNCITRAL Convention on International Commercial Mediation and Conciliation. University of Missouri School of Law Legal Studies Research Paper No. 2014-28
Tan R (2020) Investor-state arbitration meets mediation: the Singapore Convention on Mediation as Game-Changer. 29 September 2020 Kluwer Mediation Blog. http://arbitrationblog.kluwerarbitration.com/2020/09/29/investor-state-arbitration-meets-mediation-the-singapore-convention-on-mediation-as-game-changer/

Uniform mediation act and official comments (2003) J Disp Resol 1:47
Welsh N (2001) Making deals in court-connected mediation: what's justice got to do with it? Wash Univ Law Q 79:787
Winslade J, Monk G, Cotter A (1998) A narrative approach to the practice of mediation. Negot J 14(1):21

Books and Book Chapters

Abramson HI (2004) Mediation representation; advocating in a problem-solving process. National Institute for Trial Advocacy
Abramson H (2019) New Singapore Convention on cross-border mediated settlements: key choices. In: Titi C, Gómez KF (eds) Mediation in international commercial and investment disputes. Oxford University Press
Alexander N (2009) International and comparative mediation: legal perspectives. Wolters Kluwer
Alexander N (2010) International and comparative mediation: legal perspectives, 4th edn. Wolters Kluwer
Barnes BE (2007) Culture, conflict, and mediation in the Asian Pacific. University Press of America
Baruch Bush RA, Folger JP (2004) The promise of mediation: the transformative approach to conflict, 2nd edn. Jossey-Bass Publishers
Beer JE, Packard CC, Stief E (2012) The mediator's handbook, 4th edn. New Society Publishers
Boulle L, Colatrella MT Jr, Picchioni AP (2008) Mediation: skills and techniques. LexisNexis
Brekoulakis S, Lew JDM, Mistelis L (2016) The evolution and future of international arbitration. Wolters Kluwer
Cloke K (2001) Mediating dangerously. Jossey-Bass
Coe JJ Jr (2010) Concurrent Med-Arb (CMA) – some further reflections on a work in progress. In: Franck SD, Joubin-Bret A (eds) Investor-state disputes: prevention and alternatives to arbitration II. UNCTAD, pp 46–47
De Girolamo D (2020) The opening statement in mediation: a Goffman analysis. In: Moscati MF, Palmer M, Roberts M (eds) Comparative dispute resolution. Edward Elgar
Fisher R, Ury W, Patton B (1997) Getting to yes: negotiating an agreement without giving in, 2nd edn. Random House Business Books
Folberg J, Golann D, Stipanowich TJ (2016) Resolving disputes: theory, practice, and law, 3rd edn. Wolters Kluwer
Golann D (2009) Mediating legal disputes: effective strategies for neutrals and advocates. American Bar Association
Golann D, Aaron MC (2010) Using evaluations in mediation. In: Carbonneau TE, Jaeggi JA (eds) AAA handbook on mediation. JurisNet
Hardy S, Rundle O (2010) Mediation for Lawyers. CCH Australia
Irvine C, Farrington L (2016) Mediation and emotions: perception and regulation. In: Conway H, Stannard J (eds) The emotional dynamics of law and legal discourse. Hart
Joubin-Bret A, Knörich J (eds) (2010) Investor–state disputes: prevention and alternatives to arbitration. United Nations
Leoveanu A, Erac A (2019) ICC mediation/ paving the way forward in mediation. In: Titi C, Gómez KF (eds) International commercial and investment disputes. Oxford University Press
Lewicki RJ, Saunders DM, Barry B (2015) Negotiation, 7th edn. McGraw-Hill Education
Lundmark T (2012) Charting the divide between common and civil law. Oxford University Press
Martin AT (2011) International mediation: an evolving market. In: Rovine AW (ed) Contemporary issues in international arbitration & mediation: the Fordham Papers (2010). Brill
McIlwrath M, Savage J (2010) International arbitration and mediation: a practical guide. Kluwer Law International

Menkel-Meadow C, Love LP, Schneider AK (2020) Mediation: practice, policy, and ethics, 3rd edn. Wolters Kluwer
Moore CW (2014) The mediation process, 8th edn. Jossey-Bass
Nitschke F (2019) The ICSID conciliation rules in practice. In: Titi C, Gómez KF (eds) Mediation in international commercial and investment disputes. Oxford University Press
Nolan-Haley J (2012) Evolving paths to justice: assessing the EU directive on mediation. In: Rovine AW (ed) Contemporary issues in international arbitration and mediation: the Fordham papers. Brill Nijhoff
O'Sullivan G (2018) The Mediator's Toolkit: formulating and asking questions for successful outcomes. New Society Publishers
Pepperdine University Strauss Institute for Dispute Resolution (2009) Mediation: the art of facilitating settlement. Pepperdine University
Sammut G, Bauer MW (2020) Agenda setting, framing and mass mediation in the psychology of social influence. Cambridge University Press
Schreuer C (2011) From ICSID annulment to appeal half way down the slippery slope. In: The law and practice of international courts and tribunals, vol 10. Brill
Schreuer C, Malintoppi L, Reinisch A, Sinclair A (2009) The ICSID Convention: a commentary, 2nd edn. Cambridge University Press
Smith MS (2005) Single-text negotiation. Beyond intractability. Accessed 15 October 2021
Spencer D, Brogan M (2006) Mediation law and practice. Cambridge University Press
Stitt A (2004) Mediation: a practical guide. Routledge-Cavendish
Strasser F, Randolph P (2005) Mediation: a psychological insight into conflict resolution. Continuum
Tümpel H, Sudborough C (2011) ICC's ADR rules 2001-2010: current practices, case examples and lessons learned. In: Housz AI (ed) ADR in business, practice and issues across countries and cultures, vol II. Kluwer
Winslade J, Monk G (2000) Narrative mediation. Wiley, p XII

Official Reports

Gora K (2008) Therapeutic mediation. Second Mediation Days Conference, Slovenia
ICSID. The ICSID Caseload – Statistics [2020-2]
ICSID. Investor-state mediation (Icsid.worldbank.org). https://icsid.worldbank.org/en/Pages/process/adr-mechanisms%2D%2Dmediation.aspx
ICSID. Overview of conciliation under the ICSID Convention (Icsid.worldbank.org). https://icsid.worldbank.org/en/Pages/process/ICSID-Convention-Conciliation.aspx
United Nations Commission on International Trade Law Forty-ninth session New York, 27 June-15 July 2016, Report of Working Group II (Arbitration and Conciliation) on the work of its sixty-fourth session, A/CN.9/867
United Nations Commission on International Trade Law Working Group II (Dispute Settlement) Sixty-fifth session, Vienna, 12–23 September 2016, Settlement of commercial disputes: International commercial conciliation: preparation of an instrument on enforcement of international commercial settlement agreements resulting from conciliation, Note by the Secretariat. https://undocs.org/en/A/CN.9/WG.II/WP.198
United Nations Commission on International Trade Law. Report of Working Group II (Arbitration and Conciliation) on the work of its sixty-third session (Vienna, 7–11 September 2015) A/CN.9/861, paragraph 35
United Nations Treaty Collection (Treaties.un.org, 2021). https://treaties.un.org/pages/ViewDetails.aspx?src=TREATY&mtdsg_no=XXII-4&chapter=22&clang=_en

Websites and News Articles

European Commission for the Efficiency of Justice (2019) European handbook for mediation lawmaking. https://rm.coe.int/cepej-2019-9-en-handbook/1680951928, pp 19–23

Hochman SA (2012) A mediator's proposal – whether, when, and how it should be used. Mediate.com. https://www.mediate.com/articles/HochmanS1.cfm

Leathes M (2011) Stop Shovelling smoke! Give users a classic definition of mediation - Kluwer Mediation Blog. (Kluwer Mediation Blog, 2011) http://mediationblog.kluwerarbitration.com/2011/09/01/stop-shovelling-smoke-give-users-a-classic-definition-of-mediation/

Lehman P, Page NR (2007) Enhancing mediator neutrality through question-asking. Mediate.com. https://www.mediate.com/articles/pageLehman.cfm

Limbury A (2019) Brainstorming. Kluwer Mediation Blog. http://mediationblog.kluwerarbitration.com/2019/10/22/brainstorming/

Quality Assurance. International Mediation Institute. https://imimediation.org/about/quality-assurance/

Ratliff B (2018) Pre-mediation conferences. ADR Times available at https://www.adrtimes.com/pre-mediation-conferences/

Repicky T (2011) How to talk and listen effectively in mediation. Mediate.com. https://www.mediate.com/articles/RepickyT1.cfm

Rule C (2018) Reframing. Mediate.com. https://www.mediate.com/articles/Colin-Rule-Reframing.cfm

Spangler B (2003) Reality-testing. BeyondIntractability.org. https://www.beyondintractability.org/essay/reality_testing

Voyles R (n.d.) Managing an imbalance of power. Mediate.com. https://www.mediate.com/articles/voylesR3.cfm

Warnlof J (n.d.) The premediation conference: an underused step towards resolution. The Mediation Society available at https://mediationsociety.org/the-pre%C2%ADmediation-conference-an-underused-step-towards-resolution/

What is mediation? What happens in a mediation? (Jamsadr.com). https://www.jamsadr.com/mediation-defined/

Young P (2003) Overcoming impasse in mediation: a short literature review. Mediate.com. https://www.mediate.com/articles/young13.cfm?nl=56

Yu Chong S (2019) Singapore Convention Series: why is there no 'seat' of mediation?, 1 February 2019. Kluwer Mediation Blog. http://mediationblog.kluwerarbitration.com/2019/02/01/singapore-convention-series-why-is-there-no-seat-of-mediation/

Chapter 4
Mediating Sovereign Debt Disputes

As described in Chap. 2, creditors are increasingly resorting to the dispute resolution provisions provided in investment treaties to resolve their claims against debtor governments. These treaties generally provide for ICSID arbitration proceedings. Consequently, in recent years creditors have filed several such claims but the proceedings never reached the merits. Ultimately, several sovereign debt disputes were resolved outside of court and arbitral proceedings but in settlement discussions. Successful settlements are often the result of mediation proceedings. Accordingly, Chap. 3 provided a detailed description of the mediation process and the techniques used by mediators.

This Chapter will now focus on mediation as a tool for resolving sovereign debt-related investor-state disputes. Sections 4.1 and 4.2 will examine, respectively, the advantages and disadvantages of mediating sovereign debt disputes. Section 4.3 will explore some of the practical considerations involved in mediating sovereign debt disputes such as commencing the proceedings, choosing a set of rules to govern the procedure and selecting the mediator. Section 4.4 will then identify the reasons for resistance to mediating sovereign debt disputes and will make suggestions for overcoming these obstacles.

4.1 Advantages of Mediating Sovereign Debt Disputes

Let us turn now to the use of mediation for resolving sovereign debt disputes, and specifically the possible advantages of doing so. To begin, mediation could redress several of the criticisms aimed at the use of investment arbitration in this domain. For example, critics have claimed that investor-state arbitrations often lead to purportedly inconsistent awards, which in the context of sovereign lending could undermine

C. M. Sudborough, *Mediating Sovereign Debt Disputes*, EYIEL Monographs - Studies in European and International Economic Law 35,
https://doi.org/10.1007/978-3-031-46787-5_4

market confidence.[1] Since mediation is more focused on the parties' interests than an analysis of their legal rights and since it is aimed at producing a contractual agreement between them rather than a decision interpreting the law, there is no reason to be concerned about an unpredictable body of law emanating from mediation of sovereign debt disputes.[2] Furthermore, since mediation maintains the parties' power over the outcome, this element of control should further assuage creditors' concerns about arbitrary judicial decisions or arbitral awards that increase the market risk of purchasing sovereign bonds.[3]

Another popular critique of the use of investment arbitration generally takes aim at the alleged exclusive club of investment arbitrators whose continued 'club membership', or repeated selection to investment arbitration tribunals, is contended to favor the interests of investors.[4] Mediation can also redress this concern. Unlike the decision-making role of the arbitrator, the responsibility of the mediator is to facilitate the parties' negotiations using various tools for fostering open communication, trust and problem-solving creativity to ensure that the parties' negotiations are fruitful.[5] Thus, the impartiality (both real and perceived) of the mediator is critical for the parties' confidence in the mediator and active cooperation in the process.[6] Accordingly, a mediator has little to gain from favoring the interests of creditors or States' interests as it would undermine the success of his or her career.[7]

A third criticism of investment arbitration proceedings that might be redressed by mediation targets the enormous investment in time and cost which, particularly in the context of sovereign default, diverts government funds needed for public services during a time of economic crisis.[8] This reproach is especially biting from a public policy perspective in the context of sovereign debt disputes where the sovereign State must often employ austerity policies on its citizens in order to pay off its debts.[9] Although a direct comparison of costs is not yet possible given that insufficient data is available on investor-state mediations, it is possible to compare the statistics for the relative cost of international commercial arbitration and mediation as an indicator.[10] Mediation proceedings differ from arbitration proceedings in that they do not focus on fact-finding and discovery, witness testimony, reading and writing lengthy legal briefs and judgments as well a series of formal procedural steps and hearings.[11]

[1] Gómez (2018), pp. 4–21; Titi (2016), pp. 383–384; Gaillard (2008), pp. 1–3; World Investment Report 2015: Reforming International Investment Governance (2015), pp. 127–163.

[2] United Nations Conference Trade and Development (UNCTAD) (2018).

[3] Guide on Investment Mediation; Titi (2019).

[4] Eberhardt et al. (2018).

[5] Moore (2014), pp. 43–84.

[6] Id.

[7] Id.

[8] Titi (2019); Pohl (2018), p. 46; Bottini et al. (2020), pp. 251–253.

[9] Blackman and Mukhi (2010), p. 53; Alderman et al. (2016).

[10] Waters (2015) and Tümpel and Sudborough (2011).

[11] Titi (2019); ICSID, 'Overview of An Arbitration Under the ICSID Convention'.

Rather, mediation centers on facilitating the parties' negotiations and creative problem-solving (i.e. mostly verbal communications either directly between the parties or via the mediator) and then securing agreement on the terms of the settlement, which is usually drafted by the parties and their counsel.[12] Moreover, contrary to the panels of three arbitrators common in high-value and complex commercial arbitrations, the norm is to engage only one mediator irrespective of the complexity of the claims or the amount in dispute, thus diminishing the portion of the costs relating to the third party's fees and expenses.[13] In light of the differences in the process, international commercial mediations tend to last a few months (depending on the mediator and the parties' availabilities to schedule meetings) rather than years which is generally the pace of multifaceted, international arbitrations.[14] Consequently, the mediation invoice is almost certain to be lighter than in an investment arbitration which saves precious public funding for debt-laden States often in the midst of austerity regimes.

Aside from answering to the criticisms of investment arbitration as a dispute resolution tool in the sovereign debt context, mediation also provides additional benefits that are not available in other dispute resolution mechanisms. First, unlike judicial or arbitral proceedings, mediation allows sovereign bondholders and the defaulting State to preserve or rebuild a positive relationship by engaging in a dialogue that could lead to a mutually beneficial solution.[15] This is particularly important for both creditors and indebted governments as it might lead on the one hand to a greater pay-out for creditors than a potential loss in litigation or arbitration and on the other hand it gives a greater chance of renewed investment and financing for States in economic crisis.[16] Mediation provides States and creditors the possibility to strike a new deal by allowing them to include issues in their bargain that go beyond the mere issue of compensation payment.[17]

Second, as mediation focuses on the parties' mutual interests, it gives the parties an opportunity to craft a solution that goes beyond the black and white legal remedy of win or lose.[18] Judicial and arbitral proceedings do not allow the bondholders and the issuing sovereigns to explore their broader interests although there might be many cases in which they are unexpectedly similar. For example, both parties might share an interest in expediting the settlement of the dispute. For the State, an efficient settlement would limit the damage to its reputation on the financial markets, and for the creditors it would save time and costs in the collection process.[19]

---

[12] Moore (2014), pp. 43–84.

[13] Tümpel and Sudborough (2011).

[14] Id.

[15] Welsh and Schneider (2012).

[16] Joubin-Bret and Knörich (2010), p. 33.

[17] Id.

[18] Titi (2019) and Welsh and Schneider (2012).

[19] Joubin-Bret and Knörich (2010), p. 32.

Third, as mediation does not involve jurisdictional requirements or oblige parties to indicate legal standing for participating in the proceedings, it allows a broader range of participants to be involved in the process, should the disputing parties agree.[20] In the context of sovereign debt disputes in which important policy issues related to debt restructuring, economic crisis, austerity measures and bailout programs are at stake, it may be necessary to involve participants who represent other stakeholder groups to express their interests for consideration in the negotiations making it more likely that the settlement agreement will be accepted more widely by the electorate.[21]

For all the reasons explained in this section, specifically the potential for mediation to redress various criticisms of arbitration in ISDS, the particular value of the cost-efficiency of mediation proceedings in the context of sovereign debt as well as the relationship-building nature of mediation and its flexibility to take into account the unique policy and business interests of government parties and their creditors; mediation is a viable and attractive option for resolving sovereign debt disputes.

4.2 Disadvantages of Mediating Sovereign Debt Disputes

Like litigation or arbitration, mediation is not a panacea for sovereign debt disputes. To employ mediation in the most optimal manner, it is necessary to prepare for its potential disadvantages. One of the first obstacles that mediation faces in being used more systematically in the investor-state and sovereign debt context is that it remains essentially theoretical.[22] To date, although there have been a handful of investor-state conciliation cases, only one investor-state mediation case has been confirmed and the outcome is unknown.[23] Without more cases to demonstrate a proven track record and make statistics available, it is difficult to market mediation as a dispute resolution tool. This in turn makes it all the more difficult for one party to convince another to participate in mediation where no prior mediation clause exists as wary parties may decline due to lack of familiarity with the process.[24]

[20] 2012 IBA Investor-State Mediation Rules art 2–3.

[21] 2014 United Nations Commission on International Trade Law (UNCITRAL) Rules on Transparency in Treaty-based Investor-State Arbitration.

[22] Titi (2019).

[23] Correspondence with the ICC International Centre for ADR (According to the Centre, the Request for Mediation was filed pursuant to Article 3 of the ICC Mediation Rules (which applies when there is no prior agreement to mediate between the parties) pursuant to the applicable BIT which provided for the opportunity to amicably resolve disputes. After the Centre submitted notice of the Request filed by the requesting party investor, the responding State party agreed to refer the dispute to ICC Mediation Rules together with the IBA Rules for Investor-State Mediation); Nitschke (2019).

[24] Titi (2019).

Furthermore, investor-state mediation is often scoffed at by members of the litigation and arbitration community who view it as being a waste of time.[25] Rationalizing this cynical point of view, sceptics point to the statistics on Conciliation Proceedings under the ICSID Convention and Additional Facility Rules, wherein the small number of cases have for the most part failed to result in a settlement agreement.[26] However, reference to these statistics is misleading since they refer to ICSID-specific conciliation proceedings and not mediation proceedings specifically which, as mentioned above, present important differences.[27] In reality, ICSID conciliation proceedings are far more akin to non-binding, rights-based arbitration proceedings than interest-based mediation proceedings because they focus on an evaluative, fact-finding process that involves the conciliator (s) requesting documents, hearing witnesses, making site visits and issuing recommendations.[28] Instead, 'pure' mediation proceedings seek to facilitate the parties' negotiations by focusing on their interests.[29] Moreover, commercial mediations have in fact a greater rate of success than ICSID conciliation proceedings, with the great majority of cases reaching settlement.[30]

Another challenge for mediating sovereign debt disputes is the political risk and institutional obstacles for States.[31] Negotiations during a mediation can be obfuscated for States by the constraints of existing laws and regulations as well as political issues, involvement of lobbyists, and harsh publicity. For instance, it might be more damaging for a politician's career to enter into a voluntary, early settlement with immediate compensation to foreign bondholders than to be subjected to an arbitral award imposing a similar cost on the State some years later.[32] Further, voluntary settlements can generate internal, organizational conflicts wherein discords may arise as to whether the protection of foreign creditors' investment rights is of greater importance than the safeguard of the State's economic sovereignty or any number of the State's other governing powers.[33] Moreover, domestic creditors may perceive such a mediated settlement between the State and its foreign creditors as unfair, special treatment that puts the domestic creditors at a disadvantage.[34] Finally, a successful mediation requires that there be at least one representative having the mandate to negotiate on behalf of the government to reach a settlement. Should

---

[25] Id; Michael Reisman (2009), p. 26; Legum (2007).

[26] ICSID, 'The ICSID Caseload – Statistics' (2017/2) 8,13; Nitschke (2019).

[27] Nitschke (2019); Fawehinmi and Zlatanska (2016), pp. 146–152; Joubin-Bret and Knörich (2010); Shane (1995), pp. 1–9.

[28] Id.

[29] Shane (1995), pp. 1–9.

[30] 'CEDR News: Mediation Market Grows By 5%: The 2016 Mediation Audit' (2016); Martin (2011).

[31] Titi (2019), pp. 36–38; Sharpe (2014), pp. 43–45; Joubin-Bret and Knörich (2010), pp. 32.

[32] Joubin-Bret and Knörich (2010), pp. 32.

[33] Id.

[34] Id.

several government departments become involved in the dispute it may be difficult to identify one agent with the authority to negotiate the settlement on behalf of all.[35] Overall, there is no simple answer to the political and institutional obstacles to mediating sovereign debt disputes. To some degree, the remedy may lie in adopting a different mind-set, i.e. one that shifts the focus away from the short-term agendas of individual political actors and more on the long-term benefits for the State and its people. Moreover, some of these State-specific issues might also be resolved with the help of the mediator.

Another barrier to mediating sovereign debt disputes is that it seemingly runs counter to the current trend for increased transparency in ISDS, as evidenced by the adoption in 2014 of the UNCITRAL Rules on Transparency in Treaty-based Investor-State Arbitration.[36] Transparency standards now necessitate that ISDS arbitration proceedings be rendered more public in a number of ways such as making freely available the notice of arbitration, the response, the claims and counterclaims, submitted documents and exhibits as well as any decisions made by the arbitral tribunal.[37] To further the inclusiveness of ISDS proceedings, non-disputing parties (such as concerned interest groups) may now also apply to the arbitral tribunal to make submissions for the arbitral tribunal's consideration.[38] Consequently, should sovereign debt disputes now be redirected from ISDS arbitration proceedings with enhanced transparency standards to less transparent mediation proceedings, there is a risk that this would detract from the legitimacy of any settlement agreement stemming therefrom and thus render the process less attractive. Therefore, it is important that similar increased transparency standards also apply to sovereign debt mediation proceedings.[39]

Perhaps the most frequently cited obstacle to the more widespread use of mediation in ISDS and, concomitantly sovereign debt disputes, is the lack of an enforcement mechanism akin to the New York Convention.[40] Although mediated settlement agreements are legally binding contracts, parties fear that without a means of ensuring immediate enforcement of the settlement deal, they will be required to engage in further legal proceedings should one of the parties fail or refuse to carry out performance of the mediated accord.[41] In the context of sovereign debt disputes, creditors may understandably be skeptical of any voluntary dispute resolution outcome resulting in a new contract since the purpose of their claim against the debtor State is to seek compensation from the sovereign for its incomplete performance of the original bond agreement in the first place. However, the parties can circumvent this issue by requesting an arbitral tribunal to render an award that

---

[35] Legum (2007).

[36] Brown and Winch (2019).

[37] 2014 UNCITRAL Rules on Transparency Articles 1–8; Brown and Winch (2019).

[38] Id.

[39] Brown and Winch (2019), pp. 321–338.

[40] Abramson (2019), Mellersh (2017) and Brennan (2015).

[41] Gómez (2019); Abramson (2019); Mellersh (2017); Brennan (2015).

embodies the terms of their accord, known as an 'award by consent'.[42] An award by consent would thus effectively transform the parties' settlement agreement into an arbitral award enforceable under the ICSID Convention or the New York Convention.[43] In addition, the recently adopted Singapore Convention, discussed in Sect. 3.8 above, provides for the recognition and enforcement of mediated settlement agreements resolving international commercial disputes, similar to the framework established by the 1958 New York Convention for the recognition and enforcement of arbitral awards.[44] As discussed in Chap. 3, despite the fact that the Singapore Convention does not expressly state that it applies to investor-state disputes, such disputes have not been expressly excluded from its scope either, suggesting that investment disputes such as those arising out of sovereign bonds could benefit from its enforcement provisions.[45]

This section has identified some disadvantages to mediating sovereign debt disputes, namely in terms of convincing skeptics in light of the paucity of statistics on investment mediation and the ICSID conciliation track record, the political risk for government stakeholders to take responsibility for settlement agreements, concerns regarding transparency of ISDS and uncertain enforcement of investment mediation settlement agreements. However, as discussed herein, there are various nuances to understanding these disadvantages that lessen their impact, such as reference to international commercial mediation statistics, influencing the political arena to employ a more long-term mindset and the potential of an enforcement mechanism for investment mediation settlement agreements pursuant to the Singapore Convention.

4.3 Practical Considerations of Mediating Sovereign Debt Disputes

This section will now turn to some practical aspects of mediating sovereign debt disputes, such as how mediation can be introduced into the sovereign default dispute resolution process as well as various procedural considerations including whether to engage in *ad hoc* or institutional proceedings and the selection of a competent mediator.

---

[42] ICSID Convention article 43 ('If the parties file with the Secretary-General the full and signed text of their settlement and in writing request the Tribunal to embody such settlement in an award, the Tribunal may record the settlement in the form of its award'); 2021 ICC Arbitration Rules, Article 33 ('If the parties reach a settlement after the file has been transmitted to the arbitral tribunal in accordance with Article 16, the settlement shall be recorded in the form of an award made by consent of the parties, if so requested by the parties and if the arbitral tribunal agrees to do so').

[43] Id.

[44] Singapore Convention; Schnabel (2019).

[45] Tan (2020).

4.3.1 Commencing Sovereign Debt Mediation Proceedings

The first procedural question is how to commence mediation proceedings between sovereign bondholders and States in default. There are several possibilities. The most effective means of ensuring that the parties commence mediation proceedings is to have a pre-existing agreement to mediate that would obligate the parties to participate at least until the first meeting with the mediator. This agreement could be included as a mediation clause directly in the sovereign bond contract or in the language of the applicable investment treaty.[46] Such a clause could deny the parties the right to file for judicial or arbitral proceedings until the first mediation meeting has taken place or at least require that mediation proceedings be initiated in parallel to arbitration proceedings.[47] For example, Clause C of the ICC Mediation Rules creates an obligation to refer a dispute to mediation under the ICC Mediation Rules whilst permitting parallel arbitration proceedings if required, whereas Clause D states that the parties may not commence arbitration proceedings, if necessary, until an agreed period has elapsed following the filing of the request for mediation. The advantage of such a compulsory, prior mediation agreement is that it forces the parties to at least attempt mediation, which in turn gives the parties the greatest chance of reaching settlement.[48] However, the mediation clause could also provide for non-compulsory mediation in which the parties would be invited to consider mediation prior to filing for judicial or arbitral proceedings but not be obligated to do so.[49] Even where no mediation clause exists, the parties could nevertheless enter into a subsequent agreement to mediate.[50] However, in such a case there is no guarantee that they will reach such an agreement. Therefore, the party seeking to propose mediation to the other party would probably benefit from filing the request for mediation through an institution that could help persuade the other party to accept the proposal by explaining the mediation process and ensuring that it is a neutral, productive and time and cost efficient process.[51]

---

[46] Waibel (2013), pp. 162–167; Trans-Pacific Partnership Agreement (TPP) (2016) Article 9.18.

[47] Id art 9.18 (Provides that the parties cannot file for arbitration before 6 months have passed since filing a request for amicable dispute resolution proceedings as described in Article 9.18.).

[48] Tümpel and Sudborough (2011), p. 269.

[49] 2014 ICC Mediation Rules Clause B (requires the parties to discuss and consider submitting their dispute to the ICC Mediation Rules without obliging the parties to commence mediation proceedings).

[50] 2012 IBA Investor-State Mediation Rules art 1(a) (states that the IBA Mediation Rules can apply where the parties have so agreed even after the dispute arises).

[51] Tümpel and Sudborough (2011), p. 270.

4.3.2 Choice of Procedural Rules in Sovereign Debt Mediation Proceedings

Another question to answer is what procedural rules would govern the mediation proceedings. In any dispute resolution proceedings, including mediation, the parties have the choice whether to conduct the proceeding *ad hoc* or under the administration of an institutional body. In *ad hoc* proceedings, the parties will have to determine all aspects themselves, such as the governing rules, the selection of the mediator, the division of costs, etc.[52] Although this approach might save on the costs of fees to an administering institution, the parties are likely to spend a considerable amount of time seeking to resolve unexpected hurdles without any guarantee that they will manage to do so, particularly once the dispute has arisen.[53] Nevertheless, parties may still involve the limited assistance of an administering institution at some point during the proceedings even where they prefer to conduct the proceedings *ad hoc*, for example as an appointing authority for the mediator.[54]

Where parties choose to conduct the mediation under the administration of an institutional body, the administering institution will be responsible for either obtaining the agreement of the parties on the various procedural issues that might arise or in making a decision in the absence of an agreement in order to ensure that the proceedings are conducted as efficiently as possible.[55] Accordingly, although the costs of such proceedings will include fees to be paid to the administering body, that institutional body will in turn have the responsibility to ensure that the overall costs of the proceedings remain low, for example by scrutinizing any expenses the mediator seeks to have reimbursed and by making decisions necessary to expedite the process, as might be the case where the parties are unable to agree on the place of the mediation meetings or seek to replace the mediator.[56]

Several institutions have published rules which could apply to mediating investor-state sovereign debt disputes. These include the International Bar Association (IBA) Rules for Investor State Mediation, the ICC Mediation Rules and the Mediation Rules of the Arbitration Institute of the Stockholm Chamber of Commerce.[57] As stated above, the ICSID Conciliation Rules provide for conciliation and not mediation proceedings.[58] Although a worthwhile exercise, the purpose of this section is not to conduct a detailed comparison of these rules, but it would be wise to examine the various options before including any particular set of rules into a dispute resolution clause or before filing for mediation with any particular institution. In

[52] McIlwrath and Savage (2010), pp. 64–67.

[53] Id.

[54] 2015 ICC Rules for the Appointment of Experts and Neutrals.

[55] McIlwrath and Savage (2010), pp. 64–67.

[56] 2014 ICC Mediation Rules Appendix Article 3.

[57] 2012 IBA Investor-State Mediation Rules; 2014 ICC Mediation Rules; 2014 Mediation Rules of the Arbitration Institute of the Stockholm Chamber of Commerce; Nitschke (2014), pp. 151.

[58] ICSID, 'Overview of Conciliation under the ICSID Convention'.

considering the choices, it would also be prudent to take the following factors into consideration: the international reputation of the institution in terms of neutrality, training, quality of services and international network, the amount of assistance provided by the administering organization to facilitate the process where procedural obstacles occur, the process for the selection of the mediator, the process for replacing the mediator if necessary, the costs and how they are allocated and controlled, the flexibility of the process where the parties envision combining mediation and other dispute resolution mechanisms such as arbitration or expertise.[59]

4.3.3 Selecting the Mediator in Sovereign Debt Mediation Proceedings

Additionally, the parties need to select a mediator. As our focus is on sovereign debt mediation, the question is what particular skills should a mediator for such disputes have? Sovereign debt disputes are specific because they involve private parties (creditors) and sovereign States. Furthermore, sovereign debt disputes involve major issues of public policy, international finance, States' international obligations, transparency and national sovereignty. As such, not all capable mediators may be suitable for mediating disputes between States and their bondholders. Fortunately, several bodies have established guidelines in selecting and evaluating the criteria of potential mediators for investment disputes, including the IBA, the ECT and the International Mediation Institute (IMI), providing a useful reference.[60] Although each body lists different useful criteria for consideration, the various competency standards listed by all of these bodies converge on the following important points: (1) thorough training and experience as a mediator; (2) experience with investor-state disputes or dispute resolution proceedings involving States or State agencies; (3) skill in handling cross-cultural negotiations; (4) international reputation and credibility and, lastly, (5) experience dealing with government representatives, politicians and/or diplomats.[61] Further, in light of the technicalities of sovereign debt disputes, it would be beneficial to engage a mediator capable of quickly understanding the complexities of international sovereign financing and investment law. The aforementioned criteria also align with various categories of criteria that have been cited in the context of commercial arbitrations, namely (1) threshold criteria as pre-conditions for appointment, (2) sought-after professional

[59] McIlwrath and Savage (2010), pp. 187–204.

[60] 2012 IBA Investor-State Mediation Rules Appendix B; Guide on Investment Mediation art 8; International Mediation Institute (IMI) (2016).

[61] Id.

qualifications, (3) personality traits that encourage the parties' trust and confidence and (4) process orientations compatible with the parties' needs and/or wishes.[62]

Although international commercial mediation continues to flourish, parties to investment disputes do not yet benefit from a recognized body of investment mediators in making their appointments. In addition, it has not yet been verified whether similar competency criteria as those listed in the preceding paragraph were the basis for selecting the proposed panel of ICSID Conciliators.[63] Hence, parties to sovereign debt disputes would be wise to not rely solely on the listing of a proposed conciliator or mediator's name in a particular institution's panel but rather to examine his or her proven mediation skills and experience in settling disputes of a similar nature in light of the aforementioned suggested criteria. Lastly, given that investor-state sovereign debt disputes require a very specific combination of skills that might not be present in one particular mediator at any given time, parties should be open to the possibility of naming co-mediators whose combined qualifications could be particularly helpful.

4.4 Overcoming Resistance to Mediating Investment Disputes

If investment mediation is to take hold, it is necessary to acknowledge the resistance various stakeholders have to mediation, particularly in this domain. As will be discussed in this section, mediation needs to improve its "brand image", particularly in investor-state dispute resolution circles. Often overlooked as a serious and worthwhile endeavor, mediation suffers from an erroneous association with conciliation, a legal culture fixated on "winning" rather than practical outcomes and the fear of political stigma by members of government for having advocated for a settlement. Accordingly, this section will examine the various types of coercive measures that can be engaged on the domestic and international levels to encourage the use of mediation in investor-state disputes.

4.4.1 Comparing the Origins and Growth of Investment Arbitration and Mediation

Ironically, investor-state arbitration was born out of international mediation/conciliation.[64] At that time, little distinction was made between the terms mediation and conciliation since the focus was instead on distinguishing amicable, nonbinding

[62] Brower II (2019), pp. 303–313.

[63] ICSID (2018).

[64] ICSID (2009a), p. 7.

mediation/conciliation processes from adversarial, binding arbitration.[65] Based on the World Bank's experience of administering conciliations for momentous investment disputes in the 1950s and 1960s, such as Iran's nationalization of its oil industry, Egypt's nationalization of the Suez Canal Company and a financial conflict between the city of Tokyo and French bond creditors, then General Counsel Aron Broches sought to institutionalize these amicable dispute resolution services.[66] This led to the creation of ICSID whose focus was then on conciliation rather than arbitration as the World Bank did not want to assume responsibility for imposing binding decisions on the parties.[67]

However, despite ICSID's equal promotion of its conciliation and arbitration services and model clauses, States demonstrated little interest in ICSID's conciliation services and preferred instead to include ICSID arbitration clauses in their contracts and treaties.[68] As a result of these clauses, there was a significant increase in the number of investment arbitrations in the late 1990's, whereas ICSID's conciliation facility remained largely dormant.[69] As of July 2021, there have been 11 concluded ICSID conciliations in all its history whereas there have been 689 ICSID arbitrations over the same period of time.[70] While this may be true, these statistics omit the possible investor-state mediations that have been administered under different sets of rules and therefore the precise numbers are unknown, given the confidential nature of mediation.[71]

Since parties have resorted more consistently to arbitration to resolve their investor-state disputes, professional and public attention has focused on arbitration as a means of resolving investment disputes to the neglect of investor-state mediation.[72] Accordingly, whereas a community consisting of arbitrators, lawyers, academics, government officials and institutions has formed to support the investment arbitration system and to hold it accountable, there is no analogous network surrounding the practice of investment mediation.[73] The body of investor-state mediation stakeholders is small with a comparatively restricted number of qualified mediators who have experience with disputes between investors and States. Furthermore, as described previously in Chap. 3, the confusion regarding the difference between mediation and conciliation, the various mediation styles and the vocabulary used to describe these practices in commercial mediation have contributed to a general misunderstanding of the benefits of mediating investment disputes.[74]

---

[65] Id; UNCITRAL Working Group II (2018), 2018A/CN.9/WG.II/WP.205, 4.

[66] Parra (2017), pp. 22–24.

[67] Id.

[68] ICSID (2020); Nitschke (2019), pp. 121–125; Parra (2017), pp. 208–257.

[69] Id.

[70] The ICSID Caseload.

[71] Claxton (2020), p. 88.

[72] Id 82–83; Nottage (2023).

[73] Shirlow (2021), pp. 461–501.

[74] See Chap. 3.

4.4.2 *Particular Benefits of Mediation Overlooked in Investment Disputes*

Despite mediation's promise to redress various criticisms of the investor-state arbitration system, and even ICSID's recently drafted Mediation Rules,[75] evidence suggests that neither investors nor States have capitalized on the opportunity to have recourse to mediation to resolve their disputes.[76] Yet mediation figures indicate high settlement rates and superior levels of user satisfaction than litigation and arbitration.[77] Moreover, mediation proceedings are generally less time-consuming and less expensive than arbitration, which is particularly advantageous in the investor-state setting where the median length of arbitration proceedings (not including possible annulment proceedings and other related proceedings) is 4 years and 4 months and where the median costs are approximately U.S.$ 3.4 to 4.2 million.[78] In addition, mediation provides a solution to concerns about private arbitrators sitting in judgment over States since the parties to the dispute have complete control over the outcome and the terms of any settlement agreement since the mediator's purpose and authority does not extend to imposing a decision upon them.[79] In terms of a policy interest to promote economic growth, mediation is more suited than arbitration for maintaining and even reestablishing long-term business relationships damaged by conflict such as is the case of investor-state relationships because the process leads the parties to act collaboratively.[80] Finally, parties who choose to reach a mediated settlement can also circumvent the damage to their reputations that results from drawn-out arbitration proceedings.[81]

It is particularly noteworthy that the arbitral tribunal in *Achmea B.V. v. The Slovak Republic*,[82] made the remarkably unusual observation to the parties at the conclusion of the hearing on the merits that in this case, a win-win settlement would have been more optimal than the win-lose outcome of a legal decision:

> a settlement in this case would be a good thing, in that the aims approximately aligned, and that the black and white solution of a legal decision in which one side wins and the other side loses is not the optimum outcome in this case... should the Parties desire to seek out somebody who might act as a mediator or reconciliator, the Secretary-General of the PCA might be in a position to assist.[83]

---

[75] 'Proposals for Amendment of the ICSID Rules' (2021), pp. 202–214.

[76] Schneider and Welsh (2021), pp. 382–386.

[77] Centre for Effective Dispute Resolution (CEDR), The Seventh Mediation Audit: A survey of commercial mediator attitudes and experience.

[78] Global Arbitration Review (2017).

[79] See Chap. 3.

[80] Id.

[81] Id.

[82] *Achmea B.V. v. The Slovak Republic.*

[83] Id paragraph 60.

Notwithstanding the tribunal's reflection on the value of an amicable solution for their dispute, the parties did not attempt mediation, choosing instead to pursue an arbitrated outcome, which eventually involved five additional rounds of written submissions, a second arbitral hearing, additional proceedings at various levels of the German court system and ultimately proceedings before the EU Court of Justice (CJEU).[84] In fact, the proceedings before the CJEU led to a judgment resulting in the effective dismantling of the intra-EU investment treaty arbitration system.[85] Although we cannot be sure that a mediation would have guaranteed a faster or better result, it is nevertheless evident that the parties were too fixated on winning through an adversarial process to see the potential benefits of an amicable settlement through mediation, at great cost not only for them but even for the scheme of intra-EU BITs.[86]

Although the confidential nature of mediation hampers the collection of data on the precise number of investor-state mediations actually taking place, administering bodies' caseload statistics, investment dispute experts and intergovernmental institutions provide coherent evidence strongly implying that parties are not sufficiently seizing the opportunity to mediate their disputes.[87] Moreover, investor-state dispute practitioners and academics indicate that, parties are not failing to seek out mediation even where the outcome of the dispute is predictable or where the dispute could easily have been settled.[88] On the institutional level, UNCITRAL Working Group III, which is working on ISDS reform, is considering mediation as a reform option. The UNCITRAL working group report found that despite "increasing efforts to promote forms of dispute settlement other than arbitration, such as mediation, still remain under-used in ISDS".[89]

This phenomenon is curious, particularly in the sovereign debt dispute context, because the historical record indicates that the litigating parties arrive at a negotiated settlement in the vast majority of cases.[90] For example, from 1976 to 2010, holdout creditors filed 120 lawsuits against debtor governments at ICSID and in the U.S. and English courts.[91] Of the 65 cases that concluded, 48 reached a negotiated settlement.[92] In other words, parties were able to negotiate an amicable settlement in almost 74% of that sample of sovereign debt disputes.[93]

---

[84] Id paragraphs 60–72.

[85] Id.

[86] Id. See also: Fan (2020), p. 327; CEDR 'The Seventh Mediation Audit'.

[87] The ICSID Caseload; Reed (2017), p. 64; European Commission (2017); UNCITRAL Working Group III, Investor-State Dispute Settlement Reform, 'Possible reform of investor-State dispute settlement – cost and duration', A/CN.9/WG.III/WP.153 (WGIII Report), s. 60.

[88] Reed (2017), p. 64.

[89] UNCITRAL Working Group III.

[90] Schumacher et al. (2021).

[91] Cruces and Samples (2016), pp. 41–42.

[92] Id.

[93] Schumacher et al. (2021).

Although this is encouraging data since it suggests that States and investors can settle their disputes, it is nevertheless unfortunate that the parties incurred the time and financial costs of investment litigation and arbitration before attempting to reach an amicable settlement rather than attempting to mediate a settlement from the start. As a consequence of ignoring the opportunity to mediate a settlement, parties are forging ahead with expensive and lengthy arbitration proceedings contrary to their best interests and at particular risk for the constituents of the debtor governments who ultimately bear the costs in the event of an adverse award.[94]

4.4.3 *Political Resistance to Investment Mediation*

The question is why parties to investment disputes do not choose to mediate, despite evidence that mediation could lead to swifter, less costly and more investment-friendly results and notwithstanding all the efforts to promote it in the investor-state arena.[95]

The first part of the answer to this question seems to be rooted in politics as evidence indicates that States are averse to mediation because they prefer to avoid accountability for having "betrayed national patrimony" by settling with investors for fear of retribution at the ballot-box.[96] Taking the arbitrations filed by sovereign debt creditors following the Argentinean default as an example, the Argentinean government very plausibly considered it would have been political suicide to negotiate a multi-million dollar payout to compensate foreign entities when Argentina's own citizens had suffered significantly greater economic loss.[97] Specifically, elected members of government are likely concerned that political opponents will seize their efforts to mediate settlements as an opportunity to swing public opinion with allegations of corruption.[98] Elected officials might also fear that the precedent of a settlement would establish a precedent encouraging other investors to make further claims.[99]

The second part of the answer to this question suggests that State agents' lack of understanding about the mediation process, costs and potential benefits are also important factors in their reticence to seek a mediated solution to investment disputes.[100] For example, a government representative may not be aware that the parties to an investor-state dispute have the option to settle some issues through mediation and leave the issues they do not wish to settle for arbitration, thereby

---

[94]Bohoslavsky (2017), p. 12.

[95]See Sect. 4.4.2.

[96]Michael Reisman (2009); Welsh and Schneider (2013), p. 87.

[97]Welsh and Schneider (2013).

[98]Chew et al. (2018), pp. 15–16.

[99]Id 12–14.

[100]Strong (2016), pp. 2037–2038.

reducing the scope and ultimately the cost of the investment arbitration proceedings.[101] If one combines governments' insufficient or possibly incorrect information about how mediation works to concerns about maintaining elected office or possible prosecution for corruption, government agents' reluctance to mediate investor-state disputes is self-explanatory. It also suggests that efforts to promote mediation need to focus on understanding these obstacles and finding ways to overcome them.

4.4.4 Promoting Investor-State Mediation

Over the past decade, there have been various efforts by both the public and the private sectors to promote investor-state mediation.[102] Such endeavors include the EU's public consultations on the amicable resolution of disputes between investors and States, the Energy Charter's practice guidelines on investment mediation and IBA Rules for Investor-State Mediation.[103] In addition, ICSID has also been seeking to promote investor-state mediation through various means including mediation-specific publications, training programs dedicated to mediating investment disputes and proposed ICSID mediation rules for all investor-state cases.[104] Most recently, at the time of writing, UNCITRAL released draft mediation rules and model clauses.[105]

4.4.4.1 Domestic Governments' Coercive Measures to Stimulate Use of Mediation

However, if one looks at domestic legal systems, where mediation has become commonplace in many jurisdictions, such as the United States, Australia, India and China, this is largely due to their governments' use of incentives and coercive measures to compel parties to mediate rather in lieu of litigation.[106] The various forms of coercive measures can be categorized in to three groups: financial incentives, mandatory instruction and mandatory mediation.[107]

States use financial incentives to urge parties to mediate or to punish parties that hinder mediation.[108] For instance, judges may waive or decrease court fees for

---

[101] See Chap. 3, Sect. 6.

[102] European Commission Directorate-General for Financial Stability, Financial Services and Capital Markets Union (2017); Guide on Investment Mediation Appendix B.

[103] Id.

[104] ICSID (2014), pp. 1–141; ICSID (2021a); ICSID (2021b), pp. 202–222; Ubilava and Nottage (2018).

[105] 2021 UNCITRAL Mediation Rules.

[106] Schonewille and Schonewille (2014); Hopt and Steffek (2013).

[107] Claxton (2020), pp. 90–98.

[108] Id 89–90.

parties whose cases settle in mediation whereas others might deny public funding to parties who fail to meet with a mediator.[109] Other jurisdictions permit judges to consider a party's refusal to attend a mediation session or to attempt mediation when awarding costs in the final judgment.[110]

Domestic legal systems also employ mandatory instruction, either by requiring lawyers or judges to advise parties about mediation when litigation is contemplated or underway, to guarantee that parties embarking in litigation understand the alternative process and potential benefits offered by mediation.[111] Alternatively, domestic jurisdictions may oblige parties to attend a compulsory information session about mediation guided by a mediator or administering institution during ongoing court proceedings.[112]

Mandatory mediation is also a tool employed by some States to compel parties to resort to mediation.[113] This is the most stringent requirement of the three categories described above because it requires parties not just to consider or be informed about mediation but to actually engage with a mediator in settlement proceedings—although it does not go so far as to require that the parties be successful in settling their dispute.[114] Mandatory mediation may be imposed by law as a prerequisite to litigation or in a court order upon a judge's determination that mediation could offer a better outcome than the court proceedings in progress.[115]

4.4.4.2 Coercive Measures to Promote Investor-State Mediation

Given the various means by which domestic legal systems have induced parties to mediate, one wonders whether similar incentive or coercive measures aimed at promoting investor-state mediation be beneficial?[116] If the most prevalent obstacle to investment mediation is State parties' fear of political retaliation, despite the risk and cost of arbitration to their own citizens, then soft methods such as promoting a

[109] De Palo et al. (2011).

[110] Id.

[111] For example: Irish Mediation Act 2017, §§ 14(1)–(3), §16(1)(b).

[112] For example: Czech Republic Mediation Act No. 202/2012 (2012); Italian Law Decree no. 69/2013 (2013); Lithuanian Law on Conciliatory Mediation in Civil Disputes No XI-1400 (2011); Luxembourg New Civil Procedure Code Articles NCPC 1251–1 to 1251-21 (2012); UK LASPO Act (2012).

[113] For example: Indian Commercial Courts Act, Commercial Division and Commercial Appellate Division of High Courts (Amendment) Bill (2018), §12A; Greek Law 4640/2019 (2019); Croatian Mediation Act (2003); Austrian Mediation Act (2003); Hungarian Mediation Act LV (2002); Malta Mediation Act, Chapter 474 as amended by Act IX (2010).

[114] Id.

[115] United States of America Administrative Dispute Resolution Act (1998), § 652(a).

[116] Welsh and Schneider (2013), p. 71; Bingham (2011); von Kumberg (2011).

better understanding of the mediation process and its benefits is unlikely to be sufficient to engender any change.[117]

Accordingly, introducing some kind of accountability measures, either directly in investment treaties or in dispute resolution proceedings, for government agents who reject mediation might be a more efficient means of ensuring that the parties attempt mediation more frequently in investor-state disputes.[118] While a political representative may consider there is relatively little risk in outsourcing dispute resolution to a panel of arbitrators, his or her point of view might change were there to be some legal or financial liability for such a decision through similar means as those used in domestic legal systems.[119] For instance, a compulsory step in the investment dispute resolution process obligating the parties to attempt mediation could provide government agents with vital political cover from accusations of weakness or corruption needed to enter into mediated settlement discussions.[120] Once embarked in the mediation, and therefore more acquainted with the process and its advantages, the State party might see more clearly the value of settling some or all of the issues in the dispute.[121]

4.4.4.3 Coercive Measures in Investment Treaties

Investment treaties present the most obvious place for establishing coercive measures to encourage or compel parties to mediate their investment disputes.[122] Historically, international investment treaties have included "cooling off" provisions obliging the disputing parties to seek an amicable solution to their dispute before initiating arbitration proceedings, and now there are an increasing number thereof specifically including mediation as one of the available "cooling off" options.[123] Some investment treaties include rules of procedure providing for a mediation window.[124]

A more far-reaching, ambitious method would be to endorse a multilateral treaty facilitating investor-state mediation specifically, which could be based on the United Nations Convention on Transparency in Treaty-based Investor-State Arbitration

---

[117] Id.

[118] Claxton (2020), p. 91.

[119] Id.

[120] Welsh and Schneider (2013), p. 71; Bingham (2011).

[121] Tümpel and Sudborough (2011), p. 269.

[122] Welsh and Schneider (2013), pp. 91–94.

[123] UNCTAD, 'International Investment Agreements Navigator'; Comprehensive and Progressive Agreement for Trans-Pacific Partnership (2018) Art. 1; Mediation Mechanism of the Mainland and Hong Kong Closer Economic Partnership Arrangement, Investment Agreement (CEPA, 2015); EU-Canada Comprehensive Economic and Trade Agreement (2016) Article 8.20.

[124] EU-Vietnam Investment Protection Agreement (text adopted by the European Commission on 17 October 2018) Art. 3.31 and Annex 10; EU-Singapore Investment Protection Agreement (signed 19 October 2018) Art. 3.4 and Annex 6.

(Mauritius Convention).[125] The Mauritius Convention is an instrument that modifies the existing dispute resolution clauses of other investment treaties to render them more transparent, while still permitting contracting States to personalize their preferences through the use of reservations.[126] Using the Mauritius Convention as inspiration, a multilateral treaty aimed at facilitating mediation or providing for compulsory mediation by altering existing investment treaties could potentially create the kind of broad impetus needed to foster a more commonplace investment mediation practice.[127]

The benefit of using a treaty as a coercive measure to promote investor-state mediation is that it empowers the state-parties to the treaty to tailor design any compulsory terms, thereby answering the need for party autonomy to a greater degree than pressure exerted by institutions and arbitrators.[128] In addition, according to this treaty method, the decision to mediate is made by treaty negotiators who are unaffected by the political risks and pressures faced by the government agents' directly involved in the investment dispute.[129] Furthermore, one of the greatest gains of using a treaty is the grander scale of impact.[130] As described above in the *Achmea* case, the influence exerted by an arbitrator recommending mediation to the parties to the dispute might draw some public interest and commentary but has yet to exert truly meaningful change in investor-state dispute resolution practice.[131] Alternatively, a multilateral treaty with a clear investor-state mediation agenda that possibly even requires mediation as a precondition to arbitration could have a profound impact bringing about structural change as well as an archetype for States seeking to introduce mediation provisions in their own investment treaties.[132]

4.4.4.4 Coercive Measures in Dispute Resolution Practice

Dispute resolution practice may provide an additional means to coerce parties to mediate investor-state disputes, either through the actions of dispute resolution providers or arbitral tribunals.

For greater impact, the two administrative bodies that handle the majority of investor state disputes, ICSID and the Permanent Court of Arbitration, could play an

[125] United Nations Convention on Transparency in Treaty-based Investor-State Arbitration (opened for signature 17 March 2015, entered into force 18 October 2017) the ("Mauritius Convention on Transparency").

[126] Id.

[127] Id; Claxton (2020), p. 92.

[128] Welsh and Schneider (2013), p. 87; ICSID (2009a), p. s. 24.

[129] Welsh and Schneider (2013), pp. 93.

[130] Claxton (2020), pp. 92.

[131] See Sect. 4.4.2.

[132] Claxton (2020), pp. 96.

active part in encouraging or compelling parties to mediate.[133] Moreover, competing administering institutions could also endorse investment mediation as they seek to attract more investor-state cases.[134] The means by which these various institutions could encourage investor-state mediation are similar to the means by which they promote commercial arbitration and mediation.[135] These methods include: (1) publishing model clauses that provide for mediation, mediation as a pre-condition to arbitration and concurrent mediation-arbitration proceedings; (2) advising parties to ongoing arbitration proceedings on mediation services; (3) facilitating the administrative aspects of the transfer of the case from arbitration to mediation; (4) establishing financial enticements for parties in arbitration proceedings to attempt mediation by waiving or discounting certain administrative costs; (5) requiring arbitral tribunals and parties to conduct proceedings in a time and cost-efficient manner through institutional rules which may for example encourage arbitrators and parties to seek to mediate all or certain issues at dispute or for arbitral tribunals to take refusals to mediate into account when deciding the allocation of costs; (6) issuing publications advising parties about the potential advantages of mediating investment disputes; and (7) publishing information about investor-state mediations administered by the institution in an anonymized fashion.[136]

Arbitral tribunals could also take measures directly by obligating parties to mediate all or certain claims or by establish that, when the tribunal or the opposing party proposes mediation, it is the parties' duty to make a good faith effort to attempt to mediate.[137] For example, where appropriate, the tribunal could (1) identify cases or individual claims that are suitable for mediation; (2) periodically remind parties to contemplate mediation during the course of the proceedings; and (3) transferring costs to a party who hinders or unreasonably repudiates a proposal to mediate either by an opposing party or by the arbitral tribunal.[138] Although some of these measures, such as the financial penalties, might not rectify the situation in the cases in which they are applied, they may influence parties to mediate in the cases that follow.[139]

4.4.4.5 Reinforcing ISDS Efficiency Requirements

Beyond investment treaties and dispute resolution practice, the ISDS system could potentially adopt coercive measures similar to those employed in domestic legal systems.[140] Recent developments suggest that stakeholders increasingly deem

[133] The ICSID Caseload; Permanent Court of Arbitration, 'Cases'.

[134] Welsh and Schneider (2012), p. 88.

[135] Id.

[136] Leoveanu and Erac (2019), p. 270.

[137] ICSID Convention Art. 4; Berger and Jensen (2017), p. 997.

[138] Id.

[139] Claxton (2020), p. 94.

[140] Id 98.

efficiency in the investor-state dispute resolution system as not simply a worthwhile endeavor but as vital to the survival of ISDS itself, and therefore parties should be compelled to resolve their disputes accordingly.[141] This suggests that mediation might be well-positioned to be included more proactively in future measures seeking to increase time and cost efficiency in investor-state disputes since mediation proceedings are significantly less time-consuming and expensive than arbitration proceedings.[142]

For example, the IBA issued a report in October 2018 on consistency, efficiency and transparency in investor-state arbitration encouraging drafters of investment treaties to make revisions that would urge parties to use alternative dispute resolution techniques.[143] Specifically, the IBA report states that "disputants should resort to international arbitration only after they are convinced that negotiations and various forms of alternative dispute settlement techniques would not be successful."[144] Shortly thereafter, a UN working group whose mission was to make recommendations for ISDS reform concluded that parties should use mediation as a substitute to arbitration to counteract the extended duration and extensive costs of ISDS proceedings.[145]

Furthermore, the findings of these studies coincided with newly-imposed requirements from dispute resolution institutions for increased procedural efficiency. For instance in 2016, the ICC International Court of Arbitration put in place a strategy of punishing arbitrators who unjustifiably delay the submission of their draft arbitration awards to the ICC Court of Arbitration after proceedings have terminated by cutting an increasing percentage of the fees as the extent of the delay increases.[146] Other administrative bodies have included efficiency obligations directly into their institutional arbitration rules, such as ICSID's rules of procedure for arbitration, mediation and conciliation.[147] Furthermore, some institutions' rules include efficiency provisions that do not require the disputants' consent such as the consolidation of

---

[141] Joubin-Bret and Knörich (2010), pp. 1–9.

[142] See Sect. 4.4.2.

[143] International Bar Association, 'Consistency, efficiency and transparency in investment treaty arbitration' (2018).

[144] Id.

[145] United Nations Commission on International Trade Law, 'Report of Working Group III (Investor-State Dispute Settlement Reform) on the work of its thirty-ninth session' (2020).

[146] International Chamber of Commerce (2016).

[147] Proposed ICSID Convention Arbitration Rules, Rs. 2(1), 31, 51(1); Proposed Additional Facility Rules of Procedure for Arbitration Proceedings, Rs. 10(1), 40, 61. 1 ICSID Working Paper #3, Proposals for Amendment of the ICSID Rules, https://icsid.worldbank.org/en/Documents/WP_3_VOLUME_1_ENGLISH.pdf; Id., Proposed Additional Facility Rules of Procedure for Mediation Proceedings, R. 17; Proposed Rules of Procedure for Conciliation Proceedings, Rs. 25, 29; proposed Additional Facility Rules of Procedure for Conciliation Proceedings, R. 33(1), 37.

multiple arbitration proceedings and the appointment of a sole arbitrator instead of a three-member panel.[148]

At the same time, the Rules on the Efficient Conduct of Proceedings in International Arbitration (Prague Rules) were published in December 2018 as a more efficient alternative to the ubiquitous IBA Rules on the Taking of Evidence in International Arbitration.[149] The Prague Rules stipulate a multitude of rules aiming to render arbitration proceedings more efficient while also investing arbitrators with the power conduct the proceedings in a "hands-on" manner to shorten their duration and decrease the costs thereof.[150] Most notably, the Prague Rules prompt arbitral tribunals to establish the boundaries of admissible evidence and to "assist the parties in reaching an amicable settlement of the dispute at any stage of the arbitration."[151] Pursuant to the Prague Rules, arbitral tribunals may apply the terms thereof on their own initiative.[152]

In sum, the UNCITRAL and IBA reports, the intensifying efficiency provisions in the rules of various institutions and the establishment of the Prague Rules exhibit a transformation in the investor-state dispute resolution system that suggests stakeholders see efficiency as a moral obligation rather than merely as an ideal.

4.4.4.6 Problems with Coercive Measures to Promote Investor-State Mediation

Notwithstanding the extensive efforts to promote mediation and the recital of its various advantages, hostility to coercive measures to implement mediation in ISDS is a persistent reality.[153] The greater degree of force contained in the measure, whether it be an incentive or a coercive one, the greater the perception that the measure is transgressing party autonomy or denying investors' access to justice where they seek to file for arbitration.[154] Moreover, parties remain doubtful about the efficiency of investment mediation because they must take the risk of "investing" their time and money without any guarantee that the mediation will succeed—meaning that they will have to add the time and monetary costs of investment arbitration proceedings to the overall "bill" should the mediation fail.[155]

[148] For example 2018 HKIAC Arbitration Rules, Art. 28.1(b) and (c); SIAC Arbitration Rules, R. 8.1(c); E.g., SIAC Arbitration Rules, Rs. 5.2 and 9.1; 2017 ICC Arbitration Rules, Arts. 12(2) and 30 and Appendix VI.

[149] 2018 Rules on the Efficient Conduct of Proceedings in International Arbitration ("Prague Rules").

[150] Id.

[151] Id 9.1.

[152] Id 1.2.

[153] Titi (2019), pp. 33–35.

[154] Anderson (2010), p. 480.

[155] Id. See also Chap. 3 describing the mediation process.

Furthermore, since the mediation process is not necessarily adapted to every dispute, coercive measures to promote mediation in all investment disputes may misguide parties away from other, better suited alternative dispute resolution processes such as expert evaluation.[156] Lastly, coercive measures to implement investment mediation proceedings does not guarantee a genuine participation in those proceedings by the parties, who could instead be simply going through the motions instead of making a good-faith attempt to seek settlement.[157] A persistent fear is that the mediation process will be used by bad-faith parties as a fishing expedition to obtain compromising information that can be used against them by the in subsequent arbitration.[158] Despite a plethora of mediation laws barring the admissibility of information obtained through mediation proceedings in separate arbitration or judicial proceedings, in practice the information gathered through the mediation process can nevertheless influence the adverse party's line of attack and conceivably lead to admissible evidence.[159]

In addition to the above-mentioned problems with the real-world application of coercive investment mediation measures, there are also hurdles to including such provisions in treaties. At the outset, with 3000 investment treaties already in force, there are few opportunities to include such mediation provisions in new treaties.[160] Although the contracting parties may renegotiate these treaties to include mediation provisions, they face the disincentives of a highly complex, lengthy and politically-sensitive process.[161]

A large, multilateral investment treaty containing obligatory mediation provisions could have a broader influence, but an unlikely option as such treaties are rare.[162] Furthermore, a multilateral treaty like the Mauritius Convention that modifies existing treaties to incorporate mediation provisions therein would also face resistance.[163] Successful drafting of the treaty would not guarantee that it would bc adopted by a broad range of States.[164] Conversely, should the initiative for such a "mediation Mauritius Convention" fail it would undermine the advances made to encourage mediation in investment dispute proceedings.[165] Finally, the choice of incentives and coercive measures employed by such a treaty would have to be calibrated carefully to ensure that the instrument would still be effective without

[156] Report of Working Group III.

[157] Claxton (2020), pp. 95–96. See also Chap. 3 describing the mediation process.

[158] Id.

[159] UNCITRAL Model Law on International Commercial Mediation; Strong (2016), p. 2055.

[160] International Centre for Settlement of Investment Disputes, 'Database of Bilateral Investment Treaties'.

[161] Vandevelde (2017), chapters 7 and 9; Beesley (2016).

[162] Central American Free Trade Agreement (CAFTA, 2004) Article 10.15; Treaty establishing the Common Market for Eastern and Southern Africa (COMESA, 1993) Article 26.

[163] Mauritius Convention on Transparency; Claxton (2020), pp. 95–96.

[164] Chew et al. (2018).

[165] Id.

being so punitive as to dissuade ratification.[166] Nonetheless, as of October 2021, UNCITRAL Working Group III, which has been entrusted with a mandate to make recommendations on ISDS reform, is in the process designing a multilateral instrument on ISDS reform that would include mediation as alternative means of dispute resolution.[167] Although the UNITRAL working group's initiative is not to create a multilateral treaty, the aim is still to design a multilateral instrument, which some viewed as being the only means of applying reform options to "the vast network of existing investment treaties".[168]

Underlying policy and commercial reasons restrain dispute resolution institutions from utilizing coercive measures to compel parties to mediate investor-state disputes.[169] As institutions compete for investment dispute cases, they will avoid employing measures that will make their administration of proceedings too oppressive.[170]

As for arbitrators, there is no immediate financial incentive for them to urge parties to forsake the arbitration (for which they are remunerated) to pursue mediation instead (and therefore forego significant income).[171] Evidently, arbitrators will also evade any conduct that the parties might perceive as interference in their autonomy, that could discourage future appointments or lead to challenges of their awards.[172] It is plausible that the *Achmea* tribunal had similar concerns as the tribunal was very careful to emphasize that its role was not to *"get involved in any way at all"* in the parties' decision to mediation."[173]

The rationale and timing of coercive measures to encourage investment mediation also present some complications. Although the various studies conducted on the benefits of investor-state mediation provided important insights, they also possessed some methodological drawbacks, including a relatively limited sample size and survey questions that failed to distinguish between commercial and investment disputes.[174]

These studies also left unanswered questions regarding the proper choice of incentive measures, the effect of obligatory measures to overcome barriers to investment mediation and the influence of various aspects of the mediation process

[166] Claxton (2020), pp. 95–96.

[167] Report of Working Group III 18–20.

[168] Id.

[169] Chew et al. (2018) and International Chamber of Commerce (ICC) (2012).

[170] China International Economic and Trade Arbitration Commission, 2017 International Investment Arbitration Rules (For Trial Implementation); Singapore International Arbitration Centre, 2017 SIAC Investment Rules; United Nations Convention on International Settlement Agreements Resulting from Mediation (New York, 2018); Chew et al. (2018); ICC 'Arbitration Involving States and State Entities Under the ICC Rules of Arbitration.

[171] Id.

[172] International Centre for Settlement of Investment Disputes (ICSID) and United Nations Commission on International Trade Law (UNCITRAL) (2021), Articles 3 and 4.

[173] *Achmea* paragraph 60.

[174] Chew et al. (2018).

such as the choice of mediation style, level of formality of process and degree of transparency on parties' decision to mediate their investor-state disputes.[175] Specifically, it is uncertain whether an increased understanding and appreciation of the value of mediation will alleviate government agents' political accountability concerns.[176]

Moreover, there is no guarantee that coercive measures employed by domestic legal systems could have the same measure of success in the investor-state context. Indeed, to date the record of accomplishment for such obligatory mediation measures in the EU has been ambivalent.[177] As has been described previously, the investor-state context presents unique hurdles and the justifications for using coercive mediation measures in the investment dispute context are distinct.[178]

This lingering ambiguity might explain the continued focus on mediator training, broadcasting fruitful investment mediation outcomes as well as lobbying efforts to highlight mediation in key discussions about ISDS reform, until the time becomes more propitious for engaging the other more concrete coercive measures described above.[179]

4.5 Conclusion

The objective of this chapter was to specifically examine mediation as a sovereign debt dispute resolution mechanism. Despite the existence of some disadvantages of mediation in this domain, mediation's capacity to redress the growing criticisms of investor-state mediation as well as to adapt to the specific needs of sovereign bond creditors and state governments indicate that mediation is a convincingly worthwhile option for resolving sovereign debt disputes. Consequently, this chapter explored and made recommendations with regard to the practical considerations of mediating sovereign debt disputes, ranging from the commencement of the proceedings, choosing the governing rules of the mediation proceedings and selecting the appropriate mediator. Lastly, this chapter addressed the various avenues for, and challenges of, promoting parties to mediate investment disputes, particularly in the context of sovereign debt disputes. In this regard, it will be particularly interesting to pay close attention to the work of the UNCITRAL Working Group III and its proposals to encourage increased mediation in ISDS.

---

[175] Chew et al. (2018).

[176] Id.

[177] Esplugues (2014) and De Palo (2018).

[178] See this chapter.

[179] ISDS Mediation Working Group (2020); Claxton (2020), p. 99.

Sources

International Conventions and Rules

Central American Free Trade Agreement (CAFTA, 2004).

China International Economic and Trade Arbitration Commission, 2017 International Investment Arbitration Rules (For Trial Implementation).

Convention on the Settlement of Investment Disputes between States and Nationals of Other States (ICSID).

EU-Canada Comprehensive Economic and Trade Agreement (2016).

EU-Singapore Investment Protection Agreement (signed 19 October 2018).

EU-Vietnam Investment Protection Agreement (text adopted by the European Commission on 17 October 2018).

International Bar Association (IBA) Rules for Investor-State Mediation (2012).

International Chamber of Commerce (ICC) Arbitration Rules (2021).

International Chamber of Commerce (ICC) Mediation Rules (2014).

International Chamber of Commerce (ICC) Rules for the Appointment of Experts and Neutrals (2015).

Mediation Mechanism of the Mainland and Hong Kong Closer Economic Partnership Arrangement, Investment Agreement (CEPA, 2015).

Mediation Rules of the Arbitration Institute of the Stockholm Chamber of Commerce (2014).

Rules on the Efficient Conduct of Proceedings in International Arbitration (Prague Rules, 2018).

Singapore International Arbitration Centre, 2017 SIAC Investment Rules.

Trans-Pacific Partnership Agreement (TPP, 2016).

Treaty establishing the Common Market for Eastern and Southern Africa (COMESA, 1993).

United Nations Commission on International Trade Law (UNCITRAL) Model Law on International Commercial Mediation (2018).

United Nations Commission on International Trade Law (UNCITRAL) Mediation Rules (2021).

United Nations Commission on International Trade Law (UNCITRAL) Rules on Transparency in Treaty-based Investor-State Arbitration (2014).

United Nations Convention on International Settlement Agreements Resulting from Mediation (Singapore Convention, 2018).

United Nations Convention on Transparency in Treaty-based Investor-State Arbitration (opened for signature 17 March 2015, entered into force 18 October 2017) the ("Mauritius Convention on Transparency").

Domestic Rules and Legislation

Austrian Mediation Act (2003).
Croatian Mediation Act (2003).
Czech Republic Mediation Act No. 202/2012 (2012).
Greek Law 4640/2019 (2019).
Hong Kong International Arbitration Centre (HKIAC) Arbitration Rules (2018).
Hungarian Mediation Act LV (2002).
Indian Commercial Courts Act, Commercial Division and Commercial Appellate Division of High Courts (Amendment) Bill (2018).
Irish Mediation Act 2017.
Italian Law Decree no. 69/2013 (2013).
Lithuanian Law on Conciliatory Mediation in Civil Disputes No XI-1400 (2011).
Luxembourg New Civil Procedure Code Articles NCPC 1251–1 to 1251-21 (2012).
Malta Mediation Act, Chapter 474 as amended by Act IX (2010).
Singapore International Arbitration Centre (SIAC) Arbitration Rules.
United States of America Administrative Dispute Resolution Act (1998), § 652(a).
UK LASPO Act (2012).

References

Articles

Anderson DQ (2010) Mandatory mediation: an oxymoron? Examining the feasibility of implementing a court mandated mediation program. Cardozo J Conflict Resol 11:479
Berger KP, Jensen JO (2017) The Arbitrator's mandate to facilitate settlement. Fordham Int Law J 40, 997
Blackman JI, Mukhi R (2010) The evolution of modern sovereign debt litigation: vultures, Alter egos, and other legal Fauna. Law Contemp Prob 73:53
Bottini G, Titi C, Chaisse J et al (2020) Excessive costs and recoverability of cost awards in investment arbitration. J World Invest Trade 21:251–253
Chew S, Reed L, Thomas JC (2018) Report: survey on obstacles to settlement of investor-state disputes. NUS Law Working Paper:22
Claxton JM (2020) Compelling parties to mediate investor-state disputes: no pressure, no diamonds? Pepperdine Disp Resol Law J 20:78
Cruces JJ, Samples TR (2016) Settling sovereign Debt's "trial of the century". Emory Int Law Rev 31(1):6
Fan K (2020) Mediation of investor state disputes. J Dispute Resol 2:327
Fawehinmi F, Zlatanska E (2016) Mediation and conciliation: in pursuit of clarity. Int J Arbitr Mediation Dispute Manag 82:146
Gaillard E (2008) Anti-arbitration trends in Latin America. New York Law J 239(108):1–3
ICSID (2014) Alternative dispute resolution in investment disputes. ICSID Rev Foreign Investment Law J 29(1)
Legum B (2007) The difficulties of conciliation in investment treaty cases: a comment on professor Jack C. Coe's "toward a complementary use of conciliation in investor-state disputes - a

preliminary sketch". Transnational Dispute Manag 1. https://www.transnational-dispute-management.com/article.asp?key=963
Michael Reisman W (2009) International investment arbitration and ADR: married but best living apart. ICSID Rev Foreign Invest Law J 24(1):185
Nitschke F (2014) The IBA's investor-state mediation rules and the ICSID dispute settlement framework. ICSID Rev 29(1):112
Pohl J (2018) Societal benefits and costs of International Investment Agreements: A critical review of aspects and available empirical evidence. OECD Working Papers on International Investment
Reed L (2017) Suite for ISDS: mediation, arbitration, appellate bodies. Korean Arbitr Rev 9:58
Schnabel T (2019) The Singapore convention on mediation: a framework for the cross border recognition and enforcement of mediated settlements. Pepperdine Dispute Resol Law J 19:1
Schneider AK, Welsh N (2021) Bargaining in the shadow of investor-state mediation: how the threat of mediation will improve Parties' conflict management. University of St Thomas Law J 17(2):373
Shane MB (1995) The difference between mediation and conciliation. Dispute Resolution J 50, 31 (3)
Strong SI (2016) Realizing rationality: an empirical assessment of international commercial mediation. Wash Lee Law Rev 73
Tan R (2020) Investor-State Arbitration Meets Mediation: The Singapore Convention on Mediation as Game-Changer'. 29 September 2020 Kluwer Mediation Blog. http://arbitrationblog.kluwerarbitration.com/2020/09/29/investor-state-arbitration-meets-mediation-the-singapore-convention-on-mediation-as-game-changer/
Welsh NA, Schneider AK (2012) Becoming "investor-state mediation". Penn State J Law Int Aff 1:86
Welsh NA, Schneider AK (2013) The thoughtful integration of mediation into bilateral investment treaty arbitration. Harv Negot Law Rev 71:87

Books and Book Chapters

Abramson H (2019) New Singapore convention on cross-border mediated settlements: key choices. In: Titi C, Gómez KF (eds) Mediation in international commercial and investment disputes. Oxford University Press, Oxford
Bingham LB (2011) Opportunities for dispute Systems Design in Investment Treaty Disputes: consensual dispute resolution at varying levels. In: Franck SD, Joubin-Bret A (eds) Proceedings of the Washington and lee University and UNCTAD joint symposium on international investment and alternative dispute resolution, held on 29 march 2010 in Lexington, Virginia, United States of America. UNCTAD, Geneva. https://unctad.org/en/Docs/webdiaeia20108_en.pdf
Brower CH II (2019) Selection of mediators. In: Titi C, Gómez KF (eds) Mediation in international commercial and investment disputes. Oxford University Press, Oxford, pp 303–313
Brown C, Winch P (2019) The confidentiality and transparency debate in commercial and investment mediation. In: Titi C, Gómez KF (eds) Mediation in international commercial and investment disputes. Oxford University Press, Oxford
Esplugues C (2014) Civil and commercial mediation in the E.U. After the transposition of the directive 2008/52/EC on mediation in civil and commercial matters. In: Esplugues C (ed) Civil and commercial mediation in Europe: cross-border mediation, Vol. II. Intersentia, Cambridge
Gómez KF (2018) Foreign direct Investment in Latin America. In: Krajewski M (ed) Research handbook on foreign direct investment. Edward Elgar, Cheltenham
Gómez KF (2019) The role of mediation in commercial disputes: reflections on some technological, ethical, and educational challenges. In: Titi C, Gómez KF (eds) Mediation in international commercial and investment disputes. Oxford University Press, Oxford

Hopt KJ, Steffek F (eds) (2013) Mediation: principles and regulation in comparative perspective. Oxford University Press, Oxford
ICSID (2009) History of the ICSID Convention: Documents Concerning the Origin and the Formulation of the Convention on the Settlement of Investment Disputes Between States anNationals of Other States Volume II-1
Joubin-Bret A, Knörich J (eds) (2010) Investor–state disputes: prevention and alternatives to arbitration. United Nations, New York
Leoveanu A, Erac A (2019) ICC mediation: paving the way forward' in mediation. In: Titi C, Gómez KF (eds) International commercial and investment disputes. Oxford University Press, Oxford
Martin AT (2011) International mediation: an evolving market. In: Rovine AW (ed) Contemporary issues in international arbitration & mediation: the Fordham Papers (2010). Brill
McIlwrath M, Savage J (2010) International arbitration and mediation: a practical guide. Kluwer Law International, Alphen aan Den Rijn
Moore CW (2014) The mediation process, 8th edn. Jossey-Bass, San Francisco
Nitschke F (2019) The ICSID conciliation rules in practice. In: Titi C, Gómez KF (eds) Mediation in international commercial and investment disputes. Oxford University Press, Oxford
Nottage LR (2023) International arbitration and Society at Large. In: Bjorklund A, Ferrari F, Kroell S (eds) Cambridge compendium of international commercial and investment arbitration. Cambridge University Press, Cambridge
Parra AR (2017) The history of ICSID. Oxford University Press, Oxford
Schonewille M, Schonewille F (eds) (2014) The variegated landscape of mediation, a comparative study of mediation regulation and practices in Europe and the world. Eleven International Publishing, The Hague
Schumacher J, Trebesch C, Enderlein H (2021) Sovereign defaults in court. J Int Econ:131
Sharpe JK (2014) Representing a respondent state in investment arbitration. In: Giorgetti C (ed) Litigating international investment disputes: a Practitioner's guide. Brill Nijhoff, Leiden
Shirlow E (2021) The promises and pitfalls of investor-state mediation. In: Sachs L, Johnson L, Coleman J (eds) Yearbook on international investment law & policy 2019. Oxford University Press, Oxford
Titi C (2016) Economic crises, sovereign debt restructurings and the shifting landscape of international investment law. In: Segura A (ed) The reform of international economic governance, 1st edn. Routledge, Milton Park
Titi C (2019) Mediation and settlement of investment disputes: between utopia and realism. In: Titi C, Gómez KF (eds) Mediation in international commercial and investment disputes. Oxford University Press, Oxford
Tümpel H, Sudborough C (2011) ICC's ADR rules, 2001-2010: current practices, case examples and lessons learned. In: Ingen-Housz A (ed) ADR in business, practice and issues across countries and cultures, Vol. II. Wolters Kluwer, Alphen aan den Rijn
Vandevelde KJ (2017) Bilateral investment treaties: history, policy and interpretation. Oxford University Press, Oxford
von Kumberg W (2011). https://unctad.org/en/Docs/webdiaeia20108_en.pdf) Making mediation mainstream: an application for investment treaty disputes. In: Franck SD, Joubin-Bret A (eds) Proceedings of the Washington and lee University and UNCTAD joint symposium on international investment and alternative dispute resolution, held on 29 march 2010 in Lexington, Virginia, United States of America. UNCTAD, Geneva, p 71
Waibel M (2013) Sovereign defaults before international courts and tribunals. Cambridge University Press, Cambridge
Waters A (2015) The costs of arbitration. Watson Farley and Williams, London

Cases

Achmea B.V. *v. The Slovak Republic (formerly Eureko B.V. v. The Slovak Republic)*, UNCITRAL PCA Case No. 2008-13, Final Award, 7 December 2012

Official Reports

Bohoslavsky JP (2017) 'Effects of foreign debt and other related financial obligations of States on the full enjoyment of all human rights, particularly economic, social and cultural rights'. *Report of the Independent Expert to the United Nations General Assembly*
De Palo G, Feasley A, Orecchini F (2011) 'Quantifying the cost of not using mediation - a data analysis'. https://www.europarl.europa.eu/document/activities/cont/201105/20110518ATT19592/20110518ATT19592EN.pdf
Energy Charter Treaty (ECT) (2016) Guide on Investment Mediation
European Commission (2017) Consultation Document, 'Prevention and amicable resolution of disputes between investors and public authorities within the single market'. https://ec.europa.eu/info/sites/info/files/2017-investment-protection-mediation-consultationdocument_en_1.pdf
European Commission Directorate-General for Financial Stability, Financial Services and Capital Markets Union 2017 'Prevention and amicable resolution of disputes between investors and public authorities within the single market' (Consultation Document), https://ec.europa.eu/info/sites/info/files/2017-investment-protection-mediation-consultationdocument_en_1.pdf
ICSID (2017/2) 'The ICSID Caseload – Statistics'
ICSID (2018) Selection and Appointment Of Conciliators - Additional Facility Conciliation. https://icsid.worldbank.org/en/Pages/process/Selection-and-Appointment-of-Commission-Members%2D%2D-AF-Conciliation.aspx
ICSID (2020/2) 'The ICSID Caseload – Statistics
ICSID (2021a) Investor-State Mediation: Interviews. https://www.youtube.com/playlist?list=PLTPAfLBOjfQIqOstW4FwKlLykep_ma3xm
ICSID (June 2021b) Proposals for amendment of the ICSID rules
ICSID, 'Database of Bilateral Investment Treaties'. https://icsid.worldbank.org/en/Pages/resources/Bilateral-Investment-Treaties-Database.aspx
ICSID, 'Overview of An Arbitration Under the ICSID Convention' https://icsid.worldbank.org/en/Pages/process/Arbitration.aspx. Accessed 15 October 2021
ICSID, 'Overview of Conciliation under the ICSID Convention'
ICSID, Proposed Additional Facility Rules of Procedure for Mediation Proceedings
ICSID, Proposed ICSID Convention Arbitration Rules
ICSID, Proposed Rules of Procedure for Conciliation Proceedings
International Centre for Settlement of Investment Disputes (ICSID) and United Nations Commission on International Trade Law (UNCITRAL) (April 2021) 'Draft Code of Conduct for Adjudicators in International Investment Disputes – Version Two', Articles 3 and 4. https://icsid.worldbank.org/sites/default/files/draft_code_of_conduct_v2_en_final.pdf
International Chamber of Commerce (ICC) (2012) 'Arbitration Involving States and State Entities Under the ICC Rules of Arbitration – Report of the ICC Commission on Arbitration and ADR'
International Mediation Institute (IMI) (2016) Competency Criteria for Investor-State Mediators. https://imimediation.org/2016/09/19/imi-introduces-competency-criteria-investor-state-mediators/
ISDS Mediation Working Group (16 June 2020) 'Unlocking Value Through Stakeholder Engagement: New Forms to Resolve Investor-State Disputes' 6, https://imimediation.org/download/104/investor-state-mediation-task-force/60233/mwgisds-2020-unlocking-value-through-stakeholder-engagement.pdf

Permanent Court of Arbitration, 'Cases'. https://pca-cpa.org/cases/. Accessed 15 October 2021
'Proposals for Amendment of the ICSID Rules' (2021) ICSID Working Paper #5
UNCITRAL Working Group II, Dispute Settlement, Report of 68th session, 5–9 February 2018, 2018A/CN.9/WG.II/WP
UNCITRAL Working Group III, Investor-State Dispute Settlement Reform, 'Possible reform of investor-State dispute settlement - cost and duration', A/CN.9/WG.III/WP.153 (WGIII Report)
United Nations Conference Trade and Development (UNCTAD) (2018) 'Improving Investment Dispute Settlement: UNCTAD Policy Tools'. http://unctad.org/en/PublicationsLibrary/diaepcb2017d8_en.pdf
World Investment Report 2015: Reforming International Investment Governance (2015) 127–163

Websites and News Articles

Alderman L, Kanter J, Yardley J et al (17 June 2016) 'Explaining Greece's Debt Crisis'. *The New York Times* https://www.nytimes.com/interactive/2016/business/international/greece-debt-crisis-euro.html
Beesley A (23 September 2016) 'TTIP talks headed for a lengthy delay' Financial Times. https://www.ft.com/content/f79588a6-81a7-11e6-8e50-8ec15fb462f4
Brennan L (February 2015) 'Do We Need a New York Convention for Mediation/Conciliation?'. https://www.mediate.com/articles/BrennanLbl20150227.cfm
'CEDR News: Mediation Market Grows By 5%: The 2016 Mediation Audit' (2016). https://www.cedr.com/news/?item=Mediation-Market-grows-by-5-percent-The-CEDR-2016-Mediation-Audit
Centre for Effective Dispute Resolution (CEDR), The Seventh Mediation Audit: A survey of commercial mediator attitudes and experience. https://www.cedr.com/docslib/The_Seventh_Mediation_Audit_(2016).pdf
De Palo G (November 2018) 'A Ten-Year-Long "EU Mediation Paradox" When an EU Directive Needs To Be More... Directive' (European Parliament Briefing Requested by the JURI Committee) https://www.europarl.europa.eu/RegData/etudes/BRIE/2018/608847/IPOL_BRI(2018)608847_EN.pdf
Eberhardt P, Olivet C, Amos T et al 2018 'Who Guards the Guardians? The Conflicting Interests of Investment Arbitrators' (Corporate Europe Observatory) https://corporateeurope.org/trade/2012/11/chapter-4-who-guards-guardians-conflicting-interests-investment-arbitrators
Global Arbitration Review (14 December 2017) 'Damages and costs in investment treaty arbitration revisited'. https://globalarbitrationreview.com/article/1151755/damages-and-costs-ininvestment treaty arbitration revisited
International Bar Association, 'Consistency, efficiency and transparency in investment treaty arbitration' (November 2018). https://www.ibanet.org/LPD/Dispute_Resolution_Section/Arbitration/Publications.aspx
International Chamber of Commerce (5 January 2016) 'ICC Court announces new policies to foster transparency and ensure greater efficiency'. https://iccwbo.org/media-wall/news-speeches/icc-court-announces-new-policies-to-foster-transparency-and-ensure-greater-efficiency/
Mellersh N (22 September 2017) 'Can we enforce mediation agreements?' (Jams International). https://www.jamsinternational.com/blog/can-we-enforce-mediation-agreements
Ubilava A, Nottage L (2018) 'ICSID's New Mediation Rules: A Small but Positive Step Forward'. Erga Omnes – SCIL Blog. https://erga-omnes.sydney.edu.au/2018/09/
UNCTAD, 'International Investment Agreements Navigator'. https://investmentpolicyhub.unctad.org/IIA/AdvancedSearchBITResults

Chapter 5
Conclusion

This aim of this book was to study whether, and how, investment mediation could offer an advantageous means for resolving sovereign debt disputes. As was discussed herein, this topic is an important area to explore for various reasons. Firstly, it fills in a gap in the academic literature, as the author of this manuscript was unable to identify any other research specifically on this topic. Secondly, given the financial suffering and negative public policy impact of prolonged economic crisis, identifying a more efficient means of resolving sovereign debt disputes could help indebted countries to rebound economically, which itself has significant social and political consequences. Thirdly, exploring how mediation could be a valuable dispute resolution mechanism could also shed light on mediation as a tool for resolving investment disputes more generally since sovereign debt disputes are a subset of investor-state disputes. Accordingly, the research question addressed in this book is: Should parties resort to mediation for resolving sovereign debt disputes, and, if so, how could such investment mediations be put into place?

To answer the research question, this volume employed a multi-faceted analytical methodology. As a first step, to identify the stakeholders, main developments, and challenges created by the intersection of the sovereign financing and investor-state dispute settlement systems, this book explored (1) the available academic literature on sovereign debt and default, investment arbitration and mediation as well as (2) case studies of the two countries most recently plagued by sovereign debt: Argentina and Greece. Building upon this literature review and these two case studies, this manuscript subsequently conducted a comparative legal analysis of the primary judicial decisions and investment arbitration awards filed by sovereign debt creditors. Lastly, this book employed a normative component that suggested how to settle sovereign debt disputes using mediation.

This book was organized in five chapters. Chapter 1 was dedicated to introducing the research topic and research methodology.

Chapter 2 established the underlying context for this book by providing an overview of the historical and legal framework of the sovereign financing system

C. M. Sudborough, *Mediating Sovereign Debt Disputes*, EYIEL Monographs - Studies in European and International Economic Law 35,
https://doi.org/10.1007/978-3-031-46787-5_5

as well as an in-depth review of the Argentine and Greek debt crises of the early 2000s and their debt renegotiation efforts. As described in this chapter, the absence of an international bankruptcy mechanism for sovereign debt along with the steady decline in sovereign immunity has undermined the debt renegotiation process and has incentivized sovereign bond creditors to refrain from voluntary participation. Instead, such non-participating creditors have employed legal strategies to recover their full investments. Speculative hedge funds that seek out distressed debt in particular, have especially sought a markedly aggressive litigation strategy of filing arbitration proceedings pursuant to investment treaties. This chapter also detailed the jurisprudence of a series of ICSID arbitration cases filed by sovereign bond creditors. As underscored by the case law, it remains still uncertain whether sovereign bonds qualify as investments for the purpose of Article 25 of the ICSID Convention and therefore the arbitrability of such claims under the investment law framework. Furthermore, as these cases never reached a decision on the merits, it is unclear what impact they could have, nor the likelihood of enforcement or the level of compensation. The fact that Argentina settled with its sovereign bond creditors after years of litigation combined with the uncertainty of arbitrating such claims ISDS system begs the question: why not consider mediation from the outset?

Therefore, Chap. 3 dedicated itself to generating a deeper understanding of the mediation process. After reviewing the multiplicity of mediation definitions, this chapter proposed a working definition for the purpose of this volume, keeping in mind the specific political and financial nature of sovereign debt disputes. Subsequently, in light of the ICSID Conciliation Rules, Chap. 3 sought to explain the important distinctions between the mediation process from conciliation, and in particular the more flexible, informal and collaborative nature of the mediation process as opposed to the more structured, formal and evaluative character of conciliation. As discussed herein, these distinctions are important as they impact the parties' relationships with the neutral and hence the success and outcome of the proceedings. Thereafter, Chap. 3 gave a detailed description of the various phases of the process, techniques and styles used by mediators and the possibility of resorting to blended styles of mediation involving a combination of mediation and arbitration, which might be useful where the circumstances are not ripe for mediation or where different aspects of the dispute require different dispute resolution mechanisms. This chapter also examined the underlying legal framework on both a domestic and international level for mediation with regards to how parties are compelled to mediate, what procedural and ethical safeguards are put in place for the proceedings and the legal effect of an eventual settlement agreement. In this regard, this chapter studied the Singapore Convention and its potential application to investment disputes. As observed in this chapter, the richly multi-faceted quality of mediation renders it a uniquely flexible process capable of adapting to the parties' needs and the circumstances surrounding the dispute. The tremendous malleability of the mediation process suggests that it could also be put to use for disputes between indebted states and their sovereign bond creditors.

As the preceding chapters demonstrated that it worthwhile to examine how mediation could resolve sovereign debt disputes in the investor-state context, the objective of Chap. 4 was to examine mediation as a sovereign debt dispute resolution mechanism. Accordingly, this chapter investigated the advantages as well as the disadvantages of mediating in this context, particularly in comparison with arbitral proceedings. The analysis in this section of the chapter was framed on either side by sovereign bond creditors' established trend of linking their claims to investment treaties and the growing public policy concerns raised by investment arbitration proceedings in terms of cost and transparency and their effect on economic recovery. Despite the existence of some disadvantages of mediation in this domain, mediation's capacity to redress the growing criticisms of investor-state mediation as well as to adapt to the specific needs of sovereign bond creditors and state governments indicate that mediation is a convincingly worthwhile option for resolving sovereign debt disputes. Consequently, this chapter explored and made recommendations with regard to the practical considerations of mediating sovereign debt disputes, ranging from the commencement of the proceedings, choosing the governing rules of the mediation proceedings and selecting the appropriate mediator. Additionally, Chap. 4 identified the obstacles that could block sovereign bond creditors and states from mediating their disputes, such as a misunderstanding and a lack of information about the mediation process as well as short-sighted political resistance. Consequently, this part of the volume considered various coercive and beneficial measures that stakeholders can put into place towards promoting mediation in the investor-state and sovereign debt dispute context. In this regard, the endeavors of UNCITRAL Working Group III to reform ISDS and its proposals to encourage increased mediation in ISDS are of particular interest going forward.

As indicated above, it is the conclusion of this book that sovereign debt disputes should be addressed in mediation proceedings. For the various reasons described in this manuscript and with the hope that the efficiency and flexibility of the mediation process will allow for a faster resolution of the disputes between debtor states and their creditors, and therefore a faster return to capital markets and economic recovery. To deepen and advance the findings of this book, the author wishes to study the impact of the UNCITRAL Working Group's reform proposals on the dynamics of mediation in the ISDS system and in particular whether this will render mediation of sovereign debt disputes more propitious.

Sources

International Conventions and Rules

Central American Free Trade Agreement (CAFTA, 2004).
Convention on the Recognition and Enforcement of Foreign Arbitral Awards (New York Convention, 1959).
Convention on the Settlement of Investment Disputes between States and Nationals of Other States (ICSID Convention, 1965).
Council Decision 2000/427/EC of 19 June 2000 in accordance with Article 122(2) of the Treaty on the adoption by Greece of the single currency on 1 January 2001 [2000] Official Journal L 167 of 7 July 2000.
Energy Charter Treaty (ECT) Guide on Investment Mediation (2016).
European Code of Conduct for Mediators (2004).
European Directive 2008/52/EC on Certain Aspects of Mediation in Civil and Commercial Matters, proposal as adopted by the European Parliament and the Council of the European Union on 21 May 2008 (EU Mediation Directive, 2008).
European Directive 2002/92/EC on Insurance Mediation (2002).
EU-Vietnam Investment Protection Agreement (2018).
International Bar Association (IBA) Guidelines on Conflicts of Interest in International Arbitration (2004).
International Bar Association (IBA) Rules for Investor-State Mediation (2012).
International Centre for the Settlement of Investment Disputes (ICSID) Additional Facility Rules (2006).
International Centre for the Settlement of Investment Disputes (ICSID) Conciliation Rules (2006).
International Centre for Settlement of Investment Disputes (ICSID) Regulations and Rules (2006).
International Chamber of Commerce (ICC) Amicable Dispute Resolution (ADR) Rules (2001).

C. M. Sudborough, *Mediating Sovereign Debt Disputes*, EYIEL Monographs - Studies in European and International Economic Law 35,
https://doi.org/10.1007/978-3-031-46787-5

International Chamber of Commerce (ICC) Mediation Guidance Notes (2014).
International Chamber of Commerce (ICC) Mediation Rules (2014).
International Chamber of Commerce (ICC) Rules for the Appointment of Experts and Neutrals (2015).
International Mediation Institute (IMI) Code of Professional Conduct (2021).
International Mediation Institute (IMI) Competency Criteria for Investor–State Mediator2016).
Trans-Pacific Partnership Agreement (TPP, 2016).
Treaty on European Union, Protocol on the Convergence Criteria Referred to in Article 109j of the Treaty Establishing the European Community (Maastricht Treaty, 1992).
Treaty establishing the European Stability Mechanism (ESM, 2012).
Treaty establishing the Common Market for Eastern and Southern Africa (COMESA, 1993).
United Nations Commission on International Trade Law (UNCITRAL) Model Law on Commercial Conciliation (2002).
United Nations Commission on International Trade Law (UNCITRAL) Model Law on International Commercial Mediation and International Settlement Agreements Resulting from Mediation (2018).
United Nations Commission on International Trade Law (UNCITRAL) Rules on Transparency in Treaty-Based Investor-State Arbitration (2014).
United Nations Conference on Trade and Development (UNCTAD) Draft Principles on Promoting Responsible Sovereign Lending and Borrowing (2011).
United Nations Convention on International Settlement Agreements Resulting from Mediation (Singapore Convention, 2018).
United Nations Convention on Transparency in Treaty-based Investor-State Arbitration (Mauritius Convention on Transparency, 2014).
Vienna Convention on the Law of Treaties (1969).
World Intellectual Property Organization, WIPO Mediation Rules (2020).

Domestic Rules and Legislation

American Arbitration Association (ABA) 2005 Model Standards of Conduct for Mediators.
Argentine Law No. 26547, art. 1, Dec. 9, 2009, B.O. 31,798.
Australian Family Law Act 1975 (Cth); Australian Family Law Regulations 1984 (Cth); French Law of 26 May 2004 Relating to Family Mediation;
Austrian Childrens Law Reform (Kindschaftsrechts-Änderungsgesetz 2001, BGBl I 135/2000).
Austrian Federal Court Rules (Amendment) 1991 N° 461, r 4(1);
Austrian Marriage Law Reform (Eherechts-Änderungsgesetz 1999 BGBl I 125/1999);
Californian Code of Civil Procedure.

French Decree No. 2003–1166 of 2 December 2003 (*Décret portant creation du diplôme d'Etat de médiateur familial*).
French Civil Procedure Code.
German Law on Marriage and the Civil Procedure Code (Familienrechts-Änderungsgesetzes 2009 – Fam-RÄG 2009).
Euoprean Directive on Mediation, Article 5.
Minnesota General Rules of Practice, Article 114;
French Civil Procedure Code, Article 131–1; German Code of Civil Procedure, S. 278 V 2;
Florida Statutes S. 44.102(2)(a) 2008, Title V, Ch. 44.
Uniform Mediation Act (2001).
United Kingdom Family Law Act 1996.
United Kingdom Pre-action Protocols.
United Kingdom Civil Procedure Rules.
United States Individuals With Disabilities Education Act (IDEA, 1990).

Bibliography

Articles

Agusti-Panareda J (2004) Power imbalances in mediation: questioning some common assumptions. Dispute Resolution J 59(2):24
Alexander N (2008a) The mediation Metamodel: understanding practice. Conflict Resolution Q 26(1):97
Alexander N (2008b) Mediation and the art of regulation. Queensland Univ Technol Law Justice J 8(1):1
Anderson DQ (2010) Mandatory mediation: an oxymoron? Examining the feasibility of implementing a court mandated mediation program. Cardozo J Conflict Resol 11:479
Baldwin E, Kantor M, Nolan M (2006) Limits to enforcement of ICSID awards. J Int Arbitr 23(1):1
Bartole S (2006) State immunity and the protection of private investors: the Argentine bonds case before Italian courts. Italian Yearb Int Law 16:165
Bederman DJ (2000) Creditors' claims in international law. Int Lawyer 34:235
Beess und Chrostin J (2012) Sovereign debt restructuring and mass claims arbitration before ICSID, the Abaclat case. Harv Int Law J 53:505–549
Bercovitch J, Kadayifci-Orellana SA (2009) Religion and mediation: the role of faith-based actors in international conflict resolution. Int Negot 14:175
Berger KP, Jensen JO (2017) The Arbitrator's mandate to facilitate settlement. Fordham Int Law J 40, 997
Bevilacqua T (2007) Voluntary intervention and other participation of third parties in ongoing international arbitrations: a survey of the current state of play. World Arbitr Mediation Rev 1(4): 32
Bjorklund AK (2011) Sovereign immunity as a barrier to the enforcement of investor-state arbitral awards: the re-politicization of international investment disputes. Am Rev Int Arbitr 21(1–4): 211
Blackaby N (2004) Public interest and investment treaty arbitration. Transnational Dispute Manag:1
Blackman JI, Mukhi R (2010) The evolution of modern sovereign debt litigation: vultures, Alter egos, and other legal Fauna. Law Contemp Prob 73:53
Blanchard S (2014) Ambiente Ufficio S.p.A. and others v. Argentine Republic, ICSID case no. ARB/08/9 (formerly Giordano Alpi and others v. Argentine Republic), decision on jurisdiction and admissibility, 2 February 2013 (Bruno Simma and Karl-Heinz Böckstiegel) and dissent Santiago Torres Bernárdez, 2 May 2013. J World Invest Trade 15:314

C. M. Sudborough, *Mediating Sovereign Debt Disputes*, EYIEL Monographs - Studies in European and International Economic Law 35,
https://doi.org/10.1007/978-3-031-46787-5

Bogdanoski T (2009) The importance and challenge of active listening in mediation. Australasian Dispute Resolution J 20(4):201
Bolton P (2004) Inside the black box: how should a sovereign bankruptcy regime be structured? Faculty Scholarship Penn Law 53:707
Bottini G (2009) Should arbitrators live on Mars? Challenge of arbitrators in investment arbitration. Suffolk Transnational Law Rev 32(2)
Bottini G, Titi C, Chaisse J et al (2020) Excessive costs and recoverability of cost awards in investment arbitration. J World Invest Trade 21:251
Boudreau MA (2012) Restructuring sovereign debt under local law: are retrofit collective action clauses Expropriatory? Harv Bus Law Rev Online:164
Bratton WW (2004) Pari Passu and a distressed Sovereign's rational choices. Emory Law J 53:823
Brutti DJ (2020) Sovereign debt crises and and vulture hedge funds: issues and policy solutions'. Boston College Law Rev 61(5):1819
Buchheit LC (2005) The role of the official sector in sovereign debt workouts. Chic J Int Law 6:333
Buchheit LC, Gulati M (2017) Restructuring Sovereign Debt after NML v. Argentina. Capital Markets Law J 12:224, 230
Buchheit LC, Gulati M, Tirado I (April 2013) 'The problem of holdout creditors in Eurozone Sovereign Debt Restructurings'. Butterworths J Int Bank Financ Law
Buera F, Nicolini JP (2019), 'The Monetary and Fiscal History of Argentina, 1960–2017'. University of Chicago, Becker Friedman Institute for Economics Working Paper, 14–17
Burgstaller M (2006) Nationality of corporate investors and international claims against the Investor's own state. J World Invest Trade 7:857
Burke-White WW (2008) The Argentine financial crisis: state liability under BITs and the legitimacy of the ICSID system. Asian J WTO Int Health Law Policy 3(1):199
Butenskey J (2017) Tango or Sirtaki ? The Argentine and Greek dance with sovereignty and a multilateral sovereign debt restructuring framework. Boston Univ Int Law J 35:157
Cardosi JM (2013) Precluding the treasure hunt: how the World Bank Group can help investors circumnavigate sovereign immunity obstacles to ICSID award execution. Pepperdine Law Rev 41(1):1
Chabot B, Santarosa V (2017) Don't cry for Argentina (or other sovereign borrowers): lessons from a previous era of sovereign debt contract enforcement. Capital Markets Law J 12(1):9
Chan K-W (2014) The relationship between international investment arbitration and sovereign debt restructuring. Contemp Asia Arbitr J 7(1):229
Cheng T-H, Trisotto R (2009) Reasons and reasoning in investment treaty arbitration. Suffolk Transnational Law Rev 32(2)
Chew S, Reed L, Christopher Thomas QC J (2018) Report: Survey on Obstacles to Settlement of InvestorState Disputes. N.U.S. - Centre for International Law Working Paper 18/01
Chia H-B, Lee-Partridge J, Chong C-L (2004) Traditional mediation practices: are we throwing the baby out with the bath water? Conflict Resol Q 21(4):451–452
Chong SY, Steffek F (2019) Enforcement of international settlement agreements resulting from mediation under the Singapore convention – private international law issues in perspective. Singapore Acad Law J 31:448
Chua E (2019) Enforcement of international mediated settlements without the Singapore convention on mediation. Singapore Acad Law J 31:572
Cibils A, Vuolo RL (2007) At Debt's door: what can we learn from Argentina's recent debt crisis and restructuring? Seattle J Soc Justice 5:755
Claxton JM (2020) Compelling parties to mediate investor-state disputes: no pressure, no diamonds? Pepperdine Disp Resol Law J 20:78
Clodfelter MA (2014) The future direction of investment agreements in the European Union. Santa Clara J Int Law 12

Coe JJ Jr (2006) Transparency in the resolution of investor-state disputes: adoption, adaptation and NAFTA leadership. Univ Kansas Law Rev 54(4):1339
Cohen JR (2014) Open-Minded Listening. Charlotte Law Rev 5(1):139
Collins D (2012) Alternative dispute resolution for stakeholders in international investment law. J Int Econ Law 15(2):673
Crawford J (2008) Treaty and contract in investment arbitration. Arbitr Int 24:351
Cross KH (2008) Arbitration as a means of resolving sovereign debt disputes. Am Rev Int Arbitr 17:335
Cruces JJ, Samples TR (2016) Settling sovereign Debt's "trial of the century". Emory Int Law Rev 31(1):6
Dale G, El-Enany N (2013) The limits of social Europe: EU law and the Ordoliberal agenda. German Law J 14:613
de Chazournes LB (2004) Transparency and amicus curiae briefs. J World Invest Trade 5(2):333
Desierto D (2012) The international court of justice in the settlement of international investment disputes. J Dispute Prevent Resolution 1(1):201
Diathessopoulos MD (2012) The alternative forms of dispute settlement and the essential difference between these and arbitration. https://ssrn.com/abstract=2026606
Dilloff NJ (2010) Tips for Successful Mediation. Maryland Bar J 43(4):62
Ding J (2016) Enforcement in international investment and trade law: history, assessment, and proposed solutions. Georgetown J Int Law 47:1137
Eidenmüller H (2002) A legal framework for national and international mediation proceedings. J Int Dispute Resol 12:15
Enderlein H, Trebesch C, von Daniels L (2012) Sovereign debt disputes: a database on government coerciveness during debt crises. J Int Money Financ (2):250
Fan K (2020) Mediation of investor state disputes. J Dispute Resol 2:327
Fawehinmi F, Zlatanska E (2016) Mediation and conciliation: in pursuit of clarity. Int J Arbitr Mediation Dispute Manag 82:146
Fisch J, Gentile CM (2004) Vultures or vanguards? The role of litigation in sovereign debt restructuring. Emory Law J 53:1043
Foster GK (2008) Collecting from sovereigns: the current legal framework for enforcing arbitral awards and court judgments against states and their instrumentalities, and some proposals for its reform. Arizona J Int Comp Law 25:665
Francioni F (2009) Access to justice, denial of justice and international investment law. Eur J Int Law 20(3):729
Franck SD (2007a) Empirically evaluating claims about investment treaty arbitration. North Carolina Law Rev:86
Franck SD (2007b) Integrating investment treaty conflict and dispute systems design. Minn Law Rev:92
Franck SD (2014) Using investor-state mediation rules to promote conflict management: an introductory guide. ICSID Rev 29(1):66
Gaillard E (2008) Anti-arbitration trends in Latin America. New York Law J 239(108):1–3
Galič A (2003) Alternative dispute resolution in Slovenia. ICC ADR Bull 6(4):71–76
Gallagher KP (2012) Financial crises and international investment agreements: the case of sovereign debt restructuring. Global Pol 3(3):362
Garcia A (2011) The role of interactional competence in mediation. Conflict Resol Q 28(2):205
García-Bolívar OE (2005) Comparing arbitrator standards of conduct in international commercial, trade and investment disputes. Dispute Resol J 60(4):300
Georgakopoulos N (2012) Lessons from Greco-multilateralism for creditors. Connecticut J Int Law 28:21
Gerbay R (2012) Confidentiality vs transparency in international arbitration: the English perspective. Transnational Dispute Manag 9. https://www.transnational-dispute-management.com/article.asp?key=1816

Golann D (2000) Variations in mediation: how–and why–legal mediators change styles in the course of a case. J Dispute Resol 2000(1):41

Golann D (2011) Beyond brainstorming: the special barriers to interest-based mediation, and techniques to overcome them. Dispute Resol Magazine 18(1):22

Gómez KF (2011) Latin American and ICSID: David vs goliath. Law and Bus Rev Americas 17: 195

Goodman CL (2007) Uncharted Waters: financial crisis and enforcement of ICSID awards in Argentina. Univ Pa J Int Econ Law 28(2):449

Greenberg EE (2015) When "yes" may actually mean "no": rethinking informed consent to ADR processes. N Y Dispute Resol Lawyer 8:1

Griffin P, Farren A (2005) How ICSID can protect sovereign bondholders? Int Financ Law Rev 24(9):21

Gustavo OM (2005) The Legal Practice Of The Recovery Of State External Debt. Ph.D Thesis. University of Geneva

Gutierrez M (2013) Case comment, flying too close to the sun: how an EMU expulsion provision will prevent the European sovereign debt crisis from becoming a modern day Greek tragedy. Houston J Int Law 35:431

Hagan S (2005) Designing a legal framework to restructure sovereign debt. Georgetown J Int Law 36:299

Hébert B, Schreger J (2017) The costs of sovereign default: evidence from Argentina. Am Econ Rev 107(10):3119–3145

Hirsch M (2016) Explaining compliance and non-compliance with ICSID awards: the Argentine case study and a multiple theoretical approach. J Int Econ Law 19(3):681

Hoffman DA (2011) Mediation and the art of shuttle diplomacy. Negot J 263:264–270

Hofmann C (2013) A legal analysis of the euro zone crisis. Fordham J Corp Finance Law 18:519

Housos K (2015) Austerity and human rights law: towards a rights based approach to austerity policy, a case study of Greece. Fordham Int Law J 39:425

Hyde CC (1922) The negotiation of external loans with foreign governments. Am J Int Law 16: 16 523

Iversen A (2019) Vulture fund legislation. Bank Financ Services Policy Report 38(5):57

Jameson JK, Bodtker AM, Porch DM et al (2009) Exploring the role of emotion in conflict transformation. Conflict Resol Q 27(2):167

Joiner J (2015) Past due: an introduction to sovereign debt, the ongoing dispute between NML capital and Argentina, and possible ramifications of the Dispute's outcome. Law Bus Rev Am 21:85

Kabra R (2015) Has Abaclat v Argentina left the ICSID with a 'Mass'ive problem? Arbitr Int 331(3):425

Kamenis SD (2014) Vulture funds and the sovereign debt market: lessons from Argentina and Greece. Hellenic Foundation Eur Foreign Policy (ELIAMEP) 13

Karamanian SL (2013) Introductory note to Abaclat & Others v. Argentine Republich: decision on jurisdiction and admissibility (ICSID). Int Leg Mater 52(3):667

Kasenetz ED (2010) Desperate times call for desperate measures: the aftermath of Argentina's state of necessity and the current fight in the ICSID. George Washington Int Law Rev 41:709

Kelly EJ, Kaminski N (2016) Importance of emotional intelligence in negotiation and mediation. Int Comp Jurisprudence 2(1):55

Kriebaum U (2013) Foreign investments and human rights: the actors and their different roles. Transnational Dispute Manag 10. https://www.transnational-dispute-management.com/article.asp?key=1925

Krueger A, Hagan S (2016) Sovereign workouts: an IMF perspective. Chic J Int Law 6(1):203

Laflin ME (2014) Preserving the integrity of mediation through the adoption of ethical rules for lawyer-mediators. Notre Dame J Law Ethics Public Policy 14(1):479

Laird I, Askew R (2005) Finality versus consistency: does investor-state arbitration need an appellate system. J Appellate Practice Process 7(2):287

Lakhani A (2015) David versus goliath and multilateral diplomatic negotiations in the 21st century: how the Greek debt crisis negotiations marked the revenge of goliath. Cardozo J Int Comp Law 24:97
Lande J (2002) Using dispute system design methods to promote good-faith participation in court-connected mediation programs. UCLA Law Rev 50
Lane PR (2012) The European sovereign debt crisis. J Econ Perspect 26(3):49
Lapavitsas C, Kaltenbrunner A, Lindo D et al (2011) Breaking up? A radical route out of the Eurozone crisis. Res Money Finance:33
Legrand J, Canning T (2007) Vulture funds rocked by decision of English high court. J Int Banking Financial Law 5:289
Legum B (2007) The difficulties of conciliation in investment treaty cases: a comment on professor Jack C. Coe's "toward a complementary use of conciliation in investor-state disputes - a preliminary sketch". Transnational Dispute Manag 1. https://www.transnational-dispute-management.com/article.asp?key=963
Lin T-Y (2012) Systemic reflections on Argentina's non-compliance with ICSID arbitral awards: a new role of the annulment Committee at Enforcement? Contemp Asia Arbitr J 5(1):1–22
Linares JC (2005) After the Argentine crisis: can the IMF prevent corruption in its lending? A model approach. Richmond J Global Law Bus 5:13
Livingood JM (ed) (2002) Reframing and its uses. Dispute Resol J 57(4):42
Lohvinenko M, Starynskyi M, Rudenko L et al (2021) Models of mediation: theoretical and legal analysis. Conflict Resol Q 39(1):51
Love LP (1997) Top ten reasons why mediators should not evaluate. Florida State Law Rev 24:937
Macias L (2012) Case comment, the Greek debt crisis: the weaknesses of an economic and monetary union. Duquesne Bus Law J 14:251
Mark W, Weidemaier C (2014) Sovereign Immunity and Sovereign Debt. Univ Ill Law Rev 67:68
Maynard S (2016) A new framework for the analysis of multi-party claims: Giovanni Alemanni and others v the Argentine Republic, ICSID case no. ARB/07/8, decision on jurisdiction and admissibility, 17 November 2014 (sir Franklin Berman, Karl-Heinz Böckstiegel, J. Christopher Thomas). J World Invest Trade 17(1):117
McAdoo B, Welsh NA (2005) Look before you leap and keep on looking: lessons from the institutionalization of court-connected mediation. Nevada Law J 5:399
Michael Reisman W (2009) International Investment Arbitration and ADR: married but best living apart. ICSID Rev Foreign Invest Law J 24(1):185
Mitchener KJ, Weidenmier MD (2009) Supersanctions and sovereign debt repayment. J Int Money Financ 29:19
Montanaro F (2015) Postova Banka SA and Istrokapital SE v Hellenic Republic: sovereign bonds and the puzzling definition of 'investment' in international investment law. ICSID Rev 3(3):549
Nelson TG (2011) Human rights and BIT protection: areas of convergence. J World Invest Trade:22
Nitschke F (2014) The IBA's investor-state mediation rules and the ICSID dispute settlement framework. ICSID Rev 29(1):112
Nolan-Haley J (2005) Self-determination in international mediation: some preliminary reflections. Cardozo J Conflict Resol 7:277
Note (2014) Mediation of investor-state conflicts. Harv Law Rev 127(8):2543
Olivares-Caminal R (2011) The Pari Passu interpretation in the Elliott case: a brilliant strategy but an awful (mid-long term) outcome? Hofstra Law Rev 40:39
Ortolani P (2017) Are bondholders investors? Sovereign debt and investment arbitration after Poštová. Leiden J Int Law 30:383
Ostransky J (2015) Sovereign default disputes in investment treaty arbitration: jurisdictional considerations and policy implications. Groningen J Int Law 3:55
Paddock JV (2002) Case comment, IMF policy and the Argentine crisis. Univ Miami Inter-Am Law Rev 34:155

Panizza U (2013) 'Do We Need a Mechanism for Solving Sovereign Debt Crises? A Rule-based Discussion'. Working paper no. 03/2013 Geneva Graduate Institute of International and Development Studies
Panizza U, Sturzenegger F, Zettelmeyer J (2009) The economics and law of sovereign debt and default. J Econ Lit 47:651
Park SK, Samples TR (2017) Tribunalizing sovereign debt: Argentina's experience with investor-state dispute settlement. Va J Transnational Law 50:1033
Permesly J, Craven M (2018) Where are we now? Investment treaty arbitration, sovereign debt, and mass claims in the post-Abaclat era. Transnational Dispute Manag 15(1):1
Picard C, Siltanen J (2013) Exploring the significance of emotion for mediation practice. Conflict Resolution Q 31:31
Pohl J (2018) Societal benefits and costs of International Investment Agreements: A critical review of aspects and available empirical evidence. OECD Working Papers on International Investment
Porzecanski A (2005) From rogue creditors to rogue debtors: implications of Argentina's default. Chic J Int Law 6:311
Power PJ (1996) Sovereign debt: the rise of the secondary market and its implications for future restructurings. Fordham Law Rev:2701
Radi Y (2013) The "human nature" of international investment law. Transnational Dispute Manag 10(1) https://www.transnational-dispute-management.com/article.asp?key=1928
Reed L (2017) Suite for ISDS: mediation, arbitration, appellate bodies. Korean Arbitr Rev 9:58
Riskin LL (2003) Decision-making in mediation: the new old grid and the new new grid system. Notre Dame Law Rev 79(1):3
Roberts KM (2007) Mediating the evaluative-facilitative debate: why both parties are wrong and a proposal for settlement. Loyola Univ Chicago Law J 39(1):187
Robyn C (2002) Trends in mediation legislation: "all for one and one for all" or "one at all"? Univ Western Aust Law Rev 30:172
Rodriguez Correa TD (2018) Sovereign Bond Disputes Caseload: Basis For Legal Strategies In International Investment Law Arbitration'. MPIL Research Paper Series
Rogoff K, Zettelmeyer J (2002) Bankruptcy procedures for sovereigns: a history of ideas, 1976-2001. Int Monetary Fund Staff Papers 49:470
Ruiz del Rio OA (1987) Arbitration clauses in international loans. J Int Arbitr 4:45
Samples TR (2014) Rogue trends in sovereign debt: Argentina, vulture funds, and Pari Passu under New York law. Northwestern J Int Law Bus 35:49
Sandrack O (1994) Is international arbitration inept to solve disputes arising out of international loan agreements? J Int Arbitr 11:33
Schilling D (2012) NML capital, ltd. v. Argentina 2011 WL 524433 (S.D.N.Y. Feb. 15, 2011). N Y Int Law Rev 25:159
Schnabel T (2019) The Singapore convention on mediation: a framework for the Cross border recognition and enforcement of mediated settlements. Pepperdine Dispute Resol Law J 19:1
Schreuer C (2004) Non-pecuniary remedies in ICSID. Arbitr Int 20(4):324
Schreuer C (2009) Revising the system of review for investment awards, BIICL available. http://www.univie.ac.at/intlaw/wordpress/pdf/99_rev_invest_awards.pdf
Schubert MF (2013) Note, when vultures attack: balancing the right to immunity against reckless sovereigns. Brooklyn Law Rev 78:1097
Schumacher J, Trebesch C, Enderlein H (2021) Sovereign defaults in Court. J Int Econ:131
Schwarcz SL (2000) Sovereign debt restructuring: a bankruptcy Reorganization approach. Cornell Law Rev:956
Schwebel SM (2007) Is mediation of foreign investment disputes plausible? ICSID Rev 22(2):237
Schweinsberg M, Thau S, Pillutla MM (2021) Negotiation impasses: types, causes and resolutions. J Manag 47(6):1430
Shane MB (1995) The difference between mediation and conciliation. Dispute Resol J 50(3):31
Shany Y (2005) Notes and comments. Contract claims V. Treaty claims: mapping conflicts between ICSID decisions on multi-sourced investment claims. Am J Int Law 99(4):835

Simma B (2011) Foreign investment arbitration: a place for human rights? Int Comp Law Q 60(3): 573
Smits R (2015) The crisis response in Europe's economic and monetary union: Overview of legal developments. Fordham Int Law J 38:1135
Snyder EC (1994) The Menem revolution in Argentina: Progress toward a hemispheric free trade area. Texas Int Law J 29:95
Spiermann O (2004) Individual rights, state interests and the Power to waive ICSID jurisdiction under bilateral investment treaties. Arbitr Int 20(2):179
Stevens M, Love B (2010) Investor-state mediation: observations on the role of institutions. In: Rovine A (ed) Contemporary issues in international Abitration and mediation, the Fordham papers 2009. Martinus Nijhoff Publishers, Leiden
Stipanowich TJ (2015) The international evolution of mediation: a call for dialogue and deliberation. Vic Univ Wellington Law Rev 46(4):1191
Stipanowich TJ (2021) Arbitration, mediation and mixed modes: seeking workable solutions and common ground on med-arb, arb-med and settlement-oriented activities by arbitrators. Harv Negotiation Law Rev 26(Spring):265
Strong S (2013a) Mass procedures in Abaclat v. Argentine Republic: are they consistent with the international investment regime? Yearb Int Arbitr 3
Strong SI (2013b) Mass procedures as a form of "regulatory arbitration" – Abaclat v. Argentine Republic and the international investment regime. J Corp Law 38(2):259
Strong SI (2014a) Use and perception of international commercial mediation and conciliation: a preliminary report on issues relating to the proposed UNCITRAL Convention on International Commercial Mediation and Conciliation. University of Missouri School of Law Legal Studies Research Paper No. 2014-28
Strong SI (2016) Realizing rationality: an empirical assessment of international commercial mediation. Washington Lee Law Rev 74(4):1973
Sudborough CM (2014) ICC's new mediation rules: mediation steps out of the shadow. Am Bar Assoc Sect Int Law Year Rev 48:181
Sussman E (2009) The New York convention through a mediation prism. Dispute Resol Magazine:15
Tabb CJ, Mabey R, Dizengoff IS (1995) Expanding the reach of alternative dispute resolution in bankruptcy: the legal and practical bases for the use of mediation and the other forms of ADR. South Carolina Law Rev 46(6):1259
Tamura K (2004) The problem of sovereign debt restructuring: holdout problem and exit consents. J Restructuring Finance 1(1):101
Ten Cate I (2013) The costs of consistency: precedent in investment treaty arbitration. Columb J Transnational Law:51
Titi C (2014) Investment arbitration in Latin America: the uncertain veracity of preconceived ideas. Arbitr Int 30(2):357
Tsoukala P (2013) Euro zone crisis management and the new social Europe. Columbia J Eur Law 20:31
Uniform Mediation Act and Official Comments (2003) J Dispute Resol 1:47–48
Vohryzek-Griest A (2010) Unjust enrichment unjustly ignored: opportunities and pitfalls in bringing unjust enrichment claims under ICSID. Loyola Los Angeles Int Comp Law Rev 31:101
von Staden A (2011) Towards greater doctrinal clarity in investor-state arbitration: the CMS, Enron, and Sempra annulment decisions. Czech Yearb Int Law 2:207
Waibel M (2007a) Opening Pandora's box: sovereign bonds in international arbitration. Am J Int Law 101:711
Waibel M (2007b) Two worlds of necessity in ICSID arbitration: CMS v. LG&E. Leiden J Int Law 20:637
Waibel M (2014) Steering sovereign debt restructurings through the CDS quicksand. J Bank Regul 15(1):14

Welsh N (2001) Making deals in court-connected mediation: What's justice got to do with it? Wash Univ Law Q 79(3):787
Welsh NA, Schneider AK (2012) Becoming "investor-state mediation". Penn State J Law Int Aff 1: 86
Welsh NA, Schneider AK (2013) The thoughtful integration of mediation into bilateral investment treaty arbitration. Harv Negot Law Rev 71:82
Winslade J, Monk G, Cotter A (1998) A narrative approach to the practice of mediation. Negot J 14(1):21
Wright MLJ (2012) Sovereign debt restructuring: problems and prospects. Harv Bus Law Rev 2: 172
Zettelmeyer J, Trebesch C, Gulati M (2013) The Greek debt restructuring: an autopsy. Econ Policy 28:513

Books and Book Chapters

Abramson HI (2004) Mediation representation; advocating in a problem-solving process. National Institute for Trial Advocacy, Boulder
Abramson H (2019) New Singapore convention on Cross-border mediated settlements: key choices. In: Titi C, Gómez KF (eds) Mediation in international commercial and investment disputes. Oxford University Press, Oxford
Alexander N (2010) International comparative mediation: legal perspectives, 4th edn. Kluwer Law International, Alphen aan Den Rijn
Alexandrov SA (2009) Enforcement of ICSID awards: article 53 and 54 of the ICSID convention. In: Binder C, Kriebaum U, Reinisch A et al (eds) International investment law for the 21st century, essays in honour of Christoph Schreuer. Oxford University Press, Oxford
Ams J, Baqir R (2020) Anna Gelpern and others, 'sovereign default'. In: Abbas A, Pienkowski A, Rogoff K (eds) Sovereign debt: a guide for economists and practitioners. Oxford University Press, Oxford
Asteriti A, Tams C (2010) Transparency and representation of the public interest in investment treaty arbitration. In: Schill S (ed) International investment law and comparative public law, 1st edn. Oxford University Press, Oxford
Azzali S (2013) Balancing confidentiality and transparency. In: Malatesta A, Sali R (eds) The rise of transparency in international arbitration, 1st edn. JurisNet
Barnes BE (2007) Culture, conflict, and mediation in the Asian Pacific. University Press of America, Lanham
Baruch Bush RA, Folger JP (2004) The promise of mediation: the transformative approach to conflict, 2nd edn. Jossey-Bass Publishers, San Francisco
Baxter TC Jr, Gross D (2014) Special immunities: central Bank immunity. In: Lastra RM, Buchheit L (eds) Sovereign Debt Management, 1st edn. Oxford University Press, Oxford
Beer JE, Caroline C (2012) Packard with Eileen Stief, The Mediator's handbook, 4th edn. New Society Publishers, Gabriola
Bingham LB (2011) Opportunities for dispute Systems Design in Investment Treaty Disputes: consensual dispute resolution at varying levels. In: Franck SD, Joubin-Bret A (eds) Proceedings of the Washington and Lee University and UNCTAD joint symposium on international investment and alternative dispute resolution, held on 29 march 2010 in Lexington, Virginia, United States of America. UNCTAD, Geneva. https://unctad.org/en/Docs/webdiaeia20108_en.pdf
Bjorklund AK (2009) State immunity and the enforcement of investor-state arbitral awards. In: Binder C, Kriebaum U, Reinisch A, Wittich S (eds) International investment law for the 21st century: essays in honour of Christoph Schreuer. Oxford University Press, Oxford

Blustein P (2005) And the money kept rolling in (and out): wall street, the IMF, and the bankrupting of Argentina. PublicAffairs, New York

Boccuzzi C Jr, Brennan M, Johnston J (2014) Defences. In: Lastra RM, Buchheit L (eds) Sovereign Debt Management, 1st edn. Oxford University Press, Oxford

Boulle L, Colatrella MT Jr, Picchioni AP (2008) Mediation : skills and techniques. LexisNexis, Bethesda

Brekoulakis S, Lew JDM, Mistelis L (2016) The evolution and future of international arbitration. Wolters Kluwer, Alphen aan den Rijn

Brower CH II (2019) Selection of mediators. In: Titi C, Gómez KF (eds) Mediation in international commercial and investment disputes. Oxford University Press, Oxford

Brown C, Winch P (2019) The confidentiality and transparency debate in commercial and investment mediation. In: Titi C, Gómez KF (eds) Mediation in international commercial and investment disputes. Oxford University Press, Oxford

Buchheit L, Daly E (2014a) Minimizing holdout creditors: carrots. In: Lastra RM, Buchheit L (eds) Sovereign Debt Management, 1st edn. Oxford University Press, Oxford

Buchheit L, Daly E (2014b) Minimizing holdout creditors: sticks. In: Lastra RM, Buchheit L (eds) Sovereign Debt Management, 1st edn. Oxford University Press, Oxford

Buckley RP, Arner DW (2011) From crisis to crisis. Kluwer Law & Business, Alphen aan den Rijn

Cloke K (2001) Mediating dangerously. Jossey-Bass, San Francisco

Coe JJ Jr (2009) Settlement of investor-state disputes through mediation – preliminary remarks on processes, problems and prospects. In: Bishop R (ed) Enforcement of arbitral awards against sovereigns. Juris Net

Coe JJ Jr (2010a) Concurrent med-arb (CMA) – some further reflections on a work in Progress. In: Franck SD, Joubin-Bret A (eds) Investor-state disputes: prevention and alternatives to arbitration II. UNCTAD, Geneva

Coe JJ Jr (2010b) Should mediation of investment disputes be encouraged, and, if so, by whom and how? In: Rovine A (ed) Contemporary issues in international Abitration and mediation, the Fordham papers 2009. Martinus Nijhoff Publishers, Leiden

De Brabandere E (2011) Pragmatism in international law: non-state actor participation in international dispute settlement. In: d'Aspremont J (ed) Participants in the international legal system. Multiple perspectives on non-state actors in international law. Routledge, Milton Park

De Brabandere E (2012) Human rights considerations in international investment arbitration. In: Fitzmaurice M, Merkouris P (eds) The interpretation and application of the European convention of human rights: legal and practical implications. Martinus Nijhoff Publishers, The Hague

De Brabandere E (2015) Investment treaty arbitration as public international law. Cambridge University Press, Cambridge

De Girolamo D (2020) The opening statement in mediation: a Goffman analysis. In: Moscati MF, Palmer M, Roberts M (eds) Comparative Dispute Resolution. Edward Elgar, Cheltenham

de Vicuña AS (2014) Restructuring in a monetary union. In: Lastra RM, Buchheit L (eds) Sovereign Debt Management, 1st edn. Oxford University Press, Oxford

Derains Y, Levy L (2011) Is arbitration only as good as the arbitrator? Status, powers and role of the arbitrator. ICC Institute of World Business Law

Dodge WS (2009) Investment treaties between developed states: the dilemma of dispute resolution. In: Rogers C, Alford R (eds) The future of investment arbitration. Oxford University Press, Oxford

Douglas Z (2009) The international law of investment claims. Cambridge University Press, Cambridge

Dumberry P, Labelle-Eastaugh E (2011) Non-state actors in international investment law: the legal personality of corporations and NGOs in the context of investor-state arbitration. In: d'Aspremont J (ed) Participants in the international legal system, 1st edn. Routledge, Milton Park

Dupuy P-M (2009) Unification rather than fragmentation of international law? The case of international investment law and human rights law. In: Dupuy P-M, Petersmann E-U, Francioni

F (eds) Human rights in international investment law and arbitration, 1st edn. Oxford Scholarship Online
Dupuy P-M, Vinuales JE (2012) Human rights and investment disciplines: integration in Progress. In: Bungenberg M, Griebel J, Hobe S, Reinisch A (eds) International Investment Law. Nomos, Glashütte
Esplugues C (2014) Civil and commercial mediation in the E.U. After the transposition of the directive 2008/52/EC on mediation in civil and commercial matters. In: Esplugues C (ed) Civil and commercial mediation in Europe: Cross-border mediation, Vol. II. Intersentia, Cambridge
Euler D, Gehring M, Scherer M (eds) (2015) Transparency in international investment arbitration. Cambridge University Press, Cambridge
Fisher R, Ury W, Patton B (1997) Getting to yes: negotiating an agreement without giving in, 2nd edn. Random House Business Books, New York
Folberg J, Golann D, Stipanowich TJ (2016) Resolving disputes: theory, practice, and law, 3rd edn. Wolters Kluwer, Alphen aan den Rijn
Franck SD (2008) Challenges facing investment disputes: reconsidering dispute resolution in international investment agreements. In: Sauvant K (ed) Appeals mechanisms in international investment disputes. Oxford University Press, Oxford
Franck SD (2013) Managing expectations: beyond formal adjudication. In: Echandi R, Sauvé P (eds) Prospects in international investment law and policy: world trade forum. Cambridge University Press, Cambridge
Franck SD, Joubin-Bret A (2011) Investor-state disputes: prevention and alternatives to arbitration: proceedings of the United Nations conference on trade and development in Lexington, Virginia, U.S.A. United Nations, New York
Gaillard E (2005) Investment treaty arbitration and jurisdiction over contract claims: the SGS cases considered. In: Weiler T (ed) International investment law and arbitration: leading cases from the ICSID, NAFTA, bilateral treaties and customary international law. Cameron May, London
Gallagher K (2013) The new vulture culture: sovereign debt restructuring and international investment rules. In: Gallagher K (ed) The clash of globalizations: essays on the political economy of trade and development policy. Anthem Press, London
Gianviti F, Krueger AO, Pisani-Ferry J et al (2010) A European mechanism for sovereign debt crisis resolution: a proposal. Bruegel, Brussels
Golann D (2009) Mediating legal disputes: effective strategies for neutrals and advocates. American Bar Association, Chicago
Golann D, Aaron MC (2010) Using evaluations in mediation. In: Carbonneau TE, Jaeggi JA (eds) AAA handbook on mediation. JurisNet
Gómez KF (2018) Foreign direct Investment in Latin America. In: Krajewski M (ed) Research handbook on foreign direct investment. Edward Elgar, Cheltenham
Gómez KF (2019) The role of mediation in commercial disputes: reflections on some technological, ethical, and educational challenges. In: Titi C, Gómez KF (eds) Mediation in international commercial and investment disputes. Oxford University Press, Oxford
Gulati M, Scott RE (2013) The three and a half minute transaction. University of Chicago Press, Chicago
Guzman M, Stiglitz JE (2016) Creating a framework for sovereign debt restructuring that works. In: Guzman M, Ocampo JA, Stiglitz JE (eds) Too Little, too late. Columbia University Press, New York
Hardy S, Rundle O (2010) Mediation for lawyers. CCH Australia, Melbourne
Hopt KJ, Steffek F (eds) (2013) Mediation: principles and regulation in comparative perspective. Oxford University Press, Oxford
Irvine C, Farrington L (2016) Mediation and emotions: perception and regulation. In: Conway H, Stannard J (eds) The emotional dynamics of law and legal discourse. Hart, Oxford
Karen Halverson Cross (2014) Sovereign Arbitration. In: Lastra RM, Buchheit L (eds) Sovereign Debt Management, 1st edn. Oxford University Press, Oxford
Klabbers J (2009) Treaty conflict and the European Union. Cambridge University Press, Cambridge

Koopmans SMG (2008) Diplomatic dispute settlement. T.M.C. Asser, The Hague
Krasner SD (2001) Problematic sovereignty. Columbia University Press, New York
Krueger A (2002) A new approach to sovereign debt restructuring. International Monetary Fund, Washington, D.C.
Kulick A (2012) Global public interest in international investment law. Cambridge University Press, Cambridge
Lastra RM (2014) The role of the International Monetary Fund. In: Lastra RM, Buchheit L (eds) Sovereign Debt Management, 1st edn. Oxford University Press, Oxford
Legum B, Mouawad C (2010) The meaning of "investment" in the ICSID convention. In: Bekker PHF, Dolzer R, Waibel M (eds) Making transnational law work in the global economy: essays in honour of Detlev Vagts, 1st edn. Cambridge University Press, Cambridge
Leoveanu A, Erac A (2019) ICC mediation: paving the way forward' in mediation. In: Titi C, Gómez KF (eds) International commercial and investment disputes. Oxford University Press, Oxford
Lewicki RJ, Saunders DM, Barry B (eds) (2015) Negotiation, 7th edn. McGraw Hill Education, Columbus
Lienau O (2014) The longer-term consequences of sovereign debt restructuring. In: Lastra RM, Buchheit L (eds) Sovereign Debt Management, 1st edn. Oxford University Press, Oxford
Lundmark T (2012) Charting the divide between common and civil law. Oxford University Press, Oxford
Lutrell S (2011) Bias challenges in investor-state arbitration: lessons from international commercial arbitration. In: Brown C, Miles K (eds) Evolution in investment treaty law and arbitration. Cambridge University Press, Cambridge
Maupin JA (2013) Transparency in international investment law: the good, the bad and the murky. In: Bianchi A, Peters A (eds) Transparency in international law. Cambridge University Press, Cambridge
Maute J (2006) Hyperinflation, currency board, and bust: the case of Argentina. Peter Lang, Frankfurt am Main
McIlwrath M, Savage J (2010) International arbitration and mediation: a practical guide. Kluwer Law International, Alphen aan Den Rijn
McLachlan C, Shore L, Weiniger M (2008) International investment arbitration: substantive principles. Oxford University Press, Oxford
Megginson WL (2018) Privatization, state capitalism, and state ownership of business in the 21st century. Now Publishers, Hanover
Menaker AJ, Paliwal SG (2015) Remedies – Damages. In: Golden J, Lamm C (eds) International financial disputes -arbitration and mediation, 1st edn. Oxford University Press, Oxford
Menkel-Meadow C, Love LP, Schneider AK (2020) Mediation: practice, policy, and ethics, 3rd edn. Wolters Kluwer, Alphen aan den Rijn
Mistelis LA (ed) (2015) Concise international arbitration, 2nd edn. Wolters Kluwer, Alphen aan den Rijn
Montt S (2009) State liability in investment treaty arbitration. Hart Publishing, Oxford
Moore CW (2014a) The mediation process, 8th edn. Jossey-Bass, San Francisco
Nitschke F (2019) The ICSID conciliation rules in practice. In: Titi C, Gómez KF (eds) Mediation in international commercial and investment disputes. Oxford University Press, Oxford
Nolan-Haley J (2012) Evolving paths to justice: assessing the EU directive on mediation. In: Rovine AW (ed) Contemporary issues in international arbitration and mediation: the Fordham papers. Brill Nijhoff, Leiden
O'Sullivan G (2018) The Mediator's toolkit: formulating and asking questions for successful outcomes. New Society Publishers, Gabriola
Oliveri EJ (1992) Latin American debt and the politics of international finance. Praeger, Connecticut
Parra AR (2017) The history of ICSID, 2nd edn. Oxford Univeresity Press, Oxford

Penusliski IM (2010) A dispute systems design diagnosis of ICSID. In: Waibel M, Kaushal A, Chung K-H et al (eds) The backlash against investment arbitration: perceptions and reality. Kluwer Law International, Alphen aan Den Rijn

Pepperdine University Strauss Institute for Dispute Resolution (2009) Mediation: the art of facilitating settlement. Pepperdine University, Malibu

Peterson LE (2011) Majority opinion in ICSID bondholders claim has broader lessons for defaulting sovereigns, fractured tribunals, shareholder groupings, and would-be claimants needing help getting ICSID claims registered. Investment Arbitration Reporter 4

Rault CJ (2017) The legal framework of sovereign debt management. In: Geiwitz A, Kebekus F, Knecht TC et al (eds) Schriften zur Restrukturierung. Nomos, Glashütte, Volume 9

Sammut G, Bauer MW (2020) The psychology of social influence. Cambridge University Press, Cambridge

Schill S (2010) International investment law and comparative public law. Oxford University Press, Oxford

Schill S, Kim Y-I (2011) Sovereign bonds in economic crisis: is the necessity defence under international law applicable in investor-state relations? A critical analysis of the decision of the German constitutional court in the Argentine bondholder cases. In: Sauvant KP (ed) Yearbook of international investment law and policy 2010–2011. Oxford University Press, Oxford

Schlemmer EC (2008) Investment, investor, nationality, and shareholders. In: Muchlinski P, Ortino F, Schreuer C (eds) The Oxford handbook of international investment law. Oxford University Press, Oxford

Schonewille M, Schonewille F (eds) (2014) The variegated landscape of mediation, a comparative study of mediation regulation and practices in Europe and the world. Eleven International Publishing, The Hague

Schreuer C (2011) From ICSID annulment to appeal half way down the slippery slope. In: The law and practice of international courts and tribunals. Brill, Leiden, Volume 10

Schreuer C, Dolzer R (2008) Interpretation and application of investment treaties. In: Principles of international investment law. Oxford University Press, Oxford

Schreuer C, Malintoppi L, Reinisch A, Sinclair A (2009) The ICSID convention: a commentary. Cambridge University Press, Cambridge

Sharp D (2014) The significance of human rights for the debt of countries in transition. In: Bohoslavsky JP, Cernic JL (eds) Making Sovereign Financing & Human Rights Work. Hart Publishing, Oxford

Sharpe JK (2014) Representing a respondent state in investment arbitration. In: Giorgetti C (ed) Litigating international investment disputes: a Practitioner's guide. Brill Nijhoff, Leiden

Shirlow E (2021) The promises and pitfalls of investor-state mediation. In: Sachs L, Johnson L, Coleman J (eds) Yearbook on International Investment law & Policy 2019. Oxford University Press, Oxford

Spencer D, Brogan M (2006) Mediation law and practice. Cambridge University Press, Cambridge

Stevens M (2009) The Power of ICSID ad hoc committees to order security when granting a stay of enforcement. In: Bishop RD (ed) Enforcement of arbitral awards against sovereigns. JurisNet

Stitt A (2004) Mediation: a practical guide. Routledge-Cavendish, Milton Park

Strasser F, Randolph P (2005) Mediation: a psychological insight into conflict resolution. Continuum, London, pp 84–85

Strong S (2014b) Use and perception of international commercial mediation and conciliation: a preliminary report on issues relating to the proposed UNCITRAL convention on international commercial mediation and conciliation. University of Missouri School of Law Legal Studies Research Paper No. 2014–28

Sturzenegger F, Zettelmeyer J (2007) Debt defaults and lessons from a decade of crises. MIT Press, Cambridge

Sussman E (2013) Capturing the benefits of arbitration for Cross border insolvency disputes. In: Rovine A (ed) Contemporary issues in international arbitration and mediation. Martinus Nijhoff, Leiden

Tawil GS (2009) Binding force and enforcement of ICSID awards: untying articles 53 and 54 of the ICSID convention. In: van den Berg AJ (ed) 50 years of the New York convention: ICCA international arbitration conference, ICCA congress series no, vol 14. Kluwer Law International, Alphen aan Den Rijn

Thrasher RD (2021) The emerging role of international investment agreements in sovereign debt restructuring. In: Thrasher RD (ed) Constraining development: the shrinking of policy space in the international trade regime. Anthem Press, London

Timothy Martin A (2011) International mediation: an evolving market. In: Rovine AW (ed) Contemporary issues in International Arbitration & Mediation: the Fordham papers (2010). Brill, Leiden

Titi C (2016) Economic crises, sovereign debt restructurings and the shifting landscape of international investment law. In: Segura A (ed) The reform of international economic governance, 1st edn. Routledge, Milton Park

Titi C (2019) Mediation and settlement of investment disputes: between utopia and realism. In: Titi C, Gómez KF (eds) Mediation in international commercial and investment disputes. Oxford University Press, Oxford

Tümpel H, Sudborough C (2011) ICC's ADR rules, 2001-2010: current practices, case examples and lessons learned. In: Ingen-Housz A (ed) ADR in business, practice and issues across countries and cultures, Vol. II. Wolters Kluwer, Alphen aan den Rijn

van Haersholte-van Hof J, Hoffmann AK (2008) The relationship between international tribunals and domestic courts. In: Muchlinski P, Ortino F (eds) The Oxford handbook of international investment law, 1st edn. Oxford University Press, Oxford

Van Harten G (2008) Investment treaty arbitration and public law. Oxford University Press, Oxford

Van Harten G (2013) Sovereign choices and sovereign constraints: judicial restraint in investment treaty arbitration. Oxford University Press, Oxford

Vandevelde KJ (2017) Bilateral investment treaties: history, policy and interpretation. Oxford University Press, Oxford

Vitale G (1995) Multilateral sovereign debt restructuring: the Paris Club and the London Club. In: Eichengreen B, Portes R (eds) Crisis? What crisis? Orderly workouts for sovereign debtors. Center for Economic Policy Research, Washington, DC

Waibel M (2010) The diplomatic channel. In: Crawford J, Pellet A, Olleson S (eds) Handbook on state responsibility, 1st edn. Oxford University Press, Oxford

Waibel M (2011) Bank insolvency and state insolvency. In: Lastra R (ed) Cross-border Bank insolvency, 1st edn. Oxford University Press, Oxford

Waibel M (2013a) Sovereign defaults before international courts and tribunals. Cambridge University Press, Cambridge

Waibel M (2013b) Tracing the origins of the UNCTAD principles. In: Bohoslavsky JP, Esposito C, Li Y (eds) Sovereign financing and international law: the UNCTAD principles on responsible sovereign lending and borrowing, 1st edn. Oxford University Press, Oxford

Waibel M, Kaushal A, Chung K-H et al (2010) The backlash against investment arbitration. Wolters Kluwer, Alphen aan den Rijn

Wälde T (2005) The Serbian loans case: a precedent for investment treaty protection of foreign debt? In: Weiler T (ed) International investment law and arbitration - leading cases from the ICSID, NAFTA, bilateral treaties and customary international law, 1st edn. Cameron May, London

Waters A (2015) The costs of arbitration. Watson Farley and Williams, London

Weidemaier WMC, McCarl R (2014) Creditors' Remedies. In: Lastra RM, Buchheit L (eds) Sovereign debt management, 1st edn. Oxford University Press, Oxford

Wells L (2010) Property rights for foreign capital: sovereign debt and private direct investment in times of crisis. In: Sauvant KP (ed) Yearbook on international investment law and policy. Oxford University Press, Oxford
Winslade J, Monk G (2000) Narrative mediation. Wiley, New York
Yannaca-Small K (ed) (2018) Arbitration under international investment agreements: a guide to the key issues. Oxford University Press, Oxford
Zettelmeyer J, Trebesch C, Gulati GM (2014) Managing holdouts: the case of the 2012 Greek exchange. In: Lastra RM, Buchheit L (eds) Sovereign Debt Management. Oxford University Press, Oxford

Cases

Abaclat and others v. Argentine Republic, ICSID Case No. ARB/07/5 Consent Award Under ICSID Arbitration Rule 43(2) 29 December 2016
Abaclat and others v. Argentine Republic, ICSID Case No. ARB/07/5 Decision on Jurisdiction and Admissibility, 4 August 2011
Abaclat and others v. Argentine Republic, ICSID Case No. ARB/07/5 Dissenting Opinion to Decision on Jurisdiction and Admissibility, 4 August 2011
Achmea B.V. v. The Slovak Republic (formerly Eureko B.V. v. The Slovak Republic), UNCITRAL PCA Case No. 2008-13, Final Award, 7 December 2012
Allied Bank Intern. v. Banco Credito Agricola, 757 F.2d 516 (1985)
Ambiente Ufficio S.p.A. and others (Case formerly known as Giordano Alpi and others) and Argentine Republic, ICSID Case No. ARB/08/9 Decision on Jurisdiction and Admissibility Dissenting Opinion of Dr. Santiago Torres Bernardez 2 May 2013
Ambiente Ufficio S.p.A. and others (Case formerly known as Giordano Alpi and others) and Argentine Republic, ICSID Case No. ARB/08/9 Order of Discontinuance of the Proceeding 28 May 2015
Ambiente Ufficio S.p.A. and others v. Argentine Republic, ICSID Case No. ARB/08/9, Decision on Jurisdiction and Admissibility, 8 February 2013
Azurix Corp. v. Argentine Republic, ICSID Case No. ARB/01/12 Decision on the Argentine Republic's Request for a Continued Stay of Enforcement of the Award, 28 December 2007
CIBC Bank & Trust Co. v. Banco Cent. Do Brasil, 886 F. Supp. 1105 (S.D.N.Y. 1995)
CMS Gas Transmission Company v. the Republic of Argentina, ICSID Case No. ARB/01/8 Decision on the Argentine Republic's Request for a Continued Stay of Enforcement of the Award, 1 September 2006
Compañía de Aguas del Aconquija S.A. and Vivendi Universal S.A. v. Argentine Republic, ICSID Case No. ARB/97/3 Decision on the Argentine Republic's Request for a Continued Stay of Enforcement of the Award, 4 November 2008
Elliott Associates, LP v Republic of Peru [1998] 12 F Supp 2d 328 (SDNY 1998)
Elliott Assocs., L.P., General Docket No. 2000/QR/92, 16 (Court of Appeal of Brussels, 8th Chamber, Sept. 26, 2000)
Enron Corporation Ponderosa Assets, *L.P. v. Argentine Republic*, ICSID Case No. ARB/01/3 Decision on the Argentine Republic's Request for a Continued Stay of Enforcement of the Award, 7 October 2008
Fedax N.V. v. The Republic of Venezuela, ICSID Case No. ARB/96/3, Award, 9 March, 1998
Fedax N.V. v. The Republic of Venezuela, ICSID Case No. ARB/96/3, Decision of the Tribunal on Objections to Jurisdiction, 11 July 1997
Giovanni Alemanni and others v. Argentine Republic, ICSID Case No. ARB/07/8 Decision on Jurisdiction and Admissibility, 14 November 2014

Giovanni Alemanni and others v. Argentine Republic, ICSID Case No. ARB/07/8 Order of the Tribunal Discontinuing the Proceeding 14 December 2015
Poštová banka, AS and Istrokapital SE v., ICSID Case No. ARB/13/8 Award of 9 April 2015
Republic of Argentina v. Weltover, Inc 504 U.S. 607 (1992)
Roseinvestco UK Ltd. v. *The Russian Federation*, SCC ARBITRATION V (079/2005), Final Award, 12 September 2010
Salini Costruttori S.p.A. and Italstrade S.p.A. v. Kingdom of Morocco, ICSID Case No. ARB/00/4 Decision on Jurisdiction, 23 July 2001
Sempra Energy International v. Argentine Republic, ICSID Case No. ARB/02/16 Decision on the Argentine Republic's Request for a Continued Stay of Enforcement of the Award, 5 March 2009
Settlement Agreement between the Republic of Argentina and the Associazione per la Tutela degli Investitori in Titoli Argentini dated 21 April 2016

Official Reports

Asonuma T, Chamon M, Erce A et al (2019) 'Costs of sovereign defaults: restructuring strategies, bank distress and the capital inflow-credit channel'. *International Monetary Fund Working Paper WP/19/69*
Alogoskoufis G (January 2012) 'Greece's sovereign debt crisis: retrospect and prospect'. *Hellenic Observatory Papers on Greece and South East Europe*, 16–17
Bohoslavsky JP (2017) 'Effects of foreign debt and other related financial obligations of States on the full enjoyment of all human rights, particularly economic, social and cultural rights'. *Report of the Independent Expert to the United Nations General Assembly*
'Database of ICSID Member States' International Centre for Settlement of Investment Disputes
De Palo G, Feasley A, Orecchini F (2011) 'Quantifying the cost of not using mediation - a data analysis'. *European Parliament Briefing*
De Palo G (2018) 'A Ten-Year-Long "EU Mediation Paradox" When an EU Directive Needs To Be More... Directive'. *European Parliament Briefing*
'Enter the troika: the European Commission, the IMF, the ECB' *European Stability Mechanism*
'European Handbook for Mediation Lawmaking' (14 June 2019) *European Commission for the Efficiency of Justice*
Gora K (2008) 'Therapeutic Mediation'. *Second Mediation Days Conference, Slovenia*
Gurria A (13 October 2014) 'The growing pains of investment treaties'. *Organization for Economic Cooperation and Development*
Hornbeck J (19 October 2004) Argentina's sovereign debt restructuring. *Congressional Research Service*
'The ICSID Caseload—Statistics (2017-2)' *International Centre for Settlement of Investment Disputes*
'The ICSID Caseload – Statistics (2020-2)' (2020) *International Centre for Settlement of Investment Disputes*
'Improving Investment Dispute Settlement: UNCTAD Policy Tools' (2018a) *United Nations Conference on Trade and Development*
'Improving Investment Dispute Settlement: UNCTAD Policy Tools' (2018b) *United Nations Conference Trade and Development*
'Investment-Related Dispute Settlement: Reflections On A New Beginning' (2014) *International Institute for Sustainable Development*
'Investor–State Disputes: Prevention and Alternatives to Arbitration' (2010) *UNCTAD Series on International Investment Policies for Development*
'Memorandum of Economic Policies of the Government of Argentina' (14 February 2000) *International Monetary Fund*

'Overview of An Arbitration under the ICSID Convention' International Centre for Settlement of Investment Disputes
'Overview of Conciliation under The Additional Facility' International Centre for Settlement of Investment Disputes
'Overview of Conciliation under the ICSID Convention' International Centre for Settlement of Investment Disputes
'Overview of Investment Treaty Clauses on Mediation' (July 2021) *International Centre for Settlement of Investment Disputes*
Pohl J, Mashigo K, Nohen A (2012) 'Dispute Settlement Provisions in International Investment Agreements: A Large Sample Survey'. *Organization for Economic Cooperation and Development*
Pouget S (1 October 2013) 'Arbitrating and mediating disputes: Benchmarking arbitration and mediation regimes for commercial disputes related to foreign direct investment'. *World Bank Policy Research Working Paper No. 6632*
'Prevention and amicable resolution of disputes between investors and public authorities within the single market' (2017) *European Commission*
'Proposals for Amendment of the ICSID Rules' (2021) *International Centre for Settlement of Investment Disputes Working Paper #5*
'The Role of the IMF in Argentina, 1991-2002' (2003) *International Monetary Fund*
'Report of Working Group II (Arbitration and Conciliation)' (2016) *United Nations Commission on International Trade Law*
'Report of Working Group III (Investor-State Dispute Settlement Reform)' (2020)' *United Nations Commission on International Trade Law*
'Second Economic Adjustment Programme for Greece – 1st Review' (2012) *European Commission on Economic and Financial Affairs*
'Second Economic Adjustment Programme for Greece – 2nd Review' (2012) *European Commission on Economic and Financial Affairs*
'Second Economic Adjustment Programme for Greece – 3rd Review' (2013) *European Commission on Economic and Financial Affairs*
'Second Economic Adjustment Programme for Greece – 4th Review' (2014) *European Commission on Economic and Financial Affairs*
'Selection and Appointment Of Conciliators: Additional Facility Conciliation' (2018) *International Centre for Settlement of Investment Disputes*
'Settlement of Commercial Disputes: Preparation of a Legal Standard on Transparency in Treaty-based Investor-State Arbitration' (20 November 2012) *United Nations Commission on International Trade Law*
'Sovereign Borrowing Outlook for OECD Countries: 2021' (2021) *Organization for Economic Development*
'Sovereign Debt Crises And Restructurings: Lessons Learnt And Proposals For Debt Resolution Mechanisms' (2012) *United Nations Conference on Trade and Development*
'Statement of Principles for a Global Approach to Multi-creditor Workouts' (2000) *International Federation of Insolvency Professionals*
Sturzenneger F, Zettelmeyer J (2005) Haircuts: estimating investor losses in sovereign debt restructurings, 1998–2005. *International Monetary Fund Working Paper No. 05–137*
'Suggested Changes to the ICSID Rules and Regulations' (12 May 2005) *Working Paper of the ICSID Secretariat*
Das US, Papaioannou MG, Trebesch C (August 2012) 'Sovereign Debt Restructurings 1950–2010: Literature Survey, Data, and Sylized Facts'. *International Monetary Fund Working Paper*
'World Investment Report 2015: Reforming International Investment Governance' (2015) *United Nations Conference on Trade and Development*, 127–163
Jean Ziegler (2015) 'Draft progress report on the activities of vulture funds and the impact on human rights' *United Nations Human Rights Advisory Committee*

Websites and News Articles

'A Synopsis of the Greek Debt Crisis' (5 July 2011) *The Denouement.* http://knightin.typepad.com/denouement/2011/07/a-synopsis-of-the-greek-debt-crisis.html

Alan Cibils, 'Argentina Could Show Greece a Way Out of Its Crisis' (3 August 2015) *Financial Justice Ireland.* http://www.socialeurope.eu/2015/08/argentina-show-greece-way-crisis/

Alderman L, Kanter J, Yardley J et al (17 June 2016) 'Explaining Greece's Debt Crisis'. *The New York Times* https://www.nytimes.com/interactive/2016/business/international/greece-debt-crisis-euro.html

Alex Chambers and Christopher Spink, 'Greece Bond Restructuring Set for Friday' (23 February 2012) *Reuters.* https://www.reuters.com/article/U.S.-greece-restructuring-idUKTRE81M1L020120223US

Angeletos GM, Azariadis C, Arkolakis C et al (21 February 2017) 'Opinion: Grexit would be catastrophic for Greece' Ekathimerini. https://www.ekathimerini.com/opinion/216374/grexit-would-be-catastrophic-for-greece/

'Argentina profile – Timeline' (1 December 2015) *BBC News* http://www.bbc.com/news/world-latin-america-18712378

'Argentina settles five outstanding investment treaty arbitration claims in historic break with its anti-enforcement stance' (14 October 2013) *Herbert Smith Freehills* https://hsfnotes.com/arbitration/2013/10/14argentina-settles-five-outstanding-investment-treaty-arbitration-claims-in-historic-break-with-its-anti-enforcement-stance/

Brennan L (February 2015) 'Do We Need a New York Convention for Mediation/Conciliation?'. *Mediate.com.* https://www.mediate.com/articles/BrennanLbl20150227.cfm

'CEDR News: Mediation Market Grows By 5%: The 2016 Mediation Audit' (2016) *CEDR.com* https://www.cedr.com/news/?item=Mediation-Market-grows-by-5-percent-The-CEDR-2016-Mediation-Audit

Chong SY (1 February 2019) 'Singapore Convention Series: Why is there no 'seat' of mediation?'. *Kluwer Mediation Blog* http://mediationblog.kluwerarbitration.com/2019/02/01/singapore-convention-series-why-is-there-no-seat-of-mediation/

Creighton A (17 July 2015) 'Greece should default on debt, take Argentina's path to recovery'. *The Australian.* https://www.theaustralian.com.au/business/greece-should-default-on-debt-take-argentinas-path-to-recovery/news-story/2d1c18fc4d003ac27f4a04a6fd638f09

'Damages and costs in investment treaty arbitration revisited' (14 December 2017) *Global Arbitration Review* https://globalarbitrationreview.com/article/1151755/damages-and-costs-ininvestment-treaty-arbitration-revisited

Donnan S (6 October 2014) 'Trade deals: Toxic talks – ddCritics claim that international arbitration has morphed into a weapon that multinationals wield to threaten and influence'. *Financial Times.* https://www.ft.com/content/27b8740e-48ce-11e4-9f63-00144feab7de

Eberhardt P, Olivet C, Amos T et al (2018) 'Who Guards the Guardians? The Conflicting Interests of Investment Arbitrators'. *Corporate Europe Observatory.* https://corporateeurope.org/trade/2012/11/chapter-4-who-guards-guardians-conflicting-interests-investment-arbitrators

'ECB announces operational details of assetbacked securities and covered bond purchase programmes' (2 October 2014) European Central Bank https://www.ecb.europa.eu/press/pr/date/2014/html/pr141002_1.en.html

Elliot L (8 July 2015) 'Could Greece emulate Argentina's success after it defaulted in 2001?'. *The Guardian* https://www.theguardian.com/world/2015/jul/08/greek-crisis-emulate-argentina-default-success

Ferrando T (27 February 2012) 'The Abaclat legacy: Investment Arbitration as an Obstacle to Greek Recovery'. *Critical Legal Thinking.* https://criticallegalthinking.com/2012/02/27/the-abaclat-legacy-investment-arbitration-as-an-obstacle-to-greek-recovery/

Foroohar R (August 2014) 'Last Tango in Buenos Aires: Argentina's debt snarl tells us how risky the global financial system still is'. *Time Magazine*

Gallagher KP, Marx D, Lachman D et al (11 July 2011) 'What Lessons Can Europe Learn From Latin America?' *Inter-American Dialogue's Latin American Advisor*. https://www.aei.org/wp-content/uploads/2011/10/LAA110711.pdf?x91208

Georgiopoulos G, Babington D (14 November 2014) 'Greece emerged from its 'Great Depression' at start of year'. *Reuters* http://uk.reuters.com/article/ukeurozone-economy-greece-idUKKCN0IY10B20141114

Graham C, Masson PR (1 November 2002) 'The IMF's Dilemma in Argentina: Time for a New Approach to Lending?'. *Brookings* http://www.brookings.edu/research/papers/2002/11/globaleconomics-graham

'Greece – Overview of economy' (undated) Nations *Encyclopedia* http://www.nationsencyclopedia.com/economies/Europe/Greece-OVERVIEW-OF-ECONOMY.html

'Greece repays ECB after tapping fresh bailout funds' (20 August 2015) *EuroNews* https://www.euronews.com/2015/08/20/greece-repays-ecb-after-tapping-fresh-bailout-funds

'Greece submits new reform plan to EU and IMF' (1 June 2015) *BBC News*. http://www.bbc.com/news/business-33062202

Hochman SA (February 2012) 'A Mediator's Proposal – Whether, When, and How It Should Be Used'. *Mediate.com*. https://www.mediate.com/articles/HochmanS1.cfm

'How The Greek Debt Reorganisation Of 2012 Changed The Rules Of Sovereign Insolvency' (2012) *Allen & Overy, LLP* https://www.allenovery.com/global/-/media/sharepoint/publications/sitecollectiondocuments/ao2020greek20debt20reorganisation20of202012.pdf?la=en-gb&hash=652BA6B85F0E71B73BE3AF3EA721DA19

'IMF Reaches Staff-Level Agreement with Greece on €30 Billion Stand-By Arrangement' (2 May 2010) *IMF Survey Magazine* http://www.imf.org/external/np/sec/pr/2010/pr10176.htm

'IMF Survey: Europe and IMF Agree €110 Billion Financing Plan With Greece' (2 May 2010) *IMF Survey online* http://www.imf.org/external/pubs/ft/survey/so/2010/car050210a.htm

Inman P (24 May 2015a) 'Greece warns it is set to default on debt repayment loans'. *The Guardian*. http://www.theguardian.com/world/2015/may/24/greecewarns-it-is-set-to-default-on-debt-repayment-loans

Inman P (9 June 2015b) 'Greek exit would trigger Eurozone collapse, says Alexis Tsipras'. *The Guardian*. http://www.theguardian.com/bU.S.iness/2015/jun/09/greekexit-would-trigger-eurozone-collapse-says-alexis-tsipras

Jones M (22 February 2018) 'Government debt levels to hit new global high this year' *S&P Reuters*. https://www.reuters.com/article/governments-debt-sp/government-debt-levels-to-hit-new-global-high-this-year-sp-idU.S.L8N1QC70R

Krauss C (10 June 2000) 'One-Day National Strike Freezes Much of Argentina'. *The New York Times*. http://web.archive.org/web/20140613141320/http://www.nytimes.com/2000/06/10/world/one-day-nationalstrike-freezes-much-of-argentina.html

Krugman P (9 July 2015) 'Argentine Lessons for Greece'. *The New York Times*. https://krugman.blogs.nytimes.com/2015/07/09/argentine-lessons-for-greece/

Leathes M (2011) Stop Shovelling Smoke! Give Users A Classic Definition Of Mediation - Kluwer Mediation Blog'. *Kluwer Mediation Blog*. http://mediationblog.kluwerarbitration.com/2011/09/01/stop-shovelling-smoke-give-users-a-classic-definition-of-mediation/

Lehman P, Page NR (September 2007) 'Enhancing Mediator Neutrality Through Question-Asking'. *Mediate.com*. https://www.mediate.com/articles/pageLehman.cfm

Leivada D (10 September 2015) 'Greek Unemployment Figures Show No Sign of Decline'. *Huffington Post*. http://www.huffingtonpost.com/entry/greece-unemploymentrate_U.S._55efa2fce4b03784e27714f4

Limbury A (22 October 2019) 'Brainstorming'. *Kluwer Mediation Blog*. http://mediationblog.kluwerarbitration.com/2019/10/22/brainstorming/

Little A (3 February 2012) 'How 'magic' made Greek debt disappear before it joined the euro'. *BBC News*. http://www.bbc.com/news/world-europe-16834815

Maurer N, Musacchio A (2006) 'The Barber of Buenos Aires: Argentina's debt renegotiations'. *Harvard Business School Case 9–706-034*. https://www.hbs.edu/faculty/Pages/item.aspx?num=33251

Mellersh N (22 September 2017) 'Can We Enforce Mediation Agreements?' *JAMS ADR Blog*. http://adrpartners.rs/en/can-enforce-mediation-agreements/

Moore E (6 October 2014b) 'IMF recommends overhaul of sovereign bonds'. *Financial Times*. https://www.ft.com/content/368be778-4d41-11e4-8f75-00144feab7de

Newcombe A (25 October 2011) 'Mass Claims and the distinction between jurisdiction and admissibility'. *Kluwer Arbitration Blog*. http://kluwerarbitrationblog.com/2011/10/25/mass-claims-and-the-distinction-between-jurisdiction-and-admissibility

'Quality Assurance' (undated) *International Mediation Institute* https://imimediation.org/about/quality-assurance/

Ratliff B (3 April 2018) 'Pre-Mediation Conferences'. *ADR* Times. https://www.adrtimes.com/pre-mediation-conferences/

Repicky T (July 2011) 'How to Talk and Listen Effectively in Mediation'. *Mediate.com*. https://www.mediate.com/articles/RepickyT1.cfm

Rooney B (9 March 2012) 'Greece: Historic restructuring paves way for bailout'. *CNN Money*. http://money.cnn.com/2012/03/09/markets/greece-creditors-default/

Rule C (July 2018) 'Reframing'. *Mediate.com*. https://www.mediate.com/articles/Colin-Rule-Reframing.cfm

Schmidt B (11 November 2015) 'The distressed debt vulture now gobbling up the Cayman Islands'. *The Independent*. https://www.independent.co.uk/news/business/analysis-and-features/distressed-debt-vulture-now-gobbling-cayman-islands-a6729521.html

Shane Smith M (July 2005) 'Single-Text Negotiation'. Beyond Intractability. https://www.beyondintractability.org/essay/single-text-negotiation

Shell A (29 June 2015) 'Greek debt crisis: Everything you need to know'. *U.S.A TODAY*. http://www.usatoday.com/story/money/markets/2015/06/25/qa-greece-debtcrisis-loan/29284181/

Sotiris P (28 June 2012) 'Austerity, Limited Sovereignty and Social Devastation. Greece and the Dark Side of European Integration'. *Gesellschaftsanalyse Und Linke Praxis*. https://www.zeitschrift-luxemburg.de/austerity-limited-sovereignty-and-social-devastation-greece-and-the-dark-side-of-european-integration/

Spangler B (November 2003) 'Reality-Testing'. *BeyondIntractability.org*. https://www.beyondintractability.org/essay/reality_testing

Stevenson S (11 February 2015) 'Are the Greeks Sound Negotiators?'. *The Slate*. https://slate.com/business/2015/02/greece-debt-negotiations-are-greek-leaders-U.S.ing-sound-negotiating-techniques.html

Stevenson A (25 April 2016) 'How Argentina Settled a Billion-Dollar Debt Dispute With Hedge Funds'. *The New York Times*. https://www.nytimes.com/2016/04/25/business/dealbook/how-argentina-settled-a-billion-dollar-debt-dispute-with-hedge-funds.html

Stylopoulos E (July 2015) The ICSID Recent Decision on Greek PSI: Can Sovereign Bonds Be Protected as Investments?. *Kluwer Arbitration Blog*. http://arbitrationblog.kluwerarbitration.com/2015/07/02/the-icsid-recent-decision-on-greek-psi-can-sovereign-bonds-be-protected-as-investments/?print=print

Sudborough C (September 2015) 'The Rise of Investment Mediation'. *Corporate Disputes Magazine*

Tan R (29 September 2020) 'Investor-State Arbitration Meets Mediation: The Singapore Convention on Mediation as Game-Changer'. *Kluwer Mediation Blog*. http://arbitrationblog.kluwerarbitration.com/2020/09/29/investor-state-arbitration-meets-mediation-the-singapore-convention-on-mediation-as-game-changer/

Thomas B, Hennessey K, Holtz-Eakin D (27 January 2011) 'Commentary, What Caused the Financial Crisis?'. *Wall Street Journal*. https://www.wsj.com/articles/SB10001424052748704698004576104500524998280

'Timeline: The unfolding Eurozone crisis' (13 June 2012) *BBC News*. https://www.bbc.com/news/business-13856580

Traynor I (11 August 2015) 'Greece and lenders agree new bailout deal, finance minister says'. *The Guardian*. https://www.theguardian.com/world/2015/aug/11/greece-and-lenders-agree-new-bailout-deal-says-finance-ministry-official

Ubilava A, Nottage L (2018) 'ICSID's New Mediation Rules: A Small but Positive Step Forward'. Erga Omnes – SCIL Blog. https://erga-omnes.sydney.edu.au/2018/09/

Voyles R (undated), 'Managing an Imbalance of Power'. *Mediate.com*. https://www.mediate.com/articles/voylesR3.cfm

Warnlof J (undated) 'The Premediation Conference: An Underused Step Towards Resolution'. *The Mediation Society*. https://mediationsociety.org/the-pre%C2%ADmediation-conference-an-underused-step-towards-resolution/

'What Is Mediation? What Happens In A Mediation?' (undated) *Jamsadr.com*. https://www.jamsadr.com/mediation-defined/

Young P (July 2003) 'Overcoming Impasse in Mediation: A Short Literature Review'. *Mediate.com*. https://www.mediate.com/articles/young13.cfm?nl=56

MIX
Papier aus verantwortungsvollen Quellen
Paper from responsible sources
FSC® C105338

If you have any concerns about our products,
you can contact us on
ProductSafety@springernature.com

In case Publisher is established outside the EU,
the EU authorized representative is:
Springer Nature Customer Service Center GmbH
Europaplatz 3, 69115 Heidelberg, Germany

Printed by Libri Plureos GmbH
in Hamburg, Germany